Sustaining Change in Universities

Continuities in Case Studies and Concepts

Burton R. Clark

Society for Research into Higher Education
& Open University Press

Open University Press
McGraw-Hill Education
McGraw-Hill House
Shoppenhangers Road
Maidenhead
Berkshire
England
SL6 2QL

email: enquiries@openup.co.uk
world wide web: www.openup.co.uk

and Two Penn Plaza, New York, NY 10121-2289, USA

First published 2004

A catalogue record of this book is available from the British Library

ISBN 0 335 21590 4 (pb)   0 335 21591 2 (hb)

Library of Congress Cataloging-in-Publication Data
CIP data has been applied for

Typeset by RefineCatch Limited, Bungay, Suffolk
Printed in the UK by MPG Books Ltd, Bodmin, Cornwall

To Adele

One, yes, but also half of two
The twining year is full of thee

For the first time a really international world of learning, highly competitive, is emerging. If you want to get into that orbit, you have to do so on merit. You cannot rely on politics or anything else. You have to give a great deal of autonomy to institutions for them to be dynamic and to move fast in international competition. You have to develop entrepreneurial leadership to go along with institutional autonomy.

Clark Kerr, *Universal Issues in the Development of Higher Education*, 1993

It is worth repeating the insight that a discipline without a large number of thoroughly executed case studies is a discipline without systematic production of exemplars, and that a discipline without exemplars is an ineffective one. In social science, especially in those branches which find themselves to be weak, more good case studies could help remedy this situation.

Bent Flyvbjerg, *Making Social Science Matter*, 2002

Contents

Acknowledgements

The author of a book based on fourteen institutional case studies incurs many debts of gratitude along the way. In helping me to gain access to relevant information and to avoid gross errors of historical fact and analytical interpretation in Part I cases, I wish to thank particularly Michael Shattock, former Registrar of the University of Warwick and Visiting Professor, Centre for Higher Education Studies, University of London; Peter West, University Secretary, University of Strathclyde; Leo Goedegebuure, Executive Director, Centre for Higher Education Policy Studies, University of Twente; Perttu Vartiainen, Rector, and Jouni Kekäle, Personnel Director, University of Joensuu; and Roger Johansson, Education Planning Officer, and Tuula Bergquist, Program Director, Chalmers Lindholmen, Chalmers University of Technology.

In Part II case studies, I based my analysis of universities in Africa, Latin America and Australia on the work of other scholars: papers on the development of the University of Makerere and other African universities written by David Court, long-time expert on African higher education in The Rockefeller Foundation; outstanding fieldwork and a published paper on the Catholic University of Chile done specifically for my study by Andres Bernasconi, now Dean, Faculdad de Ciencias Juridicas y Sociales, Universidad de Talca, Chile; and a comprehensive book-length examination of the transformation of Monash University authored by Simon Marginson, now Director, Centre for Research in International Education at that university.

For assistance in the half-dozen brief case studies of US universities in Chapter 10, I am grateful to Patricia Gumport, Professor of Education, Stanford University; Lydia Snover, Assistant to the Provost for Institutional Research, Massachusetts Institute of Technology; Kathryn M. Moore, Dean, College of Education, North Carolina State University; Mary Frank Fox and Gus Giebelhaus, faculty members, Georgia Institute of Technology; and Aimee Dorr and Sherry Miranda, Dean and Finance Officer respectively, Graduate School of Education and Information Studies, and Paula Lutomirski, Associate Vice-Chancellor, UCLA. In depicting six US institutions, I have drawn repeatedly upon basic analyses found in Roger Geiger's three volumes on American research universities.

My ongoing efforts to conceptualize the modern entrepreneurial university were particularly stimulated by the insights of Michael Shattock in personal communications as well as in a stream of speeches and papers he presented during the 1980s and 1990s, and now summed effectively in his book *Managing Successful Universities.* My concluding concept of the modern self-reliant university is drawn directly from his work.

For factual and interpretative errors, I am solely responsible.

I am grateful to the UCLA Graduate School of Education and Information Studies for providing me with an office, support services, and genial colleagueship for a dozen years and more beyond formal retirement. Adele Clark has, as many times before, edited the entire manuscript with a sharp eye for soggy expression. For clarity we have jointly created simplicities amidst a minutiae of detail.

Burton R. Clark
Santa Monica, California
December 2003

Introduction

During the last quarter of the twentieth century universities around the world found themselves under increasing pressure to change the way they operate. Alert universities gradually recognized that they had to respond to proliferating new demands of government, industry and societal groups, while maintaining and improving their traditional fields of research, teaching and student learning that became more complicated with every passing year. Whatever their heritage, or individual traditional character, the pace of change dictated a more flexible and adaptable posture. But many universities seemed unable to keep apace fast-moving times. Limited in resources, mired in encrusted practices – immovable cathedrals, some would say – they would not freely step into the rapidly flowing streams of societal change. Instead, deliberately or unconsciously, they would opt for the comfort of standing still.

We can, early in the new millennium, bring the heightened concern about the fate of universities down to earth by focusing on several questions. What most needs to be done to strengthen them for the fast-moving world of the twenty-first century? The answer, as we develop in this study, is that universities need to develop flexible capabilities that permit them to weave together new and old, change and continuity, in sustainable form. Toward that general answer, we need to know three things:

- *What* organizational elements in universities come together to compose an adaptable character? In contrast to 'the traditional university', that new character can be known as 'the proactive university,' 'the innovative university,' or even, at the cutting edge, 'the entrepreneurial university'. Whatever the name, we need to know its major ingredients.
- *How* are the elements of adaptable character developed? Are there identifiable pathways by which universities negotiate a transition from the traditional to the proactive, the innovative, the entrepreneurial?
- *How* is adaptable university character sustained? Amid ever-growing complexity of purposes and tasks, can *pathways* of change become sustaining *patterns* of change?

If we determine how some universities have been reasonably successful in transforming themselves and sustaining change, their answers will surely suggest what can be done in a practical way to strengthen universities generally. We can search for concrete practices devised by change-oriented universities as they maneuver in contemporary realities of constraint and opportunity. We thereby focus seriously on the art of the possible in major university reform. We steer clear of abstract exhortations about what must be done – those that remain unconnected to the embedded realities of university life.

This is how I approached these problems in the mid-1990s when I pursued five European proactive universities to learn how they had gone about changing their character. I focused very little on so-called theory and very much on practice. I stayed away from legislators, planners, ministers, and all others who claimed that they were in the business of defining broad policy in higher education. Instead, I spent my time with those who did the work inside universities. By means of in-depth interviews, extensive document analysis, and some observation of campus life, I took the opportunity on field trips to stand beside 'practitioners' – trustees and administrators, faculty and students – to see the world as they saw it.

As I proceeded with my research, it became clear that practical wisdom was what I was after, a pragmatic rationality that bridged the difference between understanding and use. Such know-how cannot be gained by perusing national policy documents or seeking out yearly issues in the politics of systems of higher education. It is acquired by plunging into settings inside universities that directly condition and enact research, teaching and student learning. The work of higher education is highly localized: it is done in university base units as varied as departments of physics, economics and history, and in places as dissimilar as schools of medicine, education, computer science and performing arts. The best way to find out how universities change the way they operate is to proceed in research from the bottom-up and the inside-out. 'System' analysis done top-down cannot do the job. It misses the organic flow of university internal development.

Drawing upon my 1994–96 case studies, I generalized a handful of common elements and thereby introduced a body of reasonably crisp ideas induced from practice. The key elements were defined as: a diversified funding base; a strengthened steering core; an expanded outreach periphery; a stimulated academic heartland; and an integrated entrepreneurial culture. These five conceptions became a useful framework in which to couch case-study descriptions that could also attend closely to contextual specificities and institutional peculiarities. The resulting book, *Creating Entrepreneurial Universities: Organizational Pathways of Transformation*, published in 1998,[1] used institutional narratives to give concrete meaning to concepts while putting the concepts to work to provide an overarching order to the narratives.

That small volume turned out to be the right book at the right time. By the late 1990s many more universities on every continent were indeed becoming alert to their defects and sought to react more quickly as the pace of change accelerated around them. The book became internationally a relevant manual with illustrative cases. The use of 'entrepreneurial' as the key term in the organizing framework, in place of the softer 'proactive' and 'innovative,' was also provocative. Within two to three years, the book generated lively discussion in Britain and continental Europe; and, with four printings and early translation into Spanish and Chinese, it became widely distributed in Latin America and the Far East.

A major international conference convened by the Organization for Economic Cooperation and Development (OECD) in Paris in Fall, 2000, with over 300 participants from more than forty countries, not only pursued the theme of the book but also used its stated pathways of transformation to organize presentations and debate.[2] A second major international conference on university entrepreneurialism followed a year later in Fall, 2001 at the University of Zhejiang, China. This follow-on meeting on the other side of the globe included university presidents from such other major Asian societies as India, Indonesia, Malaysia, Korea, Japan and Australia.[3]

The book became somewhat controversial. Doubters about the transforming steps I presented, and then advocated, thought it was at least a stage too far. A counter-argument was voiced in concern about 'losing the soul of the university', wherever it happens to be located.[4] Exponents of this point of view believed it was better to stay closer to the status quo and not risk changes that would tamper with whatever institutional heritage existed. Jobs and privileges obviously might be on the line; income from industry might turn into 'commercialization' that would cause the university to veer from old ways that were taken as natural. With new money on the table, universities might imitate business firms, even slavishly follow dictates of 'the market'. State money still seemed clean and safe and in the service of the public good, despite the predilections of politicians and bureaucrats to specify how it should be spent even as they reduced the state share of university revenue. Who knew where non-state subsidies and new environmental connections might lead?

But doubts aside, the problem of how to transform universities by vigorous organizational action has only deepened. Given the pressures on universities in the early twenty-first century, it has clearly moved center stage. Exploratory studies and explanatory frameworks are urgently needed.

Following the publication of *Creating Entrepreneurial Universities*, I attempted to further develop my framework by writing articles and participating in relevant conferences.[5] Along the way I became convinced that a second book could advance the international discussion underway. The 2000 Paris conference had been both discouraging and encouraging – discouraging because participants who did not report on specific institutions fell into speculation about trends in whole national systems of higher education and then moved on to large thoughts about an all-Europe conception that would harmonize national systems. The system-making world of ministers was very evident: one large wish led to another. But the conference was encouraging because other participants understood that the focus was on the institutional level and came prepared with empirical accounts of how certain universities, one by one, were attempting to change themselves. These practitioners and researchers understood that university transformation requires organizational will: they sought to present agency in action. Stimulated by the institutionally-focused papers, some with exceedingly rich and provocative stories, the meeting became for me a jumping-off point for further inquiry toward bringing together old and new case studies to evolve a conceptual framework in ways that might offer new insights about initiating and sustaining change in universities.

In this second effort, the book at hand, I first follow developments in the five European universities originally studied to see what they had accomplished in the five to six years after my field visits. Their stories are extended to 2000 and beyond. Drawing on the work of others, I then bring in new cases of universities involved in major transforming efforts elsewhere in the world. These additions enlarge the empirical sample by widening the coverage of different types of universities in radically different contexts. By such means, I seek to modify my original framework and increase its international utility. I want to assert more fully and compellingly why an entrepreneurial evolution, or something like it, is necessary in different university settings.

The introduction to my 1998 study reported conclusions derived from the research at the beginning of the analysis. This approach had clear advantages: it highlighted five elemental pathways of transformation; it allowed the explicit use of these factors as a framework that could then be woven into institutional case studies. In pursuit of 'continuities in cases and concepts', I have deliberately moved in this book to a different style of narrative reporting. Here I only touch on conclusions in this introduction in order to suggest overall coherence and then let more detailed ones emerge in piecemeal fashion; the results accumulate as the analysis moves through the set of institutions. This study emphasizes that change in universities typically proceeds in a cumulative incremental fashion. I imitate the logic of that process by gradually unfolding results; emergent findings in later cases lend weight to previous findings and add new life to them.

We understand how change is sustained in universities when we face the flow of small alterations, one after another, that lead in time to a qualitative change in organizational character. Hence, I proceed through five brief case studies before moving from cases to concepts, and then move onward from the concepts to new cases and to a final assembly of concepts in the concluding chapter.

The concept of sustainability is the organizing idea in Part I. Can an entrepreneurial transformation taking place in a university be sustained? By what means? I sought answers by returning to the University of Warwick (England), University of Strathclyde (Scotland), University of Twente (The Netherlands), University of Joensuu (Finland), and Chalmers University of Technology (Sweden), to pick up where I left them at the end of the case narratives in the previous volume. Primarily by means of published university documents, I review what happened in the years leading up to 2000.

What events or processes continued or seriously modified the transform-ational pathways those universities developed between 1980 and 1995? We encounter systemic problems of contradiction and balance taken on by entrepreneurial universities as they pursued new ways and seriously disturbed the sleeping dogs of old vested interests.

Based on these later experiences, I voice new conceptions in a seemingly contradictory vocabulary: sustained transformation depends on a 'steady state' infrastructure that pushes for change. That steady state includes a 'bureaucracy of change'. Such formulations help us understand the type of organizational solidity that is regularly involved. Just as traditional uni-versities are resistant to change because of an infrastructure of rooted forms and interests – vested interests and sunk costs in spades – change-oriented universities consist of interlocked forms and interests that insist on continu-ous change, incremental and accumulative. New vested interests are inflexible about their commitment to change: true believers are plentiful. Sustainability finds concrete footing in observable frameworks. The conclud-ing chapter in Part I pulls together these new findings from the five European universities.

Part II adds the new cases that extend and modify my original conception of prime elements in modern university transformation. These new cases in university entrepreneurialism range, in three chapters, from a reinvigorated university in East Africa (University of Makerere in Uganda) that had been sorely wracked by disastrous national dictatorships, to an exemplar case of entrepreneurial action (Catholic University of Chile) leading to extensive modernization in an Latin American setting, to the institution in Australia (Monash University) widely considered the leading entrepreneurial university in that country and indeed in the Far East. Chapter 10 explores varieties of entrepreneurialism found in the massive American university system: brief accounts of developments in two leading private universities (Stanford and MIT), two flagship public universities (University of Michigan and University of California, Los Angeles), and two post-2000 pathbreaking efforts centered on North Carolina State University and the Georgia Institute of Technology. Decentralization of public and private control, great dif-ferentiation of institutional types, and inescapable competition produce an almost genetic form of entrepreneurialism. In all these new cases I develop narrative accounts from the analyses of other scholars as well as from insti-tutional documents. These accounts are experiments in developing case studies that extend and correct a particular analytical framework.

From the cases in Parts I and II, we learn that sustainable adaptive uni-versities do not depend on ephemeral personal leadership. Charismatic leaders can serve for a time but in the lifeline of universities they are here today and gone tomorrow. Lasting transformation also does not depend on a one-time burst of collective effort occasioned by a dire environmental threat; it does not wait upon a fortuitous favorable convergence of old contending interests. Rather, whatever the initial stimulus, it depends on those collective responses that build new sets of structures and processes – accompanied by allied beliefs – that steadily express a determined institutional will. Formally and informally, a stabilizing entrepreneurial constitution is woven into the fabric of the university. That constitution is rationalized by a convincing entrepreneurial narrative that fits the setting.

To find out how the constitution and accompanying beliefs become rooted in complex universities, we need to engage in case-study research that balances descriptions of institutionally unique complexities with inductive conceptualization of elements common across cases. The twin tasks are to gain some useful partial truths without simplifying too much. When successful, we forge an ethnographic compromise between warranted generalizations and institutional specificities. We thereby emphasize situationally conditioned generalizations. We assert common elements without straying far from the working knowledge of practitioners caught up in varied contexts.

The reality of university change comes in very detailed items – in complicated governance structures, multiplying streams of income, a changing array of base units that stake out different academic territories, a developing set of contradictory beliefs. Without some footing in the intermingled details of inescapable features, analysis readily slips into soggy unanalyzed abstractions, easily contested conclusions appropriate for detached theorizing and commencement-day speeches. The truth is in the details, the details of university infrastructure and the accretion of small changes that cumulatively lead to major change. Specifying change in specific sites is what gives credence to any induced generalizations.

The wonderful virtue of case studies, then, is that we can weave accounts of institutional complexities in which we get much closer to on-the-spot crucial interactions than is possible through remote statistical analysis or purported hypothesis-testing around a few abstracted variables. The dismaying downside of case studies is that a straightforward description of many organizational details can produce, in the eyes of others, a cat's cradle of boring minutiae. To minimize this downside, I have followed the maxim throughout the book that brevity is the mother of convincing communication. All the case-study reports are brief, and some are briefer than others – in both Part I and Part II some cases are presented in a simplified fashion.

When we gain detailed empirical knowledge about universities in different nations and parts of the world we also move away from the tunnel vision induced by knowledge of higher education in only one society. Such vision leads unknowingly to arrogant opinion – whether German or French or Russian or English or American – about just what a university is like as a functioning organization and how it can go about changing its character. It helps greatly to become familiar with a variety of national settings in which we find amplifying variations of a new type of university.

The final chapter sets forth 'a third way' of university-environment relations; between state and market we find the university that newly asserts self-rule and self-reliance. Much literature about the control of higher education portrays universities as either state-led or market-dictated – they either follow the commands of state patrons or adhere closely to the aggregated market demands of 'customers'. The capacity of universities to take care of themselves is entirely omitted. But major private universities are generally more self-determined than state-led or passively steered by 'the market'. Major public universities in many countries have also developed a great deal of operational autonomy, especially as they have become large and inordinately complex. They have their own ways of sheltering research, teaching and student learning from close state control. They also strongly resist market opportunism that would turn them into shopping malls. Their problem becomes how to move from passive autonomy that risks stagnation in the status quo to proactive autonomy that risks the uncertainties of change.

A growing number of entrepreneurial universities now embody a new option for institutional self-reliance. In their more active autonomy, they marry collegiality to change as well as to the status quo. Such modern institutions know the difference between a university and a state agency. They know the difference between a university and a business firm. They also know that a complex university has many 'souls', some righteous, some unrighteous; hard choices are needed to select the one and deny the other. And they know that the world does not owe them a living, that traditional posturing will not be enough. The third way of university self-development is the promise they offer.

Many observers inside and outside the academy think the concept of entrepreneurialism, however carefully explained, should not be applied to institutions of higher learning. But universities cannot stand still or retreat into the past. Change is inevitable. Universities can be engulfed by it or they can work hard to alter their character in ways that allow them to better control their own destiny. 'Entrepreneurial' is an embracing but pointed term for referencing the attitudes and procedures that most dependably lead to the modern self-reliant, self-steering university. When we also stress that entrepreneurial action comes in collegial as well as personal forms – nailing the flag of 'collegial entrepreneurship' to the masthead – we are at the core of the complicated business of changing universities in the early twenty-first century.

Part I

Sustaining Entrepreneurialism in European Universities

Part I pursues developments at the University of Warwick in England, the University of Strathclyde in Scotland, the University of Twente in Holland, the University of Joensuu in Finland, and the Chalmers University of Technology in Sweden during the last half of the 1990s. Analyzing these institutions, the original case studies described in my earlier book led to a small set of concepts that became the explanatory architecture of how they had successfully struggled between 1980 and 1995 to transform their character. With the concepts at hand we go back to the cases a half-decade later to see what happened to their transformed character. The additional observation allows us to move from transforming steps to the means of sustaining change. The analytical logic remains double-sided: we go back to the empirical realities of specific universities; we seek a few concepts that can extend insight.

Universities undergoing change are particularly complex organizations to understand. They must be observed in motion as they seek to devise new ways and combine the new with the old. Here we watch particularly for dynamics of sustainability. Along the way we note particular types of problems that change-minded universities get themselves into, especially when they attempt to be entrepreneurial while considerably under state control.

In these five cases we will see ample variation in how university autonomy is exercised. The cases also force us to recognize how much the very newness of organizational features depends on local and national contexts. Raising funds from alumni may be a common enough procedure in the United States, for example, but it is a new idea in one European setting after another and becomes a significant change-producing activity. Newness is in the eyes of the beholding context.

1

Sustainability at Warwick: a paradigmatic case

My case study of the University of Warwick in the mid-1990s, reported in *Creating Entrepreneurial Universities*, concluded that Warwick was 'an example second to none in Europe of university proactivity, one grounded in an aggressive attitude ...' As stated by Michael Shattock, the Registrar, in the late 1980s it believed 'that attack is the best form of defense, or in university language, that optimism, some risk taking and a willingness to attempt new things represent a better policy than caution, cut-backs and academic conservatism.'[1] Warwick soon became a powerful model of the contemporary reformed university; its transformation was built upon

> a strengthened administrative capacity, a buildup of discretionary funds, a vigorous periphery of outreach structures and programs, a willingness of heartland departments to join in the pursuit of new ventures and relationships, and, finally, a wrap-around entrepreneurial mentality that unites the university in a new direction of development and presents a distinctive outlook different from traditional modes. Warwick teaches us much about what organizational changes enter into the making of entrepreneurial universities.[2]

In 2000, the aggressive attitude was still decidedly evident. When Sir Brian Follett, Warwick's Vice-Chancellor (1992–2000), spoke at the previously-mentioned OECD-IMHE Conference in Paris on the element of diversified funding base, he began by likening the 'traditional statist model' to 'a monopoly purchaser interacting with a cartel'[3] – a very different view of the state–university relationship than the one offered by a continental minister of education who confidently claimed that 'the state was the university's best friend'. Sir Brian then succinctly pointed out that the British government had began to pull back from university support in the early 1980s and then continued to do so in all the years up to the present. State funding increased twofold during those two decades, but state-led expanded student intake increased threefold, changing student–teacher ratios on the average, we may note, from 10/12:1 to 15/18:1. Institutions varied from 10:1 to 30:1, and over thirty universities out of a hundred now shouldered a 20:1 ratio or more. So much for equity in general university support.

Follett noted further that the national Research Assessment Exercise (RAE) begun in 1986 and repeated in 1989, 1992, 1996 and 2000 had increasingly focused infrastructure research funds on a subset of universities – those with high scores received much more money. The state also had ceased to put up money for capital development, leaving it to the universities to borrow money from banks for this purpose. The government had opened several doors to tuition income by allowing universities to charge graduate students as well as overseas students 'at market rates,' that is, at full cost recovery if possible. Year-by-year cutting in core per-unit support – cuts the government liked to define as 'efficiency gains' – brought the UK university system down, by 2000, to approximately 60 per cent dependence upon basic funding from its main government sponsor.

Warwick was 'in the vanguard' in reducing this dependence. Its income from the core governmental allocation for teaching and research that had been 70 per cent of total income in the 1970s had fallen to 38 per cent in 1995 and then further to 27 per cent in 2000. A core allocation of 90 million euros was far surpassed by a non-core sum of 160 million euros. 'Non-government earnings' had become the financial underpinning for all that Warwick had become and for all that it wanted to be. As Follett explained further at the Paris conference:

> Without any doubt it is this stream of funding – and its associated 'profit' – which has allowed Warwick to invest in more and better staff and to build a campus infrastructure that is internationally competitive. In terms of the UK 'league tables' then the strategy has been academically successful with the entrance requirements of students ranking amongst the highest in the land and the university regularly being rated in the top six or eight of the 100 UK universities for research, teaching, and overall. In other words the end points seem to have justified the more entrepreneurial approaches adopted; we have not sacrificed the core academic values, indeed the opposite would appear to have occurred.[4]

So much for those fretting about 'losing the soul of the university' if they actively sought out non-government income.

Of course, the diversification of income did not lead to such favorable outcomes without deliberate development of other organizational features. Follett briefly pointed to the central role played by stimulated heartland departments, the linking of new outreach units to the departments, the importance of certain kinds of managerial mechanisms, and the accumulation of a supporting culture. In very untraditional terms – particularly so for European universities – the Vice-Chancellor stressed that:[5]

> The strategy is relatively simple. Encourage all sectors of the university to look outwards at possible opportunities, establish profit sharing

arrangements that stimulate each sector to maximize their turnovers/ bottom-lines, put in place managerial mechanisms which do not confound the academic virtues with the financial virtues . . . and put in place mechanisms that can take risks.

The end result is a suite of 'businesses,' most of which are based within the academic departments. The provision of graduate training, short courses for the commercial sector, recruitment of overseas students and the research grant/contract income raises three-quarters of the €160 million each year. Without doubt much of this enterprise is focused within a small number of large players – the Warwick Business School, Warwick Manufacturing Group, Economics and Law – but virtually all academic units are involved. Some of the science departments have focused part of their overall activity upon commercial linkages for research and development, others in the humanities and social sciences have focused upon recruiting overseas students. It has become part of the culture and the financial flows are critical to the survival of many of the academic units.

Quite separately, the university has developed many of its facilities for use outside the immediate undergraduate teaching year. Warwick Conferences attracts over 100,000 visitors and has a turnover of €20 million. It not only raised the quality of the 4000 student bedrooms (a high proportion of which are now 'en suite') but we have built three Management Training Centres which operate as four-star hotels and are used for short course work. Retail services have erected a supermarket, bookshops, and various other retail outlets whilst there are a couple of growing dot-com businesses.

Sir Brian concluded:[6]

Not everything works every year but that would hardly come as a surprise to any business person. Overall though the growth rate has exceeded 10% per annum and has proved remarkably robust. The surpluses generated are spent in a host of ways. More faculty than would otherwise be possible, and importantly better paid. A building programme . . . which will exceed €150 million over six years, funded 50% from the surpluses and an ability to maintain the infrastructure in good condition (from libraries to landscaping).

Will the geese continue to lay their golden eggs? I think so not because each business is secure but because the university is prepared to change rapidly as outside pressures occur. For instance, the distance-learning MBA programmes have to alter rapidly to become company oriented and use electronic means of dissemination. The management structure plus the culture suggest such changes will occur, not without some pain but without the need for radical change . . .

The objectives are also crystal clear: to be a leading teaching and research university. The evidence and the benchmarks against which we operate suggest these academic priorities are working. I can only end by saying that the system also operates collegially and the student–staff ratio, for instance, is remarkably constant across the university so [the] funds are clearly being shifted around to maximise the whole. Finally, a good example of spending money for the public good might come from the Warwick Arts Centre which each year attracts 250,000 visitors (mostly from the community, not from the university) to its 1,100 events. It is the largest such complex outside London and requires a subsidy from us of around €1 million annually.

At several points in his presentation, the Vice-Chancellor spoke about management: e.g., 'the importance of certain kinds of managerial mechanisms'; the need to 'put in place managerial mechanisms which do not confound the academic virtues with the financial virtues'. Warwick functions by means of an extremely flat structure, one shorn of organized faculties and deans – the common middle level found in most European and American universities – with the center and the departments relating directly to each other. This minimization of vertical organization puts a premium on department responsibility and especially on a well-administered center. In its transition, the university early set its face against 'full blooded financial devolution to departments', in order to 'retain a distinct measure of financial control in the centre',[7] control that is spread among a small set of interlocked central committees composed of senior faculty, senior central administrators, and some members of the lay-dominated Court. One committee closely monitors the earned-income portfolio. Another approves the filling of all staff vacancies and decides each year on an allocation of resources to departments, including the creation of new posts and the maintenance or reallocation of old ones. It also interviews the chairs of departments on annual budgeting proposals. Still another seeks to integrate academic, financial and physical plant planning. The structure of central committees put in place during the 1980s remained much the same at the end of the 1990s.[8] Change had clearly acquired a 'steady state' with observable vested interests and standard operating procedures of its own.

For Warwick, this assemblage of related committees is an operational definition of a 'partnership' between senior academics and senior administrators – the latter hired to be an unusually strong group. The proven success of this feature of management structure is the center's regularized capacity to top-slice income from various sources and then cross-subsidize with funds thus set aside to come to the aid of academic departments weakly positioned to generate income. The 'university' simply says this is accepted – and it has been – because 'we' use academic criteria and so build the university as a whole. Such capacity is an important foundation for building encompassing interests and integrating institutional identity. Such outcomes are not achieved by 'talking the talk'. A university needs sturdy mechanisms, albeit difficult to build but invaluable when once in place.

Follett's crisp account in his fifteen-minute presentation in Paris revealed important contours of Warwick's continuing entrepreneurial style. To expand on the story and to focus on what measures contributed toward sustainability, we find telling details in reports of achievements between 1995 and 2000. Year-by-year significant developments point to an ever stronger institutionalization of the transforming pathways and offer clues to how this particular university has gone about sustaining its altered character.

In 1996, for example:[9]

1 The university appointed its first development officer and planned to launch a fund-raising campaign the following year 'to generate additional regular financial support . . . from new sources'. This was a highly significant, if belated, move. When the earned income policy was established in 1982, the university had decided to 'earn' rather than 'beg for' additional income, because it did not have a large body of graduates with significant personal resources. Graduates could now in 1996 be turned into contributing alumni, and the benefits, morally and financially, would measurably outweigh the cost of investing in an alumni-development office. This was not a risk-free step. It meant clawing-back a sizable sum of money from departments. Perhaps the entire effort might prove worthless and need to be discontinued. But if Oxford and Cambridge could do it, they reasoned, and if so many American universities could do it, why not Warwick? If successful, here would be an additional form of income with a powerful form of outreach to a key population.

2 Thirty-five young Warwick research fellows who joined the university in 1995 had by now 'firmly established themselves'. Members of this exceptionally bright cohort were already obtaining research grants for their work and attracting allied fellowships for others from outside sources: this was happening in the humanities and social sciences, in philosophy, history and psychology, as well as in the sciences. The bold international recruitment effort carried off at high speed in 1994, using earned surpluses to help fund this new scheme, was now producing expected results. The five-year fellowship recipients were chosen by international competition. The talent added to the university was impressive.

3 National public assessors and private publications continued to rate Warwick's departments very favorably. The university was able to validate success in using its transformed character to prevail over its more traditional counterparts on grounds of productive faculty and able students. In the face of anticipated 'declining allocation of resources from government in real terms until beyond the end of the century', the university had created infrastructure that made possible a high degree of success as traditionally defined. Accumulating advantage could be shown across the arts, social studies including the outstanding business school, and science and technology, a growing area of institutional strength. Engineering and the Manufacturing Group were expanding in size and acclaim; physics and mathematics were growing; and a new thrust was forming in the biological sciences. An important project was clearly afoot in medicine. The foundation of a Medical Research Institute, 'a major new development for the

University', linked a small group of research scientists to the staff from five local National Health Service hospitals.

4 Warwick continued to add interdisciplinary research centers: in 1996, in the Faculty of Social Studies, for example, a new Centre for the Study of Globalization and the Regional Political Economy founded on the back of winning a national research council competition.

5 The university could point to major units in its infrastructure that had a significant impact on its local region and community. These built-in and well-developed features stretched from

   (a) the 13-year-old science park and a new Innovative Centre in a second park, with firms spilling out to remain in the locality; to
   (b) the well-established and heavily-used Arts Centre, a venue for theatre, music, and dance; to
   (c) the major complex of conference facilities, under a 'Department of Hospitality Services', which won a 'Best Academic Venue' award for the fifth conservative year; to
   (d) a rapidly growing 'Open Studies Programme' that provided local access to part-time degree programs and also offered '2 plus 2' degree programs together with over a half-dozen nearby technical colleges.

6 Not to be overlooked, the university's print services had won an award for inplant printer of the year, against competition 'from large commercial inplants throughout the UK'. Print was part of the university's retail services operation, which with £6 million annual turnover 'makes a considerable contribution to university earned income each year'. Such small increments to the earned income portfolio did indeed add up to real money.

7 The university prepared a 'Mission Statement and Strategic Plan' to establish key objectives that would 'direct the University into the 21st century'. A commitment was reaffirmed to a 'distinctive set of aims: to remain within the elite group of research-led UK Universities, thereby providing an intellectually challenging teaching environment for our students; to continue to enhance our international reputation through the extension of collaborative research and teaching activities overseas; and to strengthen further our economic and education impact on the local region'.

University mission statements are notoriously vacuous, offering glittering generalities that provide little guidance for the hard choices that have to be made on Monday morning. But Warwick's three large stated aims – one national, one international, one local – were well-grounded in its infrastructure. Its national aim was firmly implemented in an array of excellent academic departments supported by the security of diversified income. While formerly 'hard' money from the government had turned soft, nominally 'soft' money from non-traditional sources had in the aggregate become dependable. As put by Michael Shattock:

Warwick's view now is that its earned income is more to be relied on than its income from the state: the former has proven its reliability over the years and while individual income streams will fluctuate in the contributions each year the overall pattern is one of continued growth. State income, however, has proven to be much more vulnerable and much more dependent on changes over which the university has no control.[10]

The will and the means for high national standing were well in place. Concurrently, the university had in place an uncommonly strong local outreach. It had not allowed its national ambition to eliminate local service.

Warwick's international aim had become institutionalized at a steady pace, first in reaching out to foreign sites and students in the fast-developing training programs of the Manufacturing Group and then in the programs of the business school and other departments. In 1996 the university could report international links by means of 55 formal agreements with 22 universities in Europe, Africa, Latin America, Asia and North America. Over 2,300 students from over 100 countries were on campus. The momentum in such outreach virtually assured that the university would go on enhancing its international reputation. Sheer financial opportunism in dealing with foreign students and foreign sites had caused more than one UK university serious embarrassment. But because Warwick had assiduously moved into the elite circle of academic excellence, and because its traditional departments guarded their high reputation, the odds were low that financial virtues would trump the academic ones at this particular institution.

8   Institutional confidence had increasingly become a Warwick trademark. For example, as told in the national *Times Higher*.[11]

> In a rare warts-and-all examination of life on a British campus, Warwick University is to star as the subject of a seven-part fly-on-the-wall radio series starting next week. Undeterred by the obloquy heaped on the Royal Opera House after it exposed itself to the forensic scrutiny of a BBC TV crew in *The House* series, the university authorities agreed to allow Radio 4 producer Brian King virtually unlimited access to record on the campus for much of last year.

Doing so over an eight-month period during 1996, the producer then extracted from hundreds of hours of recorded material 'those things that seem to me to say something about this thing called the university. It [the program] is a very impressionistic thing. It's not a documentary. It works on a subliminal level.' Hopefully, listeners will acquire 'a much stronger sense of the themes that preoccupy those who teach, work and study in a university'.

The warts included: 'Student drunkenness, fights, vandalism, drugs and rock and roll'; a 'deliciously rancorous senate meeting when senior academics wrangle over proposals . . .'; the very successful mathematics department, against the advice of the admissions staff, massively overshooting its student recruitment target, to the consternation of well-qualified students who now had to be denied and the considerable irritation of colleagues in other departments who had to reduce their student intakes 'as a result of the mistakes made by the maths faculty'; the eternal debates in British academic departments [here the physics department] not just over which students have passed or failed but which 'class of degrees their students should receive' – a first, a high second? – that seriously affect job prospects and especially entry to graduate programs in other universities.

The university had debated at the highest level 'whether to allow the microphones in at all', but concluded that 'it was a well-managed and academically successful institution which could withstand such microscopic examination'. The vice-chancellor held that 'Warwick was not by nature a risk-averse institution and it had a fair amount of faith in itself . . . The university knows it is imperfect. It knows it has problems galore. We thought that if a university were to be portrayed on Radio 4 then Warwick should come out of it pretty well.' A passing event, to be sure, but a signifier of institutional confidence.

The university also lists specific sources of research grants, contracts and sponsorship in its annual reports, a habit in keeping with its notion of transparency whenever possible. These included, in 1996, the expected government sources of research councils, and a half-dozen major departments – Defence, Health, Social Security, Environment, Trade and Industry, Transport – beyond the core-supporting Department for Education and Employment. Additional sources included over 160 other bodies that ranged from local city councils and hospitals to such national and international entities as the European Community, the rich Wellcome Trust, the American National Science Foundation, Barclays Bank, British Petroleum, British Gas, British Telecommunications, Rolls Royce, Glaxo, SmithKline Beecham, Siemens, and Astra Pharmaceuticals. Not a bad array of friends, especially for a young university born in the early 1960s.

In 1998, four additional developing structures indicate a steadily strengthening infrastructure. The university opened 'the first on-line broadcast quality television and radio studio in a UK University'. During its first year Warwick staff and some external organizations produced over 400 radio and TV broadcasts. Directed by a Warwick graduate who had been Controller of BBC1 Television, the studio was tied in to British Telecom's national network. Here was a major step up the ladder of national influence: Warwick's academics could now more easily reach intellectual elites and general publics, at home and abroad.[12]

Second, the university now pushed hard in the field of medicine to open up a special kind of medical school. It had submitted, with the nearby University of Leicester, a joint bid to national funding sources. Expanded activities in the biological sciences department and the new medical research centre fueled this growing ambition.

Third, the university took note that graduate students ('postgraduates' in

British terminology) had grown to be more than 40 per cent of the student body. Warwick was the first university in the UK to install an American style university-wide graduate school in the early 1990s, and then took the leadership among other universities seeking to do the same in a new association formed a few years later. A decade of augmenting parts of a graduate school had given the university an edge in advanced higher education; organized and monitored masters' and doctoral programs across many academic fields proved to be advantageous for research-based teaching and learning, reputation and income. A 40 per cent graduate level is high: much higher than found typically in continental European universities which were still trying to figure out how to organize one; higher than American flagship public universities with their large undergraduate enrollments; and approaching the 50 per cent and more graduate share found in such American leading private universities as Yale, Chicago, and Stanford.[13] As in the USA, British universities talk endlessly in public about the centrality of the undergraduate realm, but all along the graduate school, so congenial for science and research, professional training, and new income sources, becomes the growing silent success. Again, Warwick was in the vanguard.

Fourth, the Alumni and Development Office had by 1998 experienced its first full year of operations: it clearly was not going to fold or fade away. Some 64,000 graduates had been identified who could be approached, possibly turned into alumni who might offer moral and financial support. The office was now asking former students 'to give regular support to the Warwick Alumni Fund'. The effort was 'the start of a long-term, indeed permanent, programme to finance the continuing development of the University'. Alumni were now viewed as a key asset: 'this extended family of graduates is perhaps the single most important long-term asset of the University and is a vital source of support, in both financial and non-financial terms'. Donors had already passed the 1,000 mark and the office was already looking forward to leveraging its work by developing a powerful alumni base of support from which it could approach major donors.[14] Again, an increment here and an increment there can in time add up to real money.

The university's steadily accumulating advantages gained by its two-decade-old commitment to entrepreneurial action continued in 1999.[15] In a striking formulation, the vice-chancellor portrayed the 'core business' of the university to be a combination of 'delivering excellent research and teaching' and '*continuing to generate significant resources ourselves in order to build for the future*' (emphasis added). Self-reliantly, Warwick would more than ever focus on supporting itself. The state cannot be relied upon: its interests and mandates are too diverse; its support, calculated by student head, had dropped 50 per cent in two decades.

The Leicester-Warwick proposal has been approved for funding and a new Medical School would be up and running in 2000. It would focus on a 'four-year accelerated medical degree for Biological Sciences graduates', that is, a graduate-level program in a country where medical training normally begins in the undergraduate years. This is 'a key milestone for Warwick', a leg-up in the biomedical complex of subjects: 'We need medicine in order to develop our biosciences research.'[16] It would help to meet regional needs in medicine: it would hook up with the National Health Service.

The alumni effort was steadily gathering momentum. Organized groups of graduates had been established in over twenty countries, and 'networking events' were held in London. The Graduates' Association established its own endowment fund; proceeds were used to help support student scholarships. As a starter, aid was being given to twenty-five students suffering financial hardship, thereby broadening access.

Income from state core support had now dropped to 27.4 per cent of total income. The contribution of earned income was now 63 per cent, virtually two-thirds; another 10 per cent or so came from fees of domestic students.

As a special note, Michael Shattock was retiring after thirty years of service, seventeen of them as Registrar. Shattock played a central role for almost two decades. He initially conceived and then implemented the Earned-Income Policy each year. He had built a staff of central administrators known for their effectiveness. Along the way he edited journals and published basic books on British higher education. Since 1982, he had jointly led a Warwick-Oxford course for training overseas university managers. Young administrators who worked with him at Warwick had taken positions in many British universities, including Birmingham, Leeds, Coventry, Exeter, Durham, Essex, and Oxford.[17] Shattock was succeeded by Jonathan Nicholls, who, after a PhD in medieval literature at Cambridge and a postdoctoral year at Harvard, moved into the Warwick administration some years earlier as an assistant registrar. Uncommon recruitment, to say the least.

When the millennium rolled around, Warwick was in a celebratory mood. Its 2000 annual report was optimistic, forward-looking, and colorfully presented.[18] The medical school was indeed now up and running, with its first small cadre of students; the university's entering undergraduate students exhibited very high A level scores; the alumni scholarship scheme had made its first awards to 'less privileged students'; the university had established an office in London, 'at the heart of Westminster', to give it and its academics 'a stronger voice in political affairs'. Income kept coming and was increasing at 10 per cent a year. A handful of new subject border-crossing institutes had been initiated, which included an applied cognitive science group and an eighteenth-century center. A new international tie seemed promising; Carnegie Mellon, an outstanding US university known for efficient, progressive management, was to develop with Warwick a joint business management center specializing in electronic commerce. Private sponsors, primarily American firms, would fund this project and it would be based at Warwick. The aim was high; 7,000 middle managers, half from overseas, trained each year to understand the potential of the internet.[19]

The wheel of fortune landed at Warwick when Tony Blair and William Jefferson Clinton came to town in December 2000. No doubt they came for political and personal reasons but they certainly honored Warwick. The university had to muster all its reputed efficiency to make this visit of notables physically possible. In just eight days the staff had to set up a White House Press Centre and four press rooms; find accommodations for 300 security personnel and 250 reporters; install four miles of cabling; and organize on-campus landing space for seven helicopters. According to university sources, more than one billion people worldwide watched the Blair-Clinton occasion on television. What messages came across? On this December day, Blair offered the highest praise for the university for being no less than 'a beacon among British universities for its dynamism, quality and entrepreneurial zeal'. Margaret Thatcher, when she was Prime Minister, had also praised Warwick as an extremely progressive UK university, the kind the country badly needed. But her praise was hardly a blessing among British dons and the chattering classes – and she did not happen to bring Ronald Reagan along. Clinton, on a visit to the UK, chose Warwick as the venue for the last policy statement of his presidency. He gave a 'historic speech on globaliza-tion' that stressed opportunities 'to create a new development agenda for the 21st century'. Clinton's choice of Warwick was 'surely a landmark moment in the history of a young university'. His visit was seen as confirming that 'with its cosmopolitan campus, international alumni base and reputation for first rate research, Warwick is set to become a world class university'.[20]

It is hard to imagine more satisfying blessings, intended and unintended, by major international figures than what Warwick received during the last month of the last year of the twentieth century.

The university's annual report for 2000 totally avoided a gray recital of routine pronouncements and institutional data. Beautifully done in soft full color, its full-page photographs did much of the talking. Here we can see Blair and Clinton, and groups of students signifying 'a global presence' and 'widening participation', pictures celebrating the university's regional role and the development of leaders for the future. And in pictorial form news of another new substantial venture – IBM was setting down at Warwick a super-computer to underpin a 'grid' for use by academics throughout Europe. Warwick announced that it was 'eagerly seizing the existing opportunities offered by new technology to transform the face of teaching and learning, research and commerce in the 21st century. Our developing e-strategy is designed to exploit the power of the internet and to change radically the way we operate and communicate as a University . . .'

Here was 'a new vision for the University in the technology century' – and also a new way of generating income – 'to use the internet to improve research, to compete more effectively in the commercial world, and to improve teaching and learning for campus-based students, distance and life-long learners, and those in professional development courses.'[21] Given this mentality, the internet 'problem' that worries so many universities would be treated as an ongoing series of opportunities: 'flexible, innovative, and ener-getic, Warwick is well placed to embrace and prosper from the internet revolution'. Institutional exuberance clearly characterized the mood at Warwick in 2000.

Conclusion

The five elements of transformation I had isolated and highlighted in *Creating Entrepreneurial Universities* became 'just that by means of their inter-action'. For transformation to take place, a plurality of altered elements must interact and support one another; this process would lead to a circle of enhancing effects. The interaction takes place incrementally over years rather than a one-time large surge. Interlinked elements and incremental flow of change became the bases of how some universities had gone about transforming themselves. I made a strong case for transformation, yes. But could the changes be sustained? Could revised university character be made to stick? As a leading case, Warwick provides illuminating answers.

Consider the details of how Warwick rolled forward during the last half of the 1990s to embed its transformation in a stabilizing set of interests. Disposable income generated from non-government support went on growing at a dependable rate, making the university a richer place than it otherwise would have been. There was no interest anywhere on campus for reversing this trend. Heartland departments, strong at Warwick, protected and developed themselves by guarding and seeking to enlarge their own economic base. The incentive to generate income led them toward one additional form of service after another; disposable returns from these activities could be used to support students, especially graduate students, and to strengthen their own faculty ranks. Central groups at the top of the steering core also had acquired legitimate power to cross-subsidize from those parts of the infrastructure positioned to bring in resources to those who had less capacity but which should be maintained in full health.

The university continued to generated new interdisciplinary centers. The powerful reach of the Manufacturing Group and the Business School built on itself. Minor items in the earned income portfolio, as in the case of Retail Services, turned up their surpluses, year by year. Any that did not, and ought, were candidates for elimination or reconstitution. The institutional sponsorship of periodic eye-catching large initiatives continued. The setting up of a comprehensive graduate school and the research fellowship addition of faculty in the first half of the 1990s were followed in the second half by the new distinctive medical school, an allied thrust in the biosciences, and the impressive and enthusiastic embrace of computerization and electronic networking. Warwick also learned quickly how to turn graduates into alumni, a group that could become a major long-term asset, morally as well as financially. And the value of more international ties, and more non-elite programs for the local region, was not underestimated. All this in a mid-size university of about 16,000 students, with heritage only four decades deep.

The proven sustainability of an entrepreneurial university culture, as revealed by Warwick, is the way that the new infrastructure served both as a maintenance and a change mechanism. A forward thrust was built into maintenance. In dynamic rather than structural terms, what became linked and interactive were forward-propelling dynamics. Successful universities can create such dynamics as well as successful business firms – a light-year better than unsuccessful firms who are here today and gone tomorrow. Naturally, universities must propel themselves forward in ways appropriate for their own societal sector and amidst their own growing complexity; they are expected to have staying power across long periods of time. Warwick serves well as a prototype of how such adaptable stability can be created in modern proactive universities.

   Warwick as an empirical model also teaches that the difference between 'traditional' and 'entrepreneurial' universities is finally not a sharp break; it is a spectrum. Entrepreneurial universities that center themselves on academic virtues can be highly effective on traditional grounds. They are hybrids; by being entrepreneurial, they do crucial traditional things better. Why do status-quo-oriented traditionalists insist on misunderstanding the value of this productive combination?

As we move onward to other universities that are very different from Warwick in educational character and societal setting, we can pursue several questions about the problems of self-determination. Do other entrepreneurially-inclined universities similarly seek to become more self-reliant by building a capacity, as put at Warwick, 'to generate significant resources ourselves in order to build for the future'? Are they also much taken with the possibilities of becoming a university that can itself decide what routes to take to effective performance in research, teaching, and student learning amidst the high uncertainties of a fast-moving world? As they seek to change, do they encounter particular problems of balancing multiple commitments? Are they able simultaneously to be effective as a regional university, a national university, and an international university? Case by case, we can search for features that elaborate a formula of sustainable change.

2

Strathclyde: sustaining change in a place of useful learning

The University of Strathclyde in Glasgow, Scotland was fully committed in the mid-1990s to an integrating conception of itself as 'a place of useful learning'. From the day it opened as a small mechanics' institute in 1796, a simple place for plain folk unlike the already ancient University of Glasgow where professors and students toted their togas; to a slowly evolving technical college anointed a Royal College in 1912, when George V noticed that Strathclyde-trained engineers were constructing the physical infrastructure of his empire in India; to the blessings of university status in the 1960s bestowed on this rocky, hillside campus surrounded by an industrial city at the time the national government was also opening up Warwick and six other institutions – the Seven Sisters – by raising them up in green fields; to the entrepreneurial transformation of the 1980s and early 1990s described in my earlier book, the useful learning ethos served as an institutional idea that linked the past and the present and projected well into the future.

As heritage, the concept was true not only to what the institution had been but, embellished in accounts of trials and triumphs, it also became the shorthand formulation of an organizational saga: 'we' had to travel a hard road – as a technological college-cum-university in an Oxford–Cambridge besotted national system, but through determination and struggle we conquered the obstacles put in our way and have become a uniquely valuable Scottish institution. The same idea provided ideological cover for a wide range of entrepreneurial activities in the 1990s. These included expanded facilities for R&D outreach, major investment in drug research infrastructure, and the growth of a self-financing graduate business school. Further, this useful learning concept spoke directly to the desires of British government and industry – and after UK devolution in 1998, to urgings of the new Scottish Parliament and Scottish Executive – that universities ought to strongly promote regional and national economic progress, and be quick about it. Strathclyde was entitled to claim that it was already doing the job in teaching and research and the appropriate infrastructure and outlook were in place. In 1999, the year the new devolved Parliament took office,

Strathclyde reminded all parties that it 'has seen its work as pivotal in the creation of a prosperous and thriving Scotland' for many years. Now, 'the new constitutional environment has given a fresh impetus to Strathclyde's historical tradition as a "place of useful learning" '. This will 'enable the University to maximize its potential as a driving force behind the creation of a new economic development agenda for Scotland'.[1]

But building an appropriate proactive style toward the end of the twentieth century had not been easy, especially strengthening the steering core. It took the better part of five years beginning about 1982 to work out through contentious trial and error the centerpiece of an entrepreneurial Strathclyde – a formal body known as the University Management Group (UMG). After 1987, UMG provided a relatively clear model for many years of a central body organized to move quickly on basic all-university matters, especially to make strategic decisions most likely to shape long-term viability. For good reason the OECD organizers of the 2000 Paris conference asked Strathclyde's head to speak about a strengthened steering core, as they had done when they invited the Warwick vice-chancellor to do so on diversification of income.

Sir John Arbuthnott, the university's vice-chancellor, also known as principal, set out immediately to highlight and explain the UMG. His account bears close reading: understanding organizational change in universities does indeed lie in the details of accomplishment, especially amid academic sensitivities about who governs:[2]

> The 'strengthened steering core' is essentially demonstrated through the operations of the University Management Group, as the key group through which all major decisions can be quickly progressed. Like most major UK universities, Strathclyde has a Senate, which is responsible for all academic matters within the university and a Court or Governing Body, which is responsible for the management of the university's resources. The University Management Group (UMG), which was established in 1987, is the key management body that undertakes the formulation of major policy and oversees the operational management of the university on behalf of Court and Senate.

The composition of UMG is basic:

> The UMG is chaired by the Principal and has a statutory membership of 10 comprising, in addition to the Principal, the Vice-Principal, the Pro-Vice Principal, a Deputy Principal, the Secretary to the University and the *five Deans of Faculty* [emphasis added]. Other senior members of the university, including from the Lay Governing Body and Students' Association also attend. The Group meets fortnightly and works to a tight, fully prepared agenda. It has its own Secretariat to prepare the business for its discussion. Decisions taken by UMG are reported to Senate and Court on a regular basis.

Sir John then highlighted how the UMG worked to integrate a university that otherwise was highly decentralized; it pulled parts together by asserting broad interests over segmental ones and had those who implement policy share in its formation:

> A significant aspect of the Strathclyde system is that the university oper-ates a devolved financial management system whereby resources are allocated to all the Faculties, the Central administration and the Library. . . . Thereafter the Line Managers for these areas – i.e. the Dean of each Faculty, the University Secretary, etc. – are fully responsible for allocation within their own management area. Membership of the UMG comprises all these budget-holders so that agreement on major policy decisions can be reached by those ultimately responsible for their implementation. UMG therefore faces the challenge of determining overall institutional strategy and policy while at the same time squaring the circle of overall institutional interests with the interests of each of the major constituencies represented on the group. While each budget-holder may defend their area, they are obliged to work towards the evolution of *a corporate view for the university as a whole* . . . [emphasis added].

This central piece of the university's machinery, firmly institutionalized and with a high degree of transparency, worked reasonably well throughout most of the 1990s:

> It is generally accepted within the university that this *modus operandi* for progressing the business of the university has served Strathclyde well for a number of years. The frequency of meetings and preparation of high quality documentation with options analysis enables key strategic decisions and major decisions on deployment of resources to be made quickly in a manner that is open and transparent. Reports of UMG discussion and decisions are disseminated throughout the university.

Most of all, the machinery forged in the university's entrepreneurial evolution is both collegial and businesslike:

> The Strathclyde UMG combines a mixture of elected academic man-agers alongside appointed managers. The Deans of Faculty, as well as the Vice-Principal and Pro-Vice Principal hold posts by election from the academic community. They work alongside those posts that are appointed, and therefore executive, such as the Principal and the Secretary of the University as well as the senior members of the Govern-ing body and the elected student representative.

University governance structure must be a compromise, particularly in its central bodies:

> The composition and operation of UMG is essentially a working com-promise between traditional collegiate university management and a fully blown business model of executive management. The traditional mode of university management – which Strathclyde operated prior to

1987 – tends to the proliferation of academic committees and depends on widespread and lengthy consultation and consensus to be reached before decisions can be taken. It also leads to a lack of clear direction for the university as a whole. However, a full business model of top-down executive management is not necessarily desirable or workable in a university, where there is an imperative to preserve both academic autonomy and freedom and where the academic community should be the driver of developments and new ideas . . .

This compromise has enabled the university to make substantial progress in adapting to the demands of financial constraints as well as to not only respond but be proactive in developments of value to the university. *UMG strongly steers the university but avoids top-down hierarchical management* [emphasis added].

This central component of the university's strengthened steering core was firmly in place in 2000, despite the university having grown to the large size of 3,500 staff to handle 26,000 students studying for university degrees and another 36,000 in part-time continuing education. When working well, the UMG mechanism minimizes the faculty–administration schism that plagues universities around the world. Elected academics are clearly placed at the center of action. The UMG is also a sturdy bit of infrastructure for promoting encompassing interests: more individuals and groups become committed to and are made responsible for the entire university – much like the interests attached to a whole nation over those of constituent states. It promotes an all-university identity – out of many, one – because it serves to create and strengthen such interests. No wonder the university was still as proud of its 'distinctive' management group in 2000 as it had been in the early and mid-1990s. It had become a mechanism that both enabled change and enacted it.

But Strathclyde's central management group, after almost fifteen years, had not proved in one lasting form a final answer to the age-old university problem of tension between central direction and devolved control. Arbuthnott pointed out in Paris that maintaining the impetus of the whole was limited in part by the simple fact that 'a number of UMG members are elected and at the end of their term of office must return to their academic areas'. When these elected faculty are serving at the center they must be ever mindful that they will return to the ranks of their home constituency. The constraints of election are ever present. According to the Vice-Chancellor, the devolved management structure that the university had in place meant 'limitations on the financial resource available to UMG for strategic overall developments'. The central group was squeezed between the steady decline in the state share of university income, in which some discretionary monies might be found, and the claims of the internal five faculties and their many departments that what monies they brought in from any and all sources fully belonged to them. Any skimming-off-the-top by the central body would have to be highly limited. Strong high-resource faculties and departments do not go gently into subsidization of weaker, low-resource segments and all-university initiatives.

The presence of elected deans and other elected faculty in the central body is likely to continue, since, as I pointed out in my earlier volume, 'central faculty involvement became a crucial step in avoiding what the academic staff would otherwise see as hard managerialism, too much top-down command'.[3] At the same time, devolved authority in the hands of deans and their faculties, highly useful in generating initiative in the many separate 'businesses' of a complex university, can steadily draw authority from the center. Thus, even a very successful Strathclyde UMG can need attention on 'restoring' the balance. With a new Principal (Andrew Hamnett) on board in 2000, the university's Strategic Plan 2001–2005, surprisingly listed 'limited central steer' first among institutional weaknesses and noted that 'the devolved Faculty structure functions well and has real benefits, but there are times when a stronger central steer is needed'.[4] The solution? Add on to the deeply institutionalized UMG a new Principal's Strategic Management Group, a more focused body for evaluating competing priorities. The new group 'is now being created to guide UMG, Senate and Court on strategic priorities. The Group will be convened by the Principal and will include the Vice-Principal, the Pro Vice-Principal and the University Secretary' – just four people, without faculty deans. The balancing act continues: now a more central executive bit of infrastructure guides the UMG itself.

As we shall see in sharper form in two cases that follow, entrepreneurial actions stir up the old status quo of compromises long worked out in the authority structure, between top, middle and bottom, essentially between the center personified as president or rector and the sub-faculties and operating units, personified as dean, department head and research center director. In the course of transformation, new academic units are introduced, new administrative offices appear, and new counterbalances have to be worked out under pressure to be more adaptive. Perfection is not attainable in an ongoing process: adjusting actions readily undershoot and overshoot any ideal state. And where the many actors stand, on what is the ideal authority structure, depends considerably on where they sit. A tugging back and forth ensues not only from perceptions of self-interest but from responsible effort to do effective work. The responsibility of department heads after all is to maximize the effectiveness of their particular units. Hence, the problem of balance on the vertical line of authority is never finally solved. It is simply handled well or poorly, from one decade to the next. Strathclyde in 2000 was still on the plus side of the ledger of balance, compared to more inert traditional universities that had little or no capacity to change. It was both willing and able to seek new ways to have it both ways – strong central steering together with devolved initiative.

How did transforming elements – the very foundation of sustainability – connect with each other during the last half of the 1990s? We will see that both the useful-learning outlook and the strengthened steering core interacted closely with changes in the university's developmental periphery and its heartland departments. The basic commitment to useful learning (and its close counterpart, 'relevant research') significantly drove departments toward actions that extended across traditional university boundaries; in return, new non-departmental operations that began on the periphery have moved easily toward heartland status, fusing heartland and periphery to an uncommon degree.

Three thrusts forged in the years immediately before 2000 highlighted the blending of heartland and periphery so desirable in universities because it abates conflict between new tendencies and old departments.

The infrastructure for drug research

By the mid-1990s Strathclyde had developed over 20 research institutes that went beyond interdisciplinarity. They were outward-oriented units that accepted 'a market-pull component' in their research planning. We may see these institutes as an experimental effort to work out the steady-state requirements of such market-oriented groups. The Strathclyde Institute for Drug Research (SIDR), underway since 1988 within the Faculty of Science, was a particularly successful instance. It was staffed by faculty and researchers drawn from five departments. Working with partner suppliers in developing countries, the institute was successful in extracting useful pharmaceutical products from natural plant materials accumulated in a 'library of plants', as well as in producing chemically synthesized compounds. The institute worked closely with the university's Research & Consultancy Service, a highly competent, professionalized administrative office that knew how to work out 'selling agreements' with pharmaceutical and biotechnical firms in, for instance, Japan and the USA. This 'long-term line of research development was one on which some central figures at the university felt it "could hang its hat" '.[5]

By 1998 the university was ready to declare that 'exploratory drug delivery – designing more effective ways of delivering drugs to treat diseases – was big business at Strathclyde'. Adding greatly to the efforts of the first institute, a second larger Institute for Biomedical Sciences was now up and running in a long-planned new building that brought together three science departments and some '200 active researchers, with a depth and range of skills unique among British universities. *There was no direct government funding for the £14M building* [emphasis added]. Instead, the university "ploughed back royalties from a number of successful drug patents – notably from Atracurium – sold off existing property and took out commercial loans." ' It also helped greatly that 'the University was able to capitalise on its reputation and expertise to raise substantial sums from partners in the pharmaceutical industry and charitable foundations'. One friendly foundation had backed the scheme as early as 1992, 'giving the University's Management Group the confidence to proceed'.[6]

'Successful discoveries with commercial potential' that flow from this second, massive investment will be 'marketed to the pharmaceutical industry' through the well-established protocols of the first institute already experienced in such difficult, chancy business affairs. The definition of 'drug research' had been expanded by 2000 to 'healthcare, drug discovery and the development of medicines – activities which have always been at the forefront of the University's success'.[7] With an applied-research focus appropriate for early decades in the twenty-first century, Strathclyde was even willing to tout its 'commercialization', rather than subscribe to ideas common among academics that commerce can only bring trouble to universities. Its 1997 and 1999 annual reports were largely given over to two topics: 'commercialization' and 'research that makes things happen'.

Department-linked incorporated spin-offs

A second major new step was underway in building steady-state infrastructure oriented toward change. Seeking sturdy ways to transfer technology from the university to industry 'via companies that have emerged from research at Strathclyde', the university had given birth to companies that could serve as dedicated arms of particular departments. Examples were: a Diagnostic Monitoring Systems Ltd (DMS), 'a company set up to commercialise the research output from the Centre for Electrical Power Engineering'; a Microlase Optical Systems Ltd, based on the work of the Department of Physics and Applied Physics; and an Integrated Environmental Solutions Ltd, based on the Department of Architecture and Building Science. Added to these were new incorporations drawing upon drug research. With their own spin-off firms at hand, departments were encouraged to become development minded, oriented to outside problems in a way that would make them both disciplinary and transdisciplinary. DMS, for example, was busy developing 'monitoring equipment for electricity substations' to export to Europe, North and South America and the Far East, equipment that 'helps to prevent random shutdowns of the grid systems which cost the electricity industry millions of pounds per year'.[8]

These spin-offs were clearly located on the developmental periphery. In no sense were they heartland departments. But they were closely interlocked with the departments. They were trial steps exploring new possibilities, department by department, and could easily be discontinued or left to fade away. Some may amount to little and not even pay for their upkeep. But some may prove significantly beneficial for the university, industry and society.

Since the early 1990s the university had committed itself to ever more vigorous efforts to find ways to close the gap between industry and universities – the technology gap, the development gap, the gap in knowledge transfer between those who produce it in universities and those who might pick it up and put it to practical use in business, government and professional life. The Strathclyde aim was high: usefulness of the highest possible order, harnessing university knowledge 'to the business of wealth creation' for society. The latest experiment underway at the end of the decade was simplicity itself. Strathclyde did not wait for industry to come seeking new ideas; it did not labor to bring university and industry together in some massive way to jointly create an independent buffer organization linking the two. Rather, it went ahead and filled the gap incrementally with specific outreach units whereby those who produced the knowledge might guide it down the development line to commercial use. The university would maintain control across the gap. And if profit were to be made, the university would be in on it, from the ground floor and in a major way.

'Closing the technology gap' was a particular concern of the university's office of Research and Consultancy Service. Started in 1984 with just one new professional officer, a highly competent staff expanded to a dozen members by the mid-1990s – and to more than twenty by 2000. They systematically handled a portfolio of patents, industrial contracts, research marketing, and the formation of new institutes and companies, including an incubator unit and connections to a nearby science park. This office, led effectively from the beginning by Hugh Thomson, was unlike a contracts-and-grants office that routinely processed a flow of papers. Highly proactive from the beginning, and still so in 2000, it is a clear and illuminating case of a cohort of non-faculty professionals actively interacting with faculty groups as part of a joint capacity to systematically do new things. Its much valued, embedded role at Strathclyde helped point my thinking to what could be called 'the bureaucracy of change', even 'the steady state of change' – conceptions I develop in Chapter 6.

Continuing professional education

A third expanding step in the building of the university's entrepreneurial infrastructure, more strongly evident in the late 1990s than before, was growth in continuing professional education and lifelong learning. Impetus in this direction in both heartland departments and newer boundary-spanning units stemmed from a combination of the university's identity as a place of useful learning, growing curricular demands from individuals, business firms and government, and the much-welcomed income thereby gained. Such expansion in students and courses was now a strategic priority in 1999:[9]

> The Government is promoting the concept of a learning society, in which people are encouraged to study at all stages of their lives. Strathclyde is a lifelong learning university: our portfolio ranges from training primary school teachers to running a Senior Studies Institute for the over 50s. The range of postgraduate and professional programmes is unrivaled in Scotland, while our Centre for Lifelong Learning provides a growing programme of continuing personal education . . . In the last two years alone, Strathclyde's income from programmes of

Continuing Professional Development has risen over 15% as individuals and employers increasingly look to upskill in mid-career.

Among registered students in 1999, continuing education enrollment exceeded 36,000, compared to an undergraduate count of approximately 14,500 and a total for several types of graduate students of about 11,000. The continuing education students were concentrated heavily in the Faculties of Education (over 16,000) and Science (over 10,000).

Beyond these three large steps in building department-periphery infrastructure, other major efforts operating on an all-university basis were also developing in the late 1990s. One was a turn to inter-university partnerships; the second, a turn to alumni.

The search for institutional partners

Since 1998, the university became quite mindful of the advantages of partnerships, particularly with other universities. Cooperation was sought that would enable partners together and individually to compete better. A new primary effort centered on linking Strathclyde and the University of Glasgow. The two universities, located in the same city, had not exactly been great friends in the past. When Strathclyde was a small private mechanics' institute its founder had even specified in his will that no one, but no one, associated with that other place should ever be given a job at his institution. However tiny, his shop proudly would escape the academic stuffiness of an ancient university. Such personal wishes naturally became less controlling as decades slid by. But the more Strathclyde grew in size and complexity, especially in the last half of the twentieth century, the more it became competitive in general funding and in specific fields of study with Scotland's second oldest university, a hallowed institution that had persisted beyond its 550th anniversary by 2000. The University of Glasgow had 'some 19,000 students in the full range of Faculties, including Theology, Medicine and Veterinary Medicine'. The would-be partnership would have to be worked out between two 'dissimilar Universities, with a long history of antagonism'.[10]

The new partnership, known as 'Synergy', was formally agreed in 1998. Pushed from both sides, in two to three years the alliance could claim: joint research centers, Biophotonics and Scottish Studies; four joint graduate programs in such disparate fields as law and creative writing; some unification of departments, as Naval Architecture with Marine Technology; a joint 'e-systems' institute, 'to engage with the full range of opportunities, from e-commerce to e system developments, arising from the Information Revolution'; and, notably, increased income 'that would not have been won by the two Universities acting alone'. These funds stemmed from new joint research grants and from state sources dedicated to 'university challenges' and 'enterprise' development. Peter West, Strathclyde's Secretary (Registrar), in a 2001 speech to European deans concluded: 'Synergy has not involved any sacrifice of institutional autonomy but has given us a distinct competitive advantage'.[11]

Beyond the major Synergy alliance with the powerful University of Glasgow, Strathclyde had gone on to develop partnerships with other universities: for example, in Scotland, Glasgow Caledonian, a local former polytechnic, one of the new wave of institutions allowed to assume a university designation in the early 1990s, in such fields as Industrial Mathematics and Journalism Studies: and Heriot-Watt, a 1960s university near Edinburgh that Strathclydians had long lauded, in 'two areas where the universities have complementary strengths, Biological Sciences and Psychology'; and, in Germany, with the University of Dortmund.[12] The autonomy and identity of each institution entering into these alliances would be kept.

These inter-university alliances were very different from the total merger that Strathclyde had embarked upon in the early 1990s when it absorbed Jordanhill, the largest teacher-training institution in the UK, and, on a second major campus, turned it into a fifth faculty. Although voluntary from both sides, the merger was destined to become a continuing problem, one that many universities in the UK – and elsewhere around the world – would simply not had take on. State-funded teacher education, a separate messy matter at best in Britain, continued to be severely constrained and bureaucracy ridden. Jordanhill had been funded by the Scottish Office Education Department responsible for elementary and secondary education, a bureaucracy inclined to exercise considerable control over the college, particularly in setting the intake numbers for pre-service teacher education (Jordanhill also offered such areas as social work and community education, as well as in-service teacher education).

Long having concentrated on professional training, but little emphasizing research – and research done on the soggy domain 'education' at that – the new faculty in its entirety was soon having problems achieving a satisfactory level of assessed research quality. It received only a '3b rating' in the national 1996 research assessment exercise (RAE) – 'a major disappointment' that 'has further weakened the financial position of the Education Faculty'. Further in-house review was underway in the late 1990s to find 'a new research strategy for the Faculty and on strengthening inter-Faculty links' – that is, to somehow better connect this faculty to the other four faculties in an uplifting fashion.[13]

Absorbing Jordanhill into a research university framework, British style, was estimated to take a decade of hard adjustment. In 2000 it remained a tough ongoing problem – the education faculty received a 4-level rating on a very limited number of staff in the 2001 RAE – one made inescapable by the insistence of the British government, through funding councils, to assign simple numbers – 2, 3, 4, 5 – in the evaluation of whole departments, even very large ones, within some 69 subject areas, with heavy consequences for core funding of research. In such a gross cockamamie system, with 2s and 3s and then eventually 4s and even higher scores serving as punishments, vicious circles of effects, intended or not, anticipated or not, are generated all over the higher education landscape, especially for essential activities such as teacher training that simply cannot be discontinued. Other universities may drop sociology or classics, for example, when those fields are weakly staffed or too much out of fashion. Or, unbelievably, even close down the physics department.[14] But Strathclyde had to steadily, continually provide schoolteachers, while the education faculty struggled to enhance their research reputation. Such are local effects of one-size-fits-all national policies, operationalized in simple quantitative indicators.

Alliances, yes; mergers, no. Strathclyde had found out the hard way. In university mergers, even more than in the business world or among public agencies, the problems of incompatible cultures and opposing priorities can be, if not devastating, difficult for all. In the Strathclyde case, the purpose of research enhancement in the education faculty counters the purpose of practical professional training. Who will pay the bill for staffing up to do both things well? Not a government that year-in and year-out goes on insisting on 'efficiency gains', that is, more work for less money.

The turn to alumni

A second highly significant all-university effort in the late 1990s was a reinvigorated turn to alumni building, sparked by one alumnus with newly-earned financial means when he donated a 'magnificent' sum of £5 million 'to create a world-class centre for entrepreneurship'. This new Hunter Centre was created to make an education in entrepreneurship accessible to all students, starting with undergraduates, and including alumni. With three strands of education, research and practice, the center was intended also as another catalyst for successful business start-ups.

Here was a striking model of what Strathclyde alumni could do with their money, once they grasped that a worthwhile cause was helping the young by supporting one's own university. The university had just completed a mildly successful Campaign 2000, started early in the 1990s, and now wanted to aim higher in generating gift income, with alumni as main source. A new Director of Development, fresh from successful work in such matters at St Hilda's College, Oxford, was hired. Quick off the mark she and her team had been meeting with alumni and reported that their support was highly encouraging. Mr Hunter gave a further £200,000 for a summer academy; at least five other alumni or friends had made contributions in the £100–250,000 range, and the general alumni fund was expanding considerably.[15] Individual donors who had given sizeable sums during the year were listed in annual reports: 125 in 1997 had become 700 two years later.

Strathclyde was learning fast by year 2000 what other UK universities were learning at a rapid rate: you can turn graduates into alumni whose combined year-by-year contribution becomes an important source of income flexibility. Whatever its relative size, this source can become dependable, even as governmental core support turns soft.

All the above programs implemented from 1996 to 2000 interconnect clearly with diversification of income. Strathclyde had reduced its dependence on governmental core support during the two decades of 1975 to 1995 from 80 to 45 per cent. Monies from governmental research councils totaled only another 4 per cent of income in the latter year, swamped by the great increase in the third, non-government stream to over 50 per cent. In the late 1990s these shares remained relatively constant: core state support hovered around 45 per cent and third-stream income slightly over one-half. Total income had also remained relatively constant; it grew only from approximately £140 million in 1995 to £143 million in 1999, after three hard years on the income side between 1996 and 1998. The university's Strategic Plan 2001–2005 stressed that 'resource constraints' had to be overcome: 'With the prospect of further reduction in public funding, the University must exploit new opportunities for income generation if it is to be more successful . . . The university simply had to develop more growth in non-Government income.' Such sources as 'continuing professional development, international programmes and endowments' may have been in the past 'useful supplements to "core" grant and tuition fee income'. But, over the next decade, 'they are likely to become essential elements'.[16]

Continuing professional development (CPD) was already a Strathclyde thing – 'Scotland's largest supplier of CPD courses, generating over a quarter of all CPD income' in Scottish higher education institutions. Now the aim was to raise that by 25 per cent. Similarly for international programs, with 'a steady flow of Overseas students to the University at both undergraduate and postgraduate level' and niche programs well mounted abroad, income here should be raised by 5 per cent per annum. The same was true for alumni giving: following upon the Tom Hunter gift, which 'was the largest endowment [gift] ever made to a Scottish university', a new development campaign would depend on 'the cultivation of strong links with our alumni'. Similarly for income from research grants: the university felt it had to deepen its research culture to 'raise income from research grants and contracts to over £30m by 2004–05', from a base of £22 million, increasing by 10 per cent per annum.[17]

The problem for Strathclyde at the beginning of the twenty-first century was overall income growth; how to obtain additional monies year by year from other than core state allocations. Income sources that had been 'useful supplements' were now becoming 'essential elements' of the university's financial foundation. A great deal was riding on the university's capacity to raise funds from non-core sources to the point where total income would steadily increase.

State support still remained crucial, however. That support came from a powerful body, the Scottish Higher Education Funding Council (SHEFC) which 'has a fundamental influence on the shape of higher education in Scotland'. Scottish universities, stressed David Newall, Strathclyde's Director of Planning, certainly enjoy greater powers than their counterparts on mainland Europe. But, without exception, the universities are crucially dependent on Government funding. 'In practice their autonomy is constrained by whatever conditions the Funding Council may attach to their grant.'[18] Strathclyde, then, was one-half state dependent and subject to being state-led – although the new director of the funding council, in 2002, stressed 'a light touch' and greater 'trust' in the capacity of the universities to sensibly steer themselves. 'Quality enhancement' was to replace 'the traditional watchdog approach to "quality assurance" '.[19]

It was from the condition of dependency and watchdog supervision that the university was attempting to evolve by making greater use of its self-controlled 'essential elements'. Its more entrepreneurial activities were designed to make that shift. State-led or self-steered? Something of each, to be sure. But ambition and will at the university encouraged the latter.

Conclusion

Transforming elements had clearly become sustaining elements at Strathclyde, as at Warwick. Close interaction among a strengthened steering core, an expanded periphery, more enterprising heartland departments, an ever stronger wrap-around institutional belief system, and a diversified income stream locked change into the institution. It is no longer an oxymoron to speak of a steady state of change. An adapted infrastructure can become a foundation that urges further proactivity.

The Strathclyde story particularly highlights the crucial importance of understanding the entrepreneurial university as a compromise between the flatter collegial controls of the traditional university and the more hierarchical controls of a managerial model that accentuates personal authority based in such key positions as rector or vice-chancellor or president at the center, and dean and department head at the middle and lower levels. The more businesslike model also emphasizes professionalization of administration. Here at Strathclyde, a half-dozen or more highly capable central administrators serve under a lead administrator, the University Secretary. The professional staff of the office of research and consultancy service had become a collective exemplar of administrators promoting change in their daily activity.

But 'entrepreneurial' definitely does not mean full adoption of the managerial approach. Sustainable entrepreneurialism in universities comes coated with collegial forms of authority, not least in British universities where academics traditionally ran their own institutions via senate control and devoted much time to committee-based administration and to elected, not appointed, personal positions. In American parlance, the new compromise becomes a form of 'shared governance'. The understanding that those who do the work of policy implementation participate in policy formation is also a basic strength of what we can call collegial entrepreneurialism, especially as compared to entrepreneurial action in business and public administration. With their extended disciplinary base, universities are indeed different.

Strathclyde also highlights the great advantage of a changing university that possesses a highly useful focus around which it stays on course. The pursued focus becomes the hard ground of an all-university identity. Universities tend to be many things, many conflicting things, and are steadily bombarded by centrifugal tendencies of specific fields straining to go their own way. It is so easy for universities to pretend they are unified and then operate in reality as a federation of semi-independent states winding down into an even looser confederative framework – a conglomerate of stand-alone faculties, major departments, large research centers, and accumulated teaching programs, all with dedicated budgets serving as sunk costs and stabilized personnel refusing to die away when their time is past. A university that sets its face strongly against the fragmenting tendency is one that steadily labors to build encompassing interests. Such integrative interest building is measurably advanced by a grounded focus that can be asserted over and over again, connecting past, present, and future. 'A place of useful learning', for Strathclyde, is the focus and the message. Sustainability of overall character and identity has been thereby greatly enhanced.

3

University of Twente: balancing on entrepreneurial seesaws in a Dutch university

My 1998 portrayal of the University of Twente as an entrepreneurial university described a developmental 'take-off' that lifted the institution out of early marginality in Dutch higher education.[1] Established in 1964 in a depressed area in eastern Holland as the country's third technological university, Twente could not possibly match the clout of such large ancient universities as Leiden and Utrecht established in the sixteenth and seventeenth centuries, or that of large institutions developed later in Amsterdam and Rotterdam. Barely able to muster 4,000 students, Twente could no more than move in their shadows. In an economic downturn, the supporting ministry could always have targeted a marginal institution for severe cuts. It was worrisome.

Leading figures in the university in the early 1980s decisively claimed and started to develop a distinctive character, one that would attract resources, students and staff, rather than risk sliding passively into an institutional goodnight. A new definition was vigorously asserted (we are *the* entrepreneurial university) – an idea that became a set of associated beliefs and then an embracing culture; vigorous work was put into strengthening the administrative core at the top and later even more strongly at the faculty and department levels; income from non-state sources was vigorously pursued through 'contract education' as well as contract research; heartland departments were stimulated to be highly proactive – such areas as chemical technology and business studies became deeply involved in raising and spending their 'own' income; and newly created outreach offices, centers and programs defined an extensive developmental periphery. The outreach capacity became a highly visible component that attracted considerable attention from other European universities. On the continental scene, Twente was one of a handful of places that were fast off the mark in figuring out how to effect technology transfer.

The boundary-spanning activity began as far back as 1979 in an exploratory effort to devise a 'structured relationship' with small and medium-size businesses in the area. A pilot plan first helped some students in one faculty to establish, upon graduation, their own firms. This effort soon became a larger, more inclusive program located in a Transfer, Research and Development office that encouraged graduates and researchers across the university to start their own knowledge-intensive company. Through trial-and-error during the 1980s, the university gradually evolved a three-step flow in the developing of such enterprises. First, new firms resided for a year in some part of the university, aided by such advantages as an interest-free loan, advice and training, a mentor, and even some courses on how to survive the early years known for their high start-up death rate. In the second stage surviving firms took up residence in an incubator center adjacent to the campus; in the third, when time and growth dictated, the firm moved into an adjacent science park. The three-step scheme, in the eyes of central officials, was not basically a planned development; rather, it had developed incrementally by experimental efforts, a 'step-by-step, organic-growth model'.

The upshot was a significant contribution to a growing perception in Europe that Twente was well located in a growing high-tech area. It was on the railway and the major highway that began in the west at the Rotterdam harbor and led eastward to the industrial cities of northern Germany. In the mid-1990s Ericsson, the giant Swedish electrical firm, moved into the science park, giving it an anchor tenant. Meanwhile, back at the university, the original technology-transfer office underwent reorganization several times over and in the mid-1990s became part of a larger Liaison Group that aimed to serve as a central actor in linking the university to much of north-eastern and northern Holland. They wanted to provide continuing education courses for professionals as well as research-focused activity. Greater international cooperation was also on the agenda.

The Twente version of an entrepreneurial university, and particularly the problems associated with it, were very much on the minds of the two central figures from the institution who spoke at the OECD Paris 2000 conference. Frans van Vught, a social scientist, was elected Rector in 1996 and re-elected for a second four-year term. Leo Goedegebuure, a close colleague drawn from the university's well-known Centre for Higher Education Policy Studies (CHEPS), served as his principal assistant. What these relatively new central officials wanted to highlight for an international audience was the ongoing task at a place like Twente of keeping 'academics and entrepreneurship' integrated. For them, 'the other side of the coin' was that:[2]

> an entrepreneurial university can become too entrepreneurial and too decentralised . . . the discretionary funding base has become substantive enough to allow the base units to follow their own course of action, without reference to the overall institution. The base units have become self-supporting groups that act as individual entrepreneurs. From a micro-institutional perspective there is nothing wrong with this. High level work is performed in close interaction with relevant outside bodies. However, from a macro-institutional perspective, the ensuing loss of synergy can be dangerous. Cross-disciplinary innovation may be stifled,

both with respect to teaching and research because individuals and research groups act predominantly within their own specializations and interests. Distances between central and decentral units are further enlarged because of diverging interests, and ultimately the institution may move towards disintegration.

These central officials felt that the university was becoming unbalanced, erring too much on the side of entrepreneurial leeway for individual faculty and the organized faculties and departments:[3]

> ... there is a subtle difference between specialization and over-specialization, between decentralization and over-decentralization and between individualism and over-individualism ... [the university] had become too fragmented ... In order to overcome the over-fragmentation and ensuing over-specialization ... the collectivity of the institution needed to be emphasized.

In the extreme, then, an entrepreneurial university may become simply a university of entrepreneurs. Saturated with go-it-alone activity – even undergraduate students were setting up their own firms and consulting services – a rugged individualism might dominate. What then of the university as a collective body, a place of unifying values? What then of more general programs for students and a culture of service for the public good? What then of the whole university as an encompassing enterprise that could muster initiatives of its own?

In one effort to restore a better balance between the center and the now-dominant base units, Twente borrowed from Strathclyde the idea of an enlarged central management group that would include the deans of faculties. After three years of experience in the late 1990s, Goedegebuure and van Vught saw the new arrangement as a vast improvement. The new Management Team 'is a useful instrument to bring the executive level and the faculties closer together ... [moving toward] a form of joint, collective decision-making that in the eyes of many is a prerequisite for effective institutional management'. But further effort would be needed to make the team more proactive and integrative. The struggle centered on having 'the deans themselves act more as representatives *and* part of the central collective decision-making structure ...'[4] Not an easy posture for deans to maintain, as we saw at Strathclyde, but one that, with continuing attention, could be reasonably sustained. If 'horse-trading' and go-it-alone tendencies among some of the deans can be kept under control, then individual deans find it difficult to escape sharing the responsibility for the institution's overall welfare. Hopefully, some deans can keep two thoughts in mind at the same time.

But working out the relationship between faculty deans and the central management group was only part of the churning in governance that pre-occupied administrators, faculty, staff and students in the late 1990s. Institutional initiatives became overlaid by unavoidable system initiatives. The Dutch government worked out a new framework law for all universities between 1995 and 1997, which was intended to impose a large shift toward vertical managerialism. The previous major lurch took place a quarter-century earlier, in 1970. Then, in the opposite direction, the traditional professor-dominated university was replaced by a radical realignment of influence; voting rights in many organizational matters were divided in a tripartite structure of one-third for faculty, one-third for students, and one-third for non-faculty employees, similar to procedures in neighboring Germany. This action was a response to strident student demands, and in Holland to the general population who believed that encrusted public institutions, including universities, suffered from embedded privileges of established elites. Fair shares, homogeneity, and equity came to the fore: 'Ordinary is extraordinary enough.' The answer laid down by ministers for the universities was to effect an extreme version of the participatory university: the 1970 state action, as put well by Hans Daalder, was 'in many ways a unique experiment in revolution from above, in response to student activism from below . . .'[5]

Twente was in 1970 a new, small university. Although removed from student turmoil in the large cities, it still got caught up in years of lengthy and contentious deliberations in departments and in central bodies in the effort to make such broad participation work. In the midst of a confusing structure that emphasized all-in participation – community, yes, leadership, no – a three-man central body was still able to turn to much stronger steering in the name of an intended entrepreneurial university. During the next twenty years, Twente worked out its own internal compromises between vertical steerage and horizontal participation, where administrative and faculty expertise slowly were given greater weight.

But the government was not satisfied in the early 1990s with the development of steering capacity in the universities. It sought another large lurch that would once and for all wipe out the tired components of the participatory university and replace them with strong top-down thrusts in a managerial university. In the 1997 law known as MUB (Modernisering Universitaire Bestuursorganisatie), every university had to compose a top supervisory body consisting of five lay members appointed by the minister. Below that body, a three-person appointed board, including the rector, would hold 'nearly all powers regarding both academic and non-academic affairs'. At the faculty level, the dean was to become the 'omnipotent ruler'. Some representative councils could be retained but without power to approve or reject: they could advise. What the government wanted, and with haste, was a 'guardianship' structure in each university where all members of the crucial governing bodies would be appointed from the top rather than elected from below.[6]

But the understandings and expectations that had been put in place in the years since 1970 did not, of course, automatically vanish. 'The elusive concept of collective responsibility' that characterized Dutch universities in general for over two decades remained. Surviving councils for staff and students, trade union representatives and student leaders wanted to maintain their previously acquired rights and influence; at Twente they even took the university to court, and lost. But through internal negotiations, two new representative councils 'landed powers for themselves that were comparable to the pre-MUB situation'. The union representatives were particularly interested not in 'major university strategy and policy' but in 'meso and micro personnel issues' in faculties and departments. The result was more convoluted decision making than ever, in which 'decisions were reached only after lengthy debates, often with a negative undertone, and the paperwork in and around the councils increased substantially. A general perception [as of 2000] of unease and ineffectiveness has been the result.'[7]

An old story. What the government wanted in its latest lurch was results; what it got were consequences – not only in a contentious balance of power between old and new structures of student and staff influence, but also in the operation of the central management team. As de Boer and Goedegebuure concluded in their 2001 assessment of the changing structure of authority within Twente, what had emerged was 'a situation of mixed governance' in which central officials and the deans had found that 'in the factual working arrangements they are very much dependent upon each other'. At best, they are subject to 'a subtle balance of power that should be handled with care'. Heavy-handed one-size-fits-all mandates from government are not the remedy: organic on-the-spot adjustment is. And, without doubt, 'full-scale managerialism is not attainable in the present situation. Mutual dependencies that derive from the basic characteristics of universities imply that collegial operation to an extent always has to be there. Command structures do not work in a university.'[8]

So it went, little peace and quiet. The steering core got strengthened, but only after much internal struggle occasioned by strong, state-led mandates on top of ones initiated from within.

A somewhat similar one-two punch also occurred in efforts to change the university's curricular structure. As reported by van Vught and Goedegebuure in their Paris 2000 address, they had, as central actors, also taken a second major step to re-emphasize 'the collectivity of the institution', by means of a global change in curricular structure. The university introduced a major–minor requirement – unique in Holland – for all students: after much gnashing of faculty teeth in the working out of details, the plan was soon undergirded with forty majors and thirty minors. The new scheme was intended to work against an existing 'philosophy that is too much geared toward specialization'. It could operate to help bridge the university's two main internal worlds of engineering and social science – or as often put, applied science and applied social science. Students majoring on the one side would be encouraged to minor on the other. They could thereby experience the 'different worlds which in their working life they would be confronted with very regularly'. Choices for students could be increased substantially at the same time as they received a broader education. The major–minor concept could also be used externally 'to give us a unique selling point, and thus enable us to take a far more visible place in the Dutch higher education landscape than has been possible previously. The initial reactions from students, employers, the Minister, and the political parties to our new educational concept all have been very positive.'

The process of putting teeth into the major–minor conception was in itself important. After endorsing the idea, many newly formed faculty groups had to work out what was sensible and feasible, especially in defining minor programs: 'More than half of the thirty-plus minor programs have been newly created "from scratch" and involved teams from different faculties. Thus, truly interdisciplinary programs have been created on the basis of innovative ideas from the faculty . . . innovations that would not have been possible if the faculty had continued to operate solely on their own turf and in their own specializations.'[9]

The major–minor scheme required much additional committee work for busy faculty members who still had their primary commitments in departmental teaching and research. And then the government stepped in with a system-wide change in curricular structure: the Dutch universities were to obey the Bologna principles, agreed to by the member nations of the European Union (EU), to 'harmonize' the broad structures of programs and degrees appearing in the various countries. The general continental pattern of a five-to-six-year 'undergraduate' program that was supposed to contain much research-led teaching and study, and crowned with a master's degree, with newly developing doctoral degrees added on top, was now to change to include a three- or four-year bachelor program for a first degree – borrowing from the UK and other 'Anglo-Saxon' nations – to be followed by a one- or two-year master's and further research work for the doctorate. The undergraduate realm would center on programs organized toward achievement of the bachelor's degree. The master's and doctoral programs would perhaps fall into a graduate level, similar to the American structure and the one emerging in Britain.

What then of Twente's major–minor scheme that had been painfully worked out to fit the traditional five- to six-year arrangement for a master's level degree, with some student research included? It would clearly have to be refashioned to fit the shorter bachelor degree years and the follow-on master's work. Back to the drawing board for faculty, administrators and students across the campus, who could not be blamed if they were to complain of reform overload.

For universities in many European countries, the EU-inspired reform, if taken seriously, will engender a wide range of consequences. Guy Neave, in an early effort to set forth those effects, unanticipated as well as anticipated, undesired and desired, notes that the widespread consensus claimed at the top among ministers will be tested 'at the chalk face' when talk gives way to implementation, particularly 'at the level of first degrees and in the area of research training'.[10]

The Twente central administrators also spoke at the 2000 Paris meeting about a third integrative effort on behalf of the university as a whole: to use information and communication technology (ICT) as a 'binding factor' both internally and externally with other universities and business firms in

Holland. The university had been seriously involved for a decade in the development and dissemination of such technology; a Telematics Research Institute on campus linked other Dutch institutes of this type with business firms. Relevant spin-off firms existed in the nearby science park. The university was working hard in the late 1990s to enlarge and strengthen this network, with an eye on positioning 'itself as *the* leading university [in Holland] in this vastly competitive area', one that could serve as a 'test-bed' for innovative ICT-applications.

How? In 2000 the university began a 'wireless-campus project . . . in which staff and students will be provided with the latest generation mobile phones to test the so-called wireless applications protocols (WAP-technology) developed by our industrial partners'.[11] Intensely committed to such unusual university-industry interaction, Twente was a long way down the road beyond the original conception, common in universities, of knowledge transfer as linear one-way movement of knowledge and technique from the university to outside agencies. Here not only was there two-way traffic in alliances within which knowledge circulated back and forth, but the university was even willing to be a testing ground for new technologies developed in industry.

The university pushed IT yet another step toward more effective teaching and learning on the campus; it also launched at the millennium an internal initiative whereby 'all education programs of all faculties over the next few years will be located within a uniform electronic learning space, making teaching more or less time and space independent'.[12] Those interested in change at this university were certainly keeping the pedal pressed to the floor.

The thoughtful analysis served up by Goedegebuure and van Vught to an international audience of university leaders, administrators, and faculty at the 2000 meeting highlighted sharply for us the unending tasks of balancing contradictory forces as traditional universities transform themselves into a more aggressive character. When they saw their own institution tilting too far toward fragmenting dominance by individual faculties and departments, they pressed home the importance of institution-wide concepts and projects as a means of restoring a useful balance – a view from the center, a needed reintegration:[13]

> The idea is *not* to centralise a strongly decentral university, for it is recognised that a decentral structure enables the base units to react and adapt to changes in our environment effectively. This should not be lost. What has been pivotal in the changes brought about is the recognition that while maintaining a decentral and loosely coupled organisational structure, a degree of central coordination and stimulation is necessary to maximize synergy. Foremost, this requires close collaboration between the executive and the academic core of the institution – the strengthened heartland.

The introduction of institution-wide projects, they felt, was an attempt 'to operationalize' the concept of collegial entrepreneurialism, a concept I highlighted in an article published earlier that year. I maintained that 'sustainable entrepreneurialism in higher education, while admitting individual expression, has to be heavily collegial or co-operative in nature'.[14] Entrepreneurship clearly has to be understood as a characteristic of groups – from research groups and departments to entire universities – as well as of individuals. Heroic leaders can sometimes serve as ice-breakers and help for awhile. Individual faculty can, in business terms, sometimes be 'product champions' who push change more forcefully than others. But in universities, where so many individuals and groups need to be consulted and involved to make things happen, collegial relations and collegial forms of authority have to be constitutive parts of the department, the institute, the more inclusive faculty, and finally the all-university center. Institutions undergoing profound change in how they operate, aware that more is just down the road, realize that institutional identity needs cultural footing in collaborative relations up and down the line, particularly at the top.

So it seemed to those located in the Rector's office at Twente. Turning collegiality toward the promotion of change needs considerable expression at the all-university level, where it is most difficult to work out and maintain.

The question of balance between the powers of the university center and the initiatives of the lower units, as depicted in the Twente 2000 presentation, puts a different light on possible conflict between 'the academic' and 'the entrepreneurial'. When base units can 'follow their own course of action, without reference to the overall institution', the heartland departments, staffed by academics, are the entrepreneurial groups; the central administrators, with an eye cocked for cross-disciplinary programs and broader education of undergraduates, become the protectors of endangered components of 'the academic'. This is just the opposite of the common perception within and outside universities that the center may become dominated by entrepreneurial 'managers' who will run affairs from the top-down, while the base units in the old heartland struggle to protect academic virtues. Just as entrepreneurial action may become characteristic of different groups and different parts of the structure, efforts to uphold academic values and virtues may also be distributed up and down the line. The question of balance of powers becomes very important. How it is worked out has powerful implications for university coherence and identity.

During the late 1990s, Twente steadily pursued overall coherence by means of stated foci. It had maintained for a decade and more that it was a university with two broad groupings of fields: applied science and applied social science. The university offered 'training courses in both technical and social disciplines'. It 'distinguishes itself by its combination of technological and social sciences, in both its education and research programmes'.[15] Now it was ready to move from two to three foci: health sciences would be 'the third cluster'. Why? One reason was that some of the educational specializations developed under the major–minor scheme opened the possibility of developing a broader area of health sciences and biomedical technology. Another was that the university already had in place a Biomedical

Technological Institute, whose activities could be strengthened. Further, a promising pipeline of students from the secondary level was in place: 'a fully-fledged third core area . . . will enable the university to offer attractive degree programmes to secondary school leavers who have followed the teaching profile Nature and Health at pre-university level'. To move the new focus along, the Faculty of Technology and Management had appointed two medical practitioners as professors and thirty students had already begun a new specialization in Medicine and Management. The university's second business school, all graduate level and self-supporting, was also offering a trial MBA program targeted at the medical sector. *And* the university was seeking external alliances with medical centers and hospitals as far across the country as Amsterdam and Leiden.[16]

Twente had acquired the habit of developing new areas of research and teaching out of existing ones, with much trial-and-error. By always combining and recombining, 'teaching clusters' and 'research foci' could also be used adaptively to provide larger organizational foci. Trial-and-error was partially steered by building on existing strengths. In 1998 the Biomedical Technological Institute was one of four institutes judged to have 'proven excellence'; it was defined as an institutional 'spearhead', and awarded extra funding.[17]

How had the income picture of the university changed during the late 1990s? My earlier analysis had shown a change between 1980 and 1995 in which: core support from the sponsoring ministry dropped from 96 to 76 per cent of total income; income from research councils remained quite minor, from 2 to 3 per cent; and monies from 'all other sources' had gone up five-fold, from 4 to 21 per cent. Five years later, in 2000, the incomes gained from these three major sources shifted a little more toward the third category. Precise comparative figures were lost because of changes in financial categories, but a trustworthy broad estimate in 2001 placed the share of other income in total income as approximately 30 per cent. This still left dependency on state core support at a two-thirds level.[18] Core support, as in other European countries, was soft in that it was more likely to go down than up in per-person and per-program subsidy.

Hence, the financial foundation remained front and center. To pay the bills and to do some new things, extra income would have to be found. 'Budgetary pressure on the University's primary tasks will continue to increase the importance of the university's own income generated from contract research and teaching. The share of own income in the total available resources is expected to increase in the next few years.'[19] But it would not be easy. Twente's home region is not blessed with the vast number of large and small firms found in the western commercial and governmental area in Holland: Enschede will never be a Rotterdam. And the university, continental-style, was still considerably led by the state; little or no income existed from interest on endowment, alumni fund-raising, royalties and licensing, and other self-controlled sources we observed at Warwick and Strathclyde in the UK. From the perspectives of its own historical development and the situation of universities in continental Europe generally, Twente had come a major distance in changing its financial base. From the perspective of entre- preneurial universities elsewhere in the world that operated with one-half and then three-quarters of their income from other than state core support, it remained limited in possessing its own discretionary funds.

A final note on seesaws of contradictory pressures: Twente clearly intends to be simultaneously a regional university, a national university, and an international university. Its mission statements speak both of focusing effort on 'the economic and social development of the Northeast Netherlands region' – a gradually expanding conception of 'region' beyond the immedi- ate locality – and of giving priority to 'internationally acknowledged research' and to 'a significant inflow of students from abroad'. Moving from talk to implementation, the new health science 'third focus' could be seen as an important new link to students and schools in the region. The spun-off Twente Business School was running full- and part-time 'commercialized' MBA courses and executive training programs primarily for a regional clien- tele, and had regional business and professional associations bring their own training programs to campus. The technology-transfer line that stretched from university to science park was a promoter of the regional economy. The national identity, in turn, was readily captured in the conception stressed since the early 1980s that the institution was, in the Dutch system, *the* entre- preneurial university, a belief that constantly pressed for a high level of proactivity, regardless of whether the claim remained a true account of comparative thrust.

Most important for those at the top of the university's steering core was further achievement of international stature: 'The UT intends to participate actively in international top level research'; it 'intends to strengthen signifi- cantly its international profile in the next few years'. It expected to do so in education as well as in research through a 'growing number of internation- ally-oriented English-language masters programmes. The UT aims for an annual intake of 500 Masters students in 2001 and prefers to develop these programmes in co-operation with its international partners.'[20] More teach- ing in English, and conversely less in Dutch, could be seen as an operational definition of an international outlook. Twente was clearly prepared to oper- ate both regionally and internationally, with the latter taking primacy, not the least because additional funds could thereby be gained.

Conclusion

Developments at Twente between 1995 and 2000 extend my generalizations that emerged from the earlier chapters on Warwick and Strathclyde. First, the pathways of transformation identified in *Creating Entrepreneurial Universities* can become the means of sustaining ongoing change. The key seems to lie in mutually supportive interaction among the elements. As interaction becomes institutionalized, producing a new 'natural' state of affairs, the university acquires a steady state that presses for continuing change. New combinations of interest groups take the stage; new sunk costs become embedded. The changed organization is both stable and mutable. A collective 'will' to change is expressed at three levels: the base unit, the faculty, and particularly the all-university.

Second, the sustained interaction of elements in the change-minded university involves balancing across contrary forces and tendencies. At least three balancing acts are required: between central steering and devolved control; between focus and comprehensiveness; and between regional, national and international orientations.

Universities in general are subject to these opposing tendencies. If they are status-quo oriented, outcomes are left to passive evolution. But the disadvantages of drift steadily increase: a standardized diffusion of resources, or an allocation based entirely on long-standing sunk costs, becomes a telling institutional weakness as other universities pull themselves together and invest selectively and adaptively in certain fields of study and, through aggressive action, add to both their total income and discretionary monies.

Entrepreneurial universities necessarily become self-conscious about the problems of balance: a more active posture brings the clash of opposing tendencies to the surface. And with their greater consciousness comes also a greater awareness that universities will swing through the years from one emphasized tendency to another, seeking balance points of having it both ways, only to overshoot the mark.

At Twente, the 2000 central administration understood the dual need for central steering and devolved control. Excessive movement toward the latter, following naturally from liberation of base units, necessitated the deliberate cultivation of encompassing interests in common curricular structures as well as the administrative framework of central steering. The university also extended its sense of macro foci, from the two broad clusters of applied science and applied social science to a three-way claim that included the health sciences as a third major commitment. To boot, in its ambitious outlook, Twente maintained that at one and the same time it was a regional, national and international university. Such universities must be confident that they can work through contradictions contained in such major commitments and hold them in a sustainable balance. In the Joensuu narrative that follows, we will see the problem of balance of regional versus national and international orientations occur in even more challenging form.

Institutional heritage can measurably deepen contemporary contradictions. Earlier states of affair are not cleanly and completely left behind: they leave enduring deposits in habits of mind and procedure. The powers and privileges laid down for students and non faculty staff at Twente during the several decades of the 'participatory university' resisted the newly-emerging, more vertical authority structure insisted upon by both state and institution. Top-down one-size-fits-all state mandates notably intruded on local accommodations worked out incrementally. Differences between the collegial and the managerial developed along criss-crossing lines.

But substantial conflict did not stop the entrepreneurial thrust. That driving force had become part of the university's transformed character, evident in both base units and central councils. The university had acquired its own steady state of change.

4

University of Joensuu: balancing sustainability in a regional Finnish university

The University of Joensuu, established in 1969, is the newest of the five universities I visited in the mid-1990s. Begun as a university upgrade of a teachers' college, it was also the institution with the weakest provenance. The Finnish government planned it to be a small outpost, to grow from fewer than 200 students toward a target of 2,000. It was located in a minor city known neither for industry nor tourism. As a 'regional university', it was charged with the preparation of schoolteachers and local civil servants in a poor rural province located close to the Russian border, several hundred miles north of Helsinki. Research would not be conducted there: Finnish science and scholarship would be better served by concentrating it in just two or three places, specifically in the old universities of Helsinki and Turku. The founding national act even skipped mention of scientific research at Joensuu, a restriction that did not pertain to all the other universities then being formed in a new regional network. To complete the circle of heavy constraints, higher education in eastern Finland got politically and officially sorted out among three competing small cities: Kuopio got medicine; Lappeenranta got technology, Joensuu got 'human sciences' as the larger shell for teacher education.

Joensuu's development over the first quarter-century took place in two main stages. Each may be seen in retrospect as a purposive lessening of the initial constraints. In the first stage, rector and faculty sought to 'academize' teacher education by developing university-type disciplinary departments, initially in secondary-school subjects and later expanding to such non-school subjects as economics and forestry. The faculty instinct for departmentalism soon led to a continental-type grouping of departments into five faculties: science, social science, humanities, and then forestry and education. In this emerging framework, neither the first rector nor the university's new, young academics had any intention of staying out of research: 'research university', in a country heavily influenced by the German Humboldtian tradition, was an oxymoron. Of course the university would do research: that was the first thing universities did. Accordingly, after much argument, a Karelian Research

Institute opened early as 'a door to research', with funds garnered from local supporters as well as from various national agencies. Local and provincial leaders wanted to see a strong multidimensional university, one that could enhance local culture and help propel regional economic development.[1]

But major constraints remained. Operating with just 2,000–3,000 students and 20 to 25 chaired professors, the institution was small and only partially comprehensive. A third rector and his immediate staff sensed that 'Joensuu was a weak university', poorly positioned in a national system where 'region-alization' had splashed seventeen universities – ten multifaculty and seven specialized – around the countryside, in a country of five million. They embarked in the last half of the 1980s on a second major stage of organizational change, one focused on achieving greater 'self-realization'. I described the moves they made up to 1995 in the framework of pathways of transformation featured in my earlier study.

The primary change was a strengthened steering core. Joensuu volun-teered to be a 'pilot institution' in the national system, for experimentation with lump-sum budgeting, from first state to university and then, radically, from university to department. New central steerage strongly promoted steerage at the base. Decentralized control was accomplished in a series of small steps that insisted upon budgetary responsibility and self-regulation throughout heartland departments. Full-voice decentralization would not only break up the old top-down bureaucratic lines but would also, it was reasoned, 'liberate' academic initiatives from the bottom-up through disciplinary impulses of various departments. The door was opened to entrepreneurial action in the heartland, especially in the sciences and the important field of forestry; these units could most readily raise money beyond the core state funding. In the new reality, additional resources would largely if not entirely belong to the active departments. The idea, the spirit, of group entrepreneurialism grew.

Considerable diversification of income followed: from 94 per cent dependence on state core support in 1985 to 66 per cent ten years later. The university raised its research council income from 2 to 16 per cent of its total income; from third-stream 'all other sources', 4 to 27 per cent. Forestry and science departments led the charge, with about one-half to three-fifths of income from other than their basic governmental funds. Support moved steadily from guaranteed allocations to competitive sources. Forestry became a major area of development, a one-department faculty that became a pro-claimed national center of excellence and a segment of the university that readily reached across the old boundaries to other Finnish and European research centers located nearby, even to the point of sharing work space. It became the center of a basic-to-applied network at the cutting edge of worldwide developments in sustainable forestry; consultancies were carried out as far away as the Amazon region of Brazil.

But the road to transformation was a rocky one. A balance between central steering and the devolved powers of the faculties and departments required ongoing attention. Early countersteps to base-unit domination and fragmentation, voiced in ideas of center-department 'dialogue' and encompassing 'information systems', seemed not strong enough to those who occupied seats at the all-university level. Subject-matter balance also remained problematic. Teacher education remained heavily dependent on the state and bulked large in undergraduate enrollment and first-degree output; the sciences and forestry gained increasing research support from different governmental and private sources and dominated graduate enrollment and the 'production' of doctoral degrees. The university also was required to annex a small teacher-training operation in Savonlinna – a second campus one hundred miles away. How to deal with it and integrate it with the main campus became a problem.

Although comprehensive compared with the medical-and-health-centered university developing in Kuopio, and the technology-centered university growing up in Lappeenranta, Joensuu's small size and regional location dictated limited subject coverage within departments as well as across them. Hard choices had to be made. With the professional areas of medicine and engineering largely ruled out, and no particular provision made for business studies, the university was largely restricted to education and forestry as two major applied areas in which to build new outreach programs. Campus and city did not establish a science park until 1990, and, hampered by economic downturn in the early 1990s, it remained a tender operation midway through the decade.

Was the glass of proactivity and institutional innovation at this small Finnish place half-full or half-empty in 1995–96? I voted for half-full. The university willed itself into taking transforming steps between 1985 and 1995 and pushed hard for self-regulation up and down the line; it had thereby become a learning organization. As passivity gave way to self-steering, top, middle and especially base units learned much about how to learn their way. Operational units were thrust into medium- and long-term planning. They had to search for profiles of activities around which they could prosper; they had to seek departmental niches in national and international domains. And, one by one, operational components had to go on learning, however painfully, how their capabilities matched up with a changing array of externally set possibilities, starting with those located in a particular geographic region. The new voice of expressing self-development sounded very different from the one uttered by the university when it had been almost totally state dependent. Then, closely-monitored state lines of control and budgeting were clearly spelled out. Although still tender, the new tone of voice tended toward expression of self-mastery: we, ourselves, have to develop this place.

Sustainable balance early twenty-first century style

Skipping ahead a few years to 1998, for reasons of promised brevity, we find a newly elected rector, Perttu Vartiainen, stressing first that the departments are still 'the cornerstone of the operation and administration of the university ... [and] the increase in external funding, in particular, has enhanced the responsibility of the heads of department in financial matter'.[2] The balancing counterforce to such decentralization had now moved beyond talk about open dialogue and integrated information systems to a more inclusive, stronger steering committee, 'to assist the Rector, its members consisting of the Vice-Rector [now only one], the director of administration and the deans', and a Savonlinna representative, a more muscular central group, similar in general format to ones we observed at Strathclyde and Twente.

In his 1998 review the Rector then went on to highlight 'A Year of Doctors':[3]

> For several years now the University has been intensifying its graduate programs. This really began to bear fruit towards the end of 1998, when the number of doctorates greatly exceeded our agreed targets. This development is a reflection of the vigour of research activity in our departments and our success in attracting external financing in the teeth of fierce competition. I was particularly pleased when, towards the end of the year, the Finnish Academy choose the Forest Ecology Research Project, which is directed by Professor Seppo Kellomaki, to be one of the new [national] Centres of Excellence in Research.

That esteemed and specially financed research enterprise was now portrayed as 'the research flagship' of the university.

The target the Rector had in mind above was thirty-eight doctorates a year on the average; in 1998, fifty-two were awarded. This increase had a firm underpinning in the university's participation in a new 'graduate schools' plan organized by discipline and extended across universities. This system was established in Finland in 1995 to remedy deficiencies of 'postgraduate' studies because they were poorly organized and lengthy – somewhat reminiscent of German higher education. Six of these new national graduate schools were now coordinated at Joensuu, notably those with specialties in chemistry, physics, biology and forestry.

At the outset of his review the following year, the Rector stressed that 1999 'was an anniversary year, a time for looking back and looking forward'. There was much to be proud of:

> Our Third Doctoral Promotion in September was a memorable high point on *our journey from the small provincial college of thirty years ago to the medium-sized international university of today* [emphasis added]. The more than a hundred promoted doctors and twelve distinguished honorary doctors, Finnish and non-Finnish, was a fitting demonstration of the fruits of our research and our graduate schools and of our diverse academic connections and community relations.

The university remained ambitious, aiming high: 'In order to be a successful university it is not enough to be a regional or even national institute of education: we are also a part of an international scholarly community and of a national and regional system of innovation.'[4]

But regional considerations were also on the rise, while basic resources of 'time, money and space' were quite limited. Traditional regional constraints would not go away. More than in our previous four cases, Joensuu had to balance itself between being a regional university, a national university, and an international university. The problem had been given a sharp edge the previous year when the higher education evaluation council of the national ministry commissioned an outside assessment of the regional role of eastern Finland universities.

The external team indicated that 'from the outset the evaluation was intended to assist the development of the universities and not to be judgmental'.[5] A non-critical approach was followed in the case of the Lappeenranta University of Technology:

> the University is to be congratulated on the extent to which it has fulfilled its original objectives and expectations. It has created a high quality university campus environment with an enrollment of over 3,500 students and a staff of over 500 ... The University has an important influence on the industrial, economic and educational life of the region, whilst not losing sight of the need to fulfill a national role and to establish an international reputation.

All was well and good: strengths greatly outweighed weaknesses. Those committee members who concentrated on this technology-focused university even added the useful reminder that 'in fulfilling its regional responsibilities, any university these days can only exist by developing a strong national and increasingly international identity'.[6]

In the case of the health-science-focused University of Kuopio, committee applause also greatly outweighed criticism: 'the original objectives for the University in the 1960's have been well met. The institution has developed in 30 years into a traditional university with high-quality international academic research ... the University of Kuopio is a nationally and internationally recognized center for health and environmental sciences.'[7]

Not so for Joensuu. Something about the institution stuck in the craw of visiting members of this committee focused on the regional role:

> Alongside teaching, a number of departments and faculties have undertaken activities linked to their research through which they have provided a source of competence for the region. For example the Faculty of Forestry has persuaded various national and international organisations to undertake projects which involve industrial co operation within the region; the national Centres of Excellence in Mathematics and Physics have had an impact on education in the region's schools, raising competency levels in key subjects relevant to a wide range of occupations and industries. The University's expertise relevant to engagement with Russia has been used by a number of regional organisations; likewise

knowledge based on education about the application of information and communication technology. *But these are exceptions; as the self-evaluation report admits 'the international links and the disciplinary-based commitments tend to dominate the regional ones in the academic values of the university'.* [Emphasis added][8]

Further: 'The Peer Review Team came to the view that the University has many separate regionally relevant initiatives, which are not systematically connected to the University through a strategic link.' Then, regarding the small campus in Savonlinna: 'the University is not yet operating as an integrated two-campus university. This is probably one important reason why it does not use, *and some times even does not understand* the opportunities which regional engagement can provide' [emphasis added]. The Swedish Agricultural University was offered as an example of a successful multi-campus university. Further, regarding external relations: 'it is insufficient to simply assert adherence to the present academically driven priorities'.[9]

The litany of complaints finally seemed to focus on two concerns. First, the university 'aspires to be an elite, broadly-based and research-orientated institution covering education, humanities, science and the social sciences'. This is an expensive aspiration; the university will have to be more selective; the needed selectivity could form up around 'a regional orientation'. Second: 'Our over-riding concern about the University of Joensuu is the absence of any meaningful strategic plan to guide its future academic development, particularly its relationship with the region.' The Committee pointed to a half-dozen items that needed to go into such a plan; for example, mechanisms to support 'the identification of the region with the University', to support 'a resource allocation process linked to strategic priorities', even to support 'the quality assurance of the strategic planning process itself'. The Committee added: 'We recognize that the tenor of this report is less positive than that provided by Burton Clark in his recent publication. However, that analysis did not consider the regional role of the university.'[10]

But many regional developments had been unfolding during the 1985–95 decade of transformation and on into the late 1990s. A primary commitment was to forestry, as observed earlier. Located in the midst of the large wooded area of eastern Finland, the university developed forest-practice connections to two locally located forestry institutes. This central outreach was regionally intensified with connections to a new practice-oriented local polytechnic heavily centered on forestry. In short, the university became the centerpiece in a network of institutions including those with regional aims and services. Joensuu viewed itself as 'the most important national centre of forestry research'; it was important internationally and locally even as it positioned itself on a national commitment.[11]

Furthermore, the science park, organized with local and regional authorities in 1990, recovered from the effects of the deep depression of the early 1990s and was expanding rapidly in size, facilities, and personnel – the latter doubled from 150 to 300 and planned to reach 800, despite a local industrial structure not favorable to university–industry collaboration. This location was not to be likened to the English midlands, or the city of Glasgow, or a place in eastern Holland on the route between Rotterdam and German industrial cities, or the metropolis of Gothenburg. The outside base for high-tech engagement outside of forestry was weak: a science park that would prosper depended on an internally generated willpower.

By 2000, the university could report that the small Savolinna campus was developing a new centre of continuing education and regional development. The main campus was developing a new unit for regional studies and another for educational information technology. Three thousand adults were participating in professional upgrading and continuing education programs in Joensuu's Continuing Education Centre, alongside another 3,000 who were taking Open University courses. And an overall working group devoted to cooperation in regional development was underway, 'consisting of local and regional authorities as well as key personnel from the Science Park, the university and from local industry'.[12]

Thus, Joensuu, a small public university, positioned itself by 2000 within the orbit of strongly emphasized national objectives in a way that allowed it to cope with the contradictions of regional, national, and international orientations. Small, ambitious Finland clearly enunciated its goal 'of becoming the leading information society in the world' – an ambition in line with the considerable 'Nokia-ization' that had already taken place. In pursuit of this overriding national objective, the Finnish government selected 'information technology, electronics, and other high-tech areas [as] the future success factors for the Finnish economy'.[13] The country's universities then become crucial instruments and their own focused growth was directly implicated:[14]

> Consequently, the Finnish government is investing a remarkable proportion of national funds in higher education and research in the fields of natural science and technology. So far, the University of Joensuu has been successful in competing for these programme funds, and the fastest growing educational and research fields at the institution are now in the applied sciences, mainly in physics, computer sciences and chemistry. Because of the national integration of industrial development policy with higher education policy, the goals of educational and research excellence and the goals associated with the regional role of the university are beginning to merge once again.

To play even a minor role in the framework of national development, the university had to ride on its reputation for academic excellence – project by project, program by program – in harsh competitions mounted by the Finnish Academy of Science and aggressive national development agencies. In short, the aspiration in this unlikely corner of Finland to be 'an elite, broadly-based and research-orientated institution' – the posture criticized by the external review committee – offered sustainable grounds for the institution's ongoing development. Within this costly commitment, selective investment in certain scientific specialties already developed as strengths in several departments had matched up with the government's main goals for its national universities. On this path, national and international orientations and commitments lead the way for the regional. To repeat what the members of the evaluation committee who visited the Lappeenranta University of Technology had pointed out: 'in fulfilling its regional responsibilities any university these days can only exist by developing a strong national and increasingly international identity'. True, certainly, in modern competitive Finland.

The evidence is sharp and clear that the national government in Finland insists, and is able to insist, that Joensuu behave foremost as a national university that is both state-dependent and still considerably state-led. We find the story in income data and performance indicators. As partially reported above, between 1980 and 1995 core support from the ministry of education had dropped from 96 to 66 per cent of total income, funds from research councils increased from 1 to about 7 per cent, and funds from 'all other sources' had become a significant item, up from 3 to 27 per cent.[15] Five years later, in 2000, the distribution among these three main sources remained much the same; comparative categories, however, were now distorted by the insertion of funds for 'practice schools' which took up 13 per cent of reported total income. Core support then approximated 75 per cent, research councils about 6 per cent, and all others about 20 per cent (from Finnish domestic sources, public and private, and foreign sources, notably the European Union at about 5 per cent).[16]

Movement toward diversified funding had continued to be led by forestry and the sciences – chemistry, physics, computer science, biology – and was, as expected, least possible in education, the humanities and the softer social sciences. For the first group, income could be sought from different wings of the academy of sciences, national development agencies, EU development funds, and business firms. For the latter, core support had to remain overwhelmingly the financial base.

Thus, despite some diversification of income, and constant striving to develop new sources, Joensuu was considerably state-dependent. As of 2000 the constraints on income diversification were many: Finland did not allow its universities to charge tuition; Joensuu had little or no endowment or reserves deposited in the bank to earn interest; under state law, patents were still awarded to individuals not institutions; and the no-tuition entitlement of qualified students dampened the possibilities of turning them, after graduation, into grateful alumni. For the university overall, the ministry of education was overwhelmingly the main source of funding.

Moreover, state dependency by 2000 led to state guidance in the form of 'performance agreements' between the ministry and the individual universities.[17] Let us follow the trail of the sequential details. The agreement between Joensuu and the ministry for 2001–2003 began with 'objectives common to all universities'. A series of commandments followed that ranged from 'the universities will develop distinctive profiles' to national numerical targets: for example, 'universities will award an average of 1,300 doctorates and 12,700 master's degrees annually'; 'an average of 5,400 students will annually study parts of their degree abroad'; 'open university instruction will be available for an average of 20,000 calculated full-time students'.

A specified 'mission' for Joensuu then followed: it 'will operate competitively in the internationalizing operational environment while strengthening its regional impact'. In short the university must be simultaneously international, national and regional. The latter form of service must not be omitted: the university 'will particularly satisfy research and educational needs in eastern Finland and provide relevant regional services in its fields'.

After mission came agreed-upon 'priorities' for the university: 'comprehensive multi-disciplinary teacher education; research into the human life span; forests, other renewable resources, and the environment; high technology; and social and cultural developments of peripheral regions and border districts'. This broad set of priorities clearly provided room for everybody – all the faculties, stretching from teacher education and the humanities and social sciences and onward to cutting-edge work in forestry and 'high technology' in the sciences.

However, the comprehensiveness was then followed in the performance agreement by 'annual target numbers' for 2001–2003, specified by major subject areas. At the postgraduate level: '59 doctorates, with the following breakdown: the humanities and theology 9, educational sciences 8, social sciences 5, psychology 2, the natural sciences 25, and forestry 10'. For undergraduate education, '700 master's degrees with the following breakdown: theology 15, the humanities 170, educational sciences 220, social sciences 95, psychology 15, the natural sciences 140, and forestry 45'. And 'by 2003, 200 undergraduates will study part of their degree abroad'. A section in the performance agreement on resources for Joensuu then specified numerical sums in such broad categories as core, project and performance-based funding, and then 'earmarked funds' for such subcategories as graduate school salary expenditure, open university instruction, and practice schools for school teacher preparation.[18]

The targeted degree numbers show the relative weight of the different major fields. The science faculty was mandated to produce just 20 per cent of first degrees but over 40 per cent of PhDs. Similarly forestry was 6 and 17 per cent. The two faculties of science and forestry were to produce 60 per cent of the doctorates. The other fields largely showed the opposite pattern. In the undergraduate realm, education and the humanities together were to produce about 55 per cent of the basic degrees, but much less – about half of that in the doctoral work. Education contrasted sharply with science: it was scheduled to award 31 per cent of first degrees and 13 per cent of doctorates; and as reported above, science was the opposite with assigned goals of 20 and 42 per cent, respectively.

Hence, any degree figures and income figures for the university as a whole were summations of numbers from various internal fields possessing different orientations and functions. And whatever the government did in the late 1980s and early 1990s to grant experimental autonomy to Joensuu had given way, in a new age of governmental surveillance and performance indicators, to a close monitoring of program development and degree production in the name of national economic effectiveness of the universities. Rector Vartiainen, at the OECD Paris 2000 Conference, indicated that he preferred the characterization of 'innovative' to the term 'entrepreneurial'.[19] He had a point. Since 'traditional' and 'entrepreneurial' are best discussed as pure types but then understood as blended on a spectrum of differences, a sector of that continuum might best be known as 'innovative traditional'. At the least, the entrepreneurial actions of universities still well-encased in state systems, like Joensuu, will be different from the practices of those universities that reduce their state dependency to 50 per cent, and then 25 per cent and lower, as a share of total income. Joensuu has operated basically as a public university closely related to national government in the past and present, and seems positioned on a state-led pathway for the near future.

Conclusion

The fourth institution of my original set of European universities, when followed to 2000, made me more aware of how transforming universities become newly involved in certain fundamental university tensions and con- tradictions. Again we find the tension between all-university encompassing interests and the partial interests of middle and lower units; the strain between comprehensive program coverage and focused effort; and the seeming contradiction between regional, national and international orienta- tions. Such tensions are inherent in modern universities. They arise because of the need to exercise initiative at multiple levels in the face of professional primacy at the base; in the inclination to support a widening array of fields of knowledge, in the face of limited resources and the advantages of selective focus; and in the societal expectation that a university should be able to face simultaneously in a number of different directions. Traditional universities satisfied with the status quo are likely to have made their peace with such fundamental contradictions. They thrashed out unspoken answers long ago. The sleeping dogs of established interests are left alone.

But transforming universities, seeking new arrangements, stir up these contradictions and bring them to the surface for conscious resolution. They then engage in actions that seem to help them to cope, to reach reasonable new balances. But in fast-changing environments, the balances are rarely final and the contradictions are stirred up anew. Coping with them not only produces new stabilizing forms; it also becomes a steady source of change.

Joensuu's major experimentation with decentralized control necessitated a great deal of follow-on effort to strengthen the means of aggregating encompassing interests into stronger center-led steerage. Balancing on this particular seesaw required steps, increasingly apparent in the late 1990s, to beef up the central coordinating bodies. Such moves are not easy to put firmly in place once departments have come to think – as the price of their expanded responsibility – that what is theirs is theirs. The quandaries of centralized versus decentralized control never go away. They are simply handled over time, from one decade to the next, in a rebalancing of interests and authority that allows the university to move ahead.

The strains between comprehensive coverage and focused effort occurred in sharp form at Joensuu. Specialized universities, like those limited largely to technology or medicine, generally have an integrating focus; comprehensive ones generally do not. But to attempt to be strong in everything is now beyond the pale, even in the richest universities. Selective investment in some fields of study becomes a necessity, particularly in a university with the small size and location of Joensuu. Various compromises are possible in this highly delicate matter. Some fields may continue to dominate undergraduate enrollment, or at least find undergraduate education to be their bread and butter; as other fields press ahead to concentrate resources and attention on doctoral work. Joensuu balances itself on this particular division of labor; education and the humanities loom large in the one realm and the increasingly strong sciences in the other.

Joensuu's coping behavior in reconciling regional, national and international orientations seems most compelling of all if we look at effect on long-term character. The answer pursued is not the one the critical review committee was looking for – to emphasize mutual identification of university and region and to take it from there. Instead, the university chose to position itself as a national university linked to national mandates of innovation and economic development – and to take it from there. The national orientation fits the institution's selective investment in a limited number of scientific specialties, some expensive, which have produced recognition of specific foci of excellence in research and teaching, student recruitment and training. The national orientation permits the assertion of international standing and the building of international collaboration. And it becomes the basis for what the university can newly bring to its region as a center of learning at the cutting edge of research and training central to the fast-paced development of a modern advanced economy.

The university was not going to give ground on this fundamental point. In the journal *Industry & Higher Education*, in 2002, the university's rector and planning officer put it plainly: 'At the heart of the regional impact of the University of Joensuu is the research and training carried out in its basic academic units. The greatest regional effect of the university is due to its internationally competitive research and education as well as to the development of strategic priority areas.'[20] If a choice had to be made, the university would indeed choose academic excellence in the traditional departments, guided by selective investment in some scientific fields – and then take it from there. From this posture, the university would find its way to further regional service.

5

Chalmers University of Technology: entrepreneurialism redeemed

When I selected it earlier, I was not sure that the Chalmers University of Technology in Sweden was a place undergoing self-willed transition. I knew that in 1994 this university had chosen to take up a unique position in the governance of Swedish higher education by adopting a new status – a 'foundation university'. One of a kind, it took a half-step or more away from the state controls that continued to apply to all other Swedish universities. The step involved a controlling board of its own, to which all income would flow. Somewhat like private universities, it would also be freer from the state system in how it allocated resources internally, appointed and rewarded personnel, devised programs and courses, and otherwise went about the business of providing research and teaching and opportunities for student learning. Intrigued by this major change, I reasoned that the university had surely not made this choice casually, that there must have been an escalating inclination – a predisposition, a trajectory – stretching back perhaps for a decade or more, which encouraged it to view as an opportunity what others saw as a problem. Chalmers would be a Swedish experiment, one partly designed from the top but largely initiated from below by institutional volition.

Once on the scene, I found a strong case of blended transforming activities. Technologically-focused Chalmers clearly demonstrated the pathways I highlighted earlier in the 1998 book, especially in their mutual connection and full interaction.[1] The *idea* that the institution should become an entrepreneurial place was openly and strongly voiced in both the *academic heartland* and the central part of the *steering core* as early as 1980, when the campus's leading professor, backed by the rector and administrative director, announced his total devotion to 'innovation' and started up an Innovation Center, a step that led in time to the building of a multi-sided extensive *developmental periphery*. The idea that was implemented, structurally and culturally, was to construct '*a plurality of special places for innovative behavior*', places that would generate a self-propelling array of initiatives. The periphery became remarkably active as it took up new units, project oriented and interdisciplinary for the most part, which bridged to industrial firms and other outside groups. Utilizing such formal lines of outreach as an incubator building, spin-off firms, and science-park affiliations, Chalmers did not fret about commercialization. One step led to another in a highly entrepreneurial fashion all through the 1980s and early 1990s: an internal seed capital (venture capital) firm, an Industrial Contact Group, high-level management training programs that flew Swedish executives to meet with internationally renowned gurus in other countries, special undergraduate courses. Significant also were Competence Centers supported nationally, which tackled problems defined by industrial firms as well as university personnel and could claim to be doing 'a new type of research'.

Undergraduates and alumni alike were swept up in an entrepreneurial 'spirit'. It was tangibly expressed in their behavior and played well in the spirited attitude of Gothenburg – a 'second city' to Stockholm – and in the competitive attitude of the west coast of Sweden against the eastern and southern sectors. Its region did not doubt that Chalmers was indeed a regional university. Local business, especially the large firms, grew to savor close ties.

Devolved budgeting had measurably strengthened mid- and lower-level steering: deans and department heads become more prominent, while collegial groupings were on call at those levels and in a reconstructed center. Funding steadily become more diversified. Core support was down to about one-half of total income in 1995, and the state mainly subsidized undergraduate programs as its support for PhD programs and research fell to about one-third. Chalmers positioned itself well for income from research councils and non-education government departments; it learned how to generate considerable revenue from 'commissioned research', and, from the source that allows the greatest discretion, 'contributions, funds, gifts'. Such rich foundations as the Wallenberg Foundation had become important contributors to Swedish universities generally and often offered major gifts for buildings and expensive equipment.

All these material, tangible developments helped the original idea evolve into a substantial set of beliefs and then into an all-embracing culture. The symbolic side of university life, always somewhat intangible, was here in full bloom, warming the place with affect. In interviews, without prompting by me, I was encouraged by faculty and student leaders to understand the special 'spirit' of the place, one quite entrepreneurial in character. Persisting well in an alumni network, that focused culture also became the ground, the bridge, for valuable moral and financial support.

Thus the leap into foundation-university status in 1994 had quite a launching. The new status could be seen as both continuous with the evolving entrepreneurial character and as offering 'new conditions for revitalization'; if 'correctly managed' it would give Chalmers 'unique potential'. The president of the university articulated the message plainly: 'The idea of the foundation conforms unusually well with the very long tradition of Chalmers working towards increased independence and searching for independent solutions. We want to do things "ourselves". We want to "assert ourselves".'[2]

Here was a true macro institutional experiment. Could an already enterprising university position itself anew to be even more aggressive in its self-development? Chalmers's new status was a hybrid institutional form in which it was still importantly state related but was also freer to self-develop and to assert distinctiveness. Was this form sustainable? Could the university develop new infrastructures that would sustain change? What had become of this experiment by 2000?

Elaborating a transformation

Unquestionably, the steering framework adopted after the 1994 shift in official status had become quite elaborate by the turn of the century. At multiple levels infrastructure served both as institutionalized steady state and enabler of change. The newly constructed *Foundation* board served as 'the supreme decision-making body', one that appointed the university board and 'manages the foundation capital'. The *University* board, in turn, managed the university's activities; the President was 'responsible for operations generally' – a strong role – and operated with the assistance of a University Management Group consisting of the president, vice-presidents, deans of nine sub-schools, and the head of a new second campus, Chalmers Lindholmen University College, defined as a 'subsidiary'. The schools had boards of their own, as well as deans; about 80 departments had boards as well as heads. Such boards could have outsiders as well as faculty, staff and students as members. Around a firm line structure, collegial participation was dense. And under devolved internal budgeting, the middle and bottom parts of the administrative arrangement – the schools and departments – possessed considerable leeway and incentive for self-development.[3]

Following upon the 1994 credo of 'doing things ourselves' and always 'searching for independent solutions', the university by 2000 had broadly expanded its 'places of initiative', spreading them throughout heartland departments and what seemed like an ever-expanding developmental periphery. The university was fast taking the shape of a heavily *networked university*, with many parts, large and small, even becoming separate legal incorporations (AB). To illustrate: as special places for innovative activities, the university had added to the original Innovation Centre a second center for newly-formed companies, plus a Chalmersinvest AB, an Innovationskapital AB, an Entrepreneurship School, and other units, all parts of 'a broader concept – the Chalmers Innovation System'. For cooperation with industry, the university developed eight or more 'centers', 'foundations' and AB incorporations, such as the Corporate Relations Centre, the Science Park Foundation, and the Lindholmen Teknikpark AB. The university could point to LightUp Technologies AB, 'a spin-off company based on research commenced in 1992 at Chalmers', which won a national company-of-the-year award as a 'seed-capital company' in biotechnology.[4]

At the millennium the university was also alive with new interdisciplinary centers and programs which drew faculty and students from different schools and departments. Prominent and promising was the Microtechnology Center (MC2); it was engaged in basic and applied research within microelectronics and aimed to be 'one of the foremost university facilities of its kind in the world'. About fifteen research groups had been formed within it, drawing upon people – over 200 faculty, staff and students – from the schools of chemical engineering, physics and engineering physics, and electrical and computer engineering. The director of the center reported not to a particular dean or department head but to the president's office – a sign of a cross-cutting unit that would receive special support and privilege. Capital funds for a major building and expensive equipment had been made available from the Wallenberg Foundation as well as from the Chalmers Foundation board. One-third of its operation was planned for 'industrial cooperation'.[5] In 2001, the university noted that such cooperation 'has had a promising start'. For one, Philips Semiconductors was 'closing down a research facility in New York and moving the equipment to the new clean room at MC2'. Industry's rising interest in associating with the new center had already gotten to the point where the university invested in another building in the city to accommodate them.[6]

A multitude of research centers receiving support from economic-development national agencies were also proliferating. NUTEK – the Swedish National Board for Industrial and Technical Development – provided long-term support for six centers in 2000; they had just undergone international external evaluation for a phase two expansion, with positive results. I visited one of these centers in 1995 and was impressed with both its vigorous leadership and its organizational freedom. The heads of these 'competence centers' are independent of deans and departments heads: they also report directly to the President's Office and can freelance somewhat across the core line authority structure. Beyond the NUTEK centers were almost thirty inter-university research programs financed by the Swedish Foundation for Strategic Research (SSF) in which Chalmers was involved; for ten programs in such varied fields as applied mathematics, production engineering, and bioinformatics, it served as 'host' university.

When a second campus was developed within the city of Gothenburg, it added and spread initiatives in a major way, especially in providing alternative educational programs. The university had become increasingly confined and cramped in campus space; its borders were relatively fixed by neighborhood opposition to 'encroachment' and established open-space requirements. In the late 1990s, it engaged in costly major rebuilding within its confined area and managed to pick up a second property not far away through an agreement with city government. It also developed a second major campus across the city's main river, in a less built-up area know as Lindholmen. Here, a university college was established as an incorporated 'wholly-owned subsidiary'. By 2000 this second entity, with over 2,000 full-time students and growing, was operating 'an engineering foundation year' as 'a preparatory programme for university studies'; plus three-year bachelor degree programs in certain engineering fields (the first major undergraduate degree in Sweden was defined as a master's degree); and its own School of Continuing and Professional Studies. Separate from the 'old' campus, Chalmers Lindholmen University College AB was engaged in its own 'internationalization', by working up a master's-level program in information technology as a collaborative project with 'universities in Germany and Finland' in which students 'will spend one term at each of the participating universities'. The university saw the development of this second campus, in a different locality, as helping to integrate 'university activities with the population of Goteburg and industry in this area', thereby 'contributing to the development of Goteburg as a knowledge city'.[7]

As new specific units at Lindholmen operated to integrate university and industry, its School of Continuing and Professional Learning was busy forging 'partnership agreements' with first, Volvo, then Saab, and then went on to explore the present and future training needs – 'the skills required' – of other firms, including small- and medium-size enterprises (SMEs). At first, with Volvo, learning how to work together was 'new for both cultures'. How to create best practices and solutions in fast-moving companies and in pre-employment training was seen as a process of 'mutual learning'. If the relationship were to be fruitful and worth expanding to other universities and firms, it had to be 'win-win'. The school would be clearly cast in the role of 'system-supplier'. For its efforts it would receive payments from industry, backed also by national and European Community (EC) funding for development projects.[8]

Educationally, Lindholmen felt it was 'building a new concept within the university system' in which training for industry could be both specific and adaptable. With coordinators and expert groups on both sides focused on always improving the up-to-date training of employees already on the job and sustaining the flow of well-trained graduates, the university would work toward new pedagogical approaches, including in e-learning – 'learning in a non-traditional environment' – and in experiential learning – 'learning from experience' – and it would mount training programs for teachers active in adult professional training. The relationship could give the university experience in how adults learn and wish to be taught; the faculty could gain better and more up-to-date knowledge about industrial applications; and students could receive a smartly 'updated education' for employment and future capacity for personal development in work settings.[9] The moving intertwined target was to develop and stabilize programs (adding new sunk costs and segmental interests), while at the same time impelling those programs to go on changing, to keep apace changing external needs. The 'partnership' bridge was the infrastructure for doing so. If it worked, it would be one part of the university that would always be tilted toward the future.

Whether in the development of the new campus or the extensive rebuilding of the older one, the university stressed assertively that its new foundation status allowed it to engage in 'direct ownership of properties'. The properties would be 'owned and managed by the wholly-owned subsidiary

Chalmers University of Technology Properties AB', an incorporated entity responsible for the provision and planning of premises. This 'subsidiary' of the 'company' became part of a network of incorporated units called the 'Chalmers Group'. The university, incorporated as the parent company, was joined by three first-tier subsidiaries – the university college, the property company, and an investment company. 'All companies in the Group are wholly owned.'[10]

This achievement pointed to an extended transformation of a historic structure. It institutionalized operational autonomy from state officialdom by turning the university into a federated system of incorporated entities. It was fundamental footing in the organizational structure of Swedish higher education for the expressed will to be independent, to search for independent solutions, to 'assert ourselves', and 'do things ourselves'.

Active networking did not stop at Chalmers's own borders but spread externally in both national and international webs. The university was increasingly engaged in the late 1990s in forming alliances with other Swedish universities and noted institutions in other countries. In Sweden the natural alliance was with the adjacent and larger and more comprehensive University of Gothenburg. Abutting each other, the two universities had long had some interchange of students. Several science departments became joint departments, mingling faculty and physical plant. Field by field, cooperation increased and pushed forward especially in 'environmental biosciences' and information technology. In 1998 closer ties were also established with another university and two university colleges in the western area of Sweden.[11]

The intent to knit the university into international networks was prominent at the turn of the millennium. Formal institutional alliances were forged with such international notables as the Massachusetts Institute of Technology (MIT) in the United States, the Swiss Federal Institute of Technology (ETH) in Zurich, the Ecole Polytechnic in Paris, the Fraunhofer group of research centers in Germany, and the University of Tokyo in Japan; and concerning university management, with Imperial College and the London School of Economics in Great Britain. Within 'a special project to reinforce Chalmers' international networks', visits were made that year to southern Germany, Taiwan, Hong Kong and Shenzen, Singapore, Japan, southern California, Boston and surrounding regions – and even to Detroit![12] Seminars exploring possible research collaborations with universities in South Africa and Mexico were underway. And the university was steadily participating in over 100 EU (European Union) projects that involved universities and industrial firms in other countries. More than those in the regional and national ones, international networks offered a changeable portfolio of commitments; new ties here often replaced, if need be, older ties there.

All these proliferating activities, and the pressing ambition to be as independent as possible, made diversified income an ever present need and problem in a technological university loaded with old and new expensive equipment. There was never enough money, but total income steadily increased and the diversification trend deepened. Between 1980 and 1995 core support from the national ministry of education and science had fallen from 67 to 55 per cent of total income. The income figures in 1997 show that overall income was up 11 per cent over the previous year and 'within the framework of this total increase there was a trend towards financing by foundations, the EU, companies and other contributors'. State dependency had decreased from 55 to 51 per cent. In 1998 total income was up 8 per cent, and the state core financing fell further to 48 per cent. The university's statement about the trend had a stronger tone: 'A shift has taken place in financing from state-funded education and research to grants and commissions from companies and the private sector. The change took place totally within research and doctoral programmes.' The beat went on. In 1999, total income was up 10 per cent; core funds from the ministry fell to 44 per cent. In 2000, total income was up 2 per cent: core funding was 45 per cent.[13]

Thus, core support as share of total income dropped 12 per cent in 15 years (1980–95) before the new 1994 status took hold: it dropped another 10 per cent in the following five years, 1995 to 2000. Equally significant, within total income, the share contributed by the Chalmers Foundation itself – separate from monies gained from trade with companies, EU, public foundations and other state agencies – rose from a minuscule 2 per cent in 1996 to 14 per cent in 2000. The university-cum-foundation was learning how to leverage its own financial resources as a source of additional income, much as private universities do with their endowments. At the end of 2001 the foundation's modest 'capital' was 2,315 million Swedish kronor (over $US 250 million, at 9 kronor to the dollar), a 'growth in equity' of 40 per cent over the initial capital of 1994, aside from the monies contributed to operations along the way.[14]

As part of its efforts to develop other sources of income, the university continued to elaborate its capacity in alumni-related fund-raising. The university had an early start in this direction: voluntary associations of graduates maintained a Chalmers identity and linkage, for example, a Chalmers Engineers' Association. Apace with its new more independent status, the university moved in the mid-1990s to a more system-based effort to turn graduates into alumni who would steadily offer moral, political and financial support. By 2001 the university could report the successful end of fund-raising for a prize-winning functioning new student union building for which, it was stressed, 2,300 benefactors had given 'donations amounting to SEK [Swedish Kronor] 61 million' (almost $US 7 million).[15]

To boot, the university also initiated a Chalmers Global Fund, developed in cooperation with a bank and slated to appear on the stock market, which would 'be directed mainly at alumni, students and employees', to build funds that would be invested globally. The university would take 'two percent of the total value of the fund at the year-end . . . to support its international work'.[16] Nothing ventured, nothing gained! Give it a shot: 'we' are all in this together.

As this fast-moving institution was elaborating its entrepreneurial character in the late 1990s, nailing down its earlier transformation and finding ways to go on changing, questions of focus and balance in subjects and programs had to be raised and given at least temporary solutions. Even in this 'technological university', with its built-in avoidance of the humanities and most of the social sciences, the remaining domain of science and technology had become sprawling and very complicated – too much for any university to cover and to afford in its entirety. How then to best explore new possibilities while protecting an essential core? Chalmers's answer was to have its top board name four 'strategic investment areas' as new operating areas in 2000 and 2001, with 'time-limited' specified financial commitments for five to seven years: microtechnology, information technology, biosciences and environmental sciences. And sums were attached to each. At the same time, the board defined 'the renewal and quality of undergraduate programs' as an even larger 'prioritized investment' – and specified a large sum for it.[17] So, the thinking was to invest selectively in new subject areas by all means, high cost and all. But a teaching heartland, centered on an undergraduate realm leading as far as the master's degree, was still basic, particularly as backed by traditional departments and the expressed desires of active student leaders.

Students have a serious voice at Chalmers. For example: the first major statement appearing in the 2001 Annual Report was by the president, the second by the chairman of the Student Union. The Union view pointed to an acute shortage of accommodations, the importance of effective reception of new students, and the need for 'increased flexibility and individualization' in undergraduate courses.

In Chalmers, as elsewhere among proactive universities, balancing between the new and the old never reaches a final solution. Here the bargain was time-limited trials for specified new ventures that, when successful, would roll forward the more established structure.

Conclusion

Chalmers had become a strong case by 2000 of how, in a European setting, to serve simultaneously as a regional, national and international university. Firstly, helped by its technological focus, it rode the wave of national intent that Swedish universities should learn how to better combine research for understanding with research and training for use. Like Strathclyde in Scotland, it was a place of science and technology – applied S & T – proud to be known for its useful learning. Here, national and regional interests could be seamlessly blended. And those interests required research and training capabilities that could lead to international standing. Chalmers became increasingly certain it could run with the best in other countries, and as evidence pointed to the international networks in which it was included.

Second, Chalmers became a heavily networked university in both its internal operations and its external relations. The internal networking is of particular interest; it consisted of an incorporated company with incorporated subsidiaries that were operationally independent but also linked as parts of one or more Chalmers 'systems'. The networking orientation encouraged new experimental ventures that also could still be related in a loosely joined system. Here was a way to move forward adaptively, while consolidating in tentative, changeable arrangements the ground that had been won. This feature of 'privateness' was not available in older state-defined structures. It comes with the assertive autonomy found elsewhere in some public–private hybrid universities developing in other parts of the world in the early twenty-first century. The emphasis is put squarely on innovative, experimental organization as the basis for sustained innovation, a pivotal point.

The way that Chalmers aggressively moved into external alliances and networks with other universities points to the importance of voluntary linkage with other institutions in arrangements that can be fairly easily modified, even discarded, in comparison with merger forms of connection that establish tighter and more permanent integration. At Chalmers the voluntary line of alliance with firms and other universities has even been pursued, quasi-independently, by such major sub-units as the new Lindholmen campus. Flexibility seemed to be gained, for all contributing parties: leave when it is in your interest to do so; stay and expand the alliance, the network, if it is useful. Mergers have been pursued at this university only in a bottom-up organic fashion by a few related departments with the nearby large University of Gothenburg.

Third, Chalmers has benefited considerably from relatively rapid change in its diversification of income. At the turn of the century, the university could appropriately point to a significant shift underway, year by year, from state core funding to support by other sources, including university acquired funds. Annual increases in total income in the 1997–2000 years, (11, 8, 10, and 2 per cent), averaged nearly 8 per cent. This level of annual increase can ease many pains of adjusting to change. It both pays the bills of slowly rising costs of fixed items and leaves money to support new initiatives. National and state governments cannot be counted on for such beneficial annual increases. They are most dependably gained through institutional initiative in diversifying the financial base. The figures for Chalmers are reminiscent of the annual growth in total income that we noted in the Warwick narrative, where the growth rate exceeded 10 per cent per annum in the late 1990s; 'surpluses' thus generated could be spent in a host of ways.

Allowing for differences in societal settings, we can hazard two guesses about thresholds and springboards in the financial foundation of universities if they are to be steadily adaptable. Universities (like nations!) need at least 2 to 3 per cent threshold average annual increase in total income to just pay the bills. As a springboard for entrepreneurial action, they need at least 5 per cent, and are blessed when they manage to experience 8 to 10 per cent or greater annual additions in their overall budget. They can then simultaneously fix buildings, mow the grass, reward faculty, revise courses, support needy students *and* invest in the future.

Last, and most important, Chalmers exhibited processes that can be summarized as *the social (organizational) development of initiative, innovation, and leadership*. To effectively 'search for independent solutions', the university spread the responsibility for that search to a vast plurality of 'places of initiative'. These places at the outset of transformation were modeled in a major Innovation Centre and then encouraged to emerge in heartland departments and many boundary-spanning units that pursued outside definitions of interdisciplinary and transdisciplinary problems and services. The argument is straightforward. In rapidly changing times with multiplying demands, initiative needs more than ever to be widely distributed within a university: from top to middle to bottom; from heartland departments in the regular academic core to offices, centers, and programs that compose an expanded periphery. In both the core and the periphery new units experiment with new ideas, especially with new forms of outreach. The spread of the power, the right, the obligation to initiate becomes the organizational footing for innovation.

Increasing the number of places that have power to initiate also develops much needed context-appropriate leadership. Leadership is then not treated as a phenomenon dependent on special personality traits, added by discerning recruitment or somehow developed in classes that claim to train leaders for all purposes. Rather, leadership is understood as something that you or I could do, if given the opportunity, the power, to exercise initiative as members of a highly motivated group. Leadership emerges on the spot, situationally developed in many places in an ongoing, organic fashion.

Chalmers has developed its own language to identify and explain these noteworthy organizational processes. The spreading of powers of initiative is seen as 'the *perpetuum mobile* of the university'. It leads to 'an increasing number of true leaders emerging at all levels'. As a result, 'leadership [is] in a constant state of development'. This is a primary reason why 'Chalmers has developed constantly'.[18]

Chalmers – an instructive case study – teaches that the question of how a university can consistently go on changing becomes a question of how it goes about trying to organizationally innovate within and about itself. Useful answers can be found in the direction of constructing multiplying centers of initiative, where a host of groups possess the will and the authority to experiment in how things get done. 'Innovation centers' are notably not 'cost centers'. The cost conception tidies up the edges of existing structures; the innovation definition emphasizes openness and the liberation of energies. From the Chalmers unusual experience, we learn that evolving 'a plurality of special places for innovative behavior' can be both a structure and a dynamic for sustaining change in a university.

6

From transformation to sustainability

If we are going to track and explain change in universities, especially entrepreneurially induced change, it is essential to cycle between case studies and
concepts. The concepts originally set forth in my 1998 book were induced
from case studies. In this second effort, those basic ideas are tested, cor-
rected, and extended by further case work, out of which new concepts as well
as amended older ones are set forth. This logic can operate among
researchers as well as within the body of work of any one scholar; notably, it
encourages interaction between researchers and practitioners in a joint
effort to develop greater practical wisdom. The intent is to probe complex
settings in a way that combines research for understanding with research for
use. A cases-concepts-cases approach can take the analysis of universities into
'the Pasteur quadrant'.

The value of entering *Pasteur's Quadrant*

In his illuminating book, *Pasteur's Quadrant*, Donald E. Stokes developed a
particularly clear depiction of a cross-cutting relationship between the goals
of research for fundamental understanding and research for practical use.
Starting with a single dimension that stretched from basic to applied
research, a common approach, Stokes found he could not effectively locate
the research of Louis Pasteur. Committed both to understanding the processes he discovered *and* to control of the effects of those processes on
humans, animals and various products, this noted scientist belonged equally
far to the left and to the right on this simple continuum. To locate Pasteur at
one point, not at two opposites, a two-dimension conception was clearly
needed, which, when heuristically dichotomized as yes and no on each
dimension, produced a fourfold table. Yes on fundamental understanding
but no on research designed for use became the Bohr quadrant of pure basic
research. Yes on use but no on understanding became the Thomas Edison
box of pure applied research; invent without bothering to explain. The box

for no on both aims went unnamed but can serve as a bin in which to dump dilatory efforts exploring particular phenomena without seeking broad explanation or applied use. Perhaps papers written in social or educational research solely to fatten a publication record would fall here! The quadrant for a double yes became the Pasteur box of '*use-inspired basic research*'. The work of John Maynard Keynes in the social sciences would clearly be included here, as well as the wandering category of 'strategic research' that 'has waited for such a framework to provide it with a conceptual home'.[1]

Led by the huge outpouring of biomedical research in the 1980s and 1990s, much scientific research, including the social sciences, has clearly turned toward the Pasteur combination. The old dichotomy between pure and applied research has slowly given way in one field after another to the realization that the pure and the applied often interact and can stimulate one another. Basic research can indeed be 'use-inspired'. And use can be served by concepts central to broad understanding. Even research on elementary and secondary education has increasingly sought, by operating close to practice, both fundamental understanding and immediate application.'[2] How to do such research becomes the critical question.

When we want to probe such complex organized systems as modern universities, especially to determine how they undergo change, institutional case studies offer a way. They provide in-depth information from which we can draw concentrated conceptual findings that provide both understanding and possible usefulness. The derived concepts can readily be turned back upon the cases to understand them in a common framework. At the same time, in the fullness of case studies we also observe the local variability of concepts and their embeddedness in the particularities that each institution possesses. Just as a picture can be worth a thousand words, a case-study narrative can be worth a thousand statistics. It presents an elaborate composite, core features interweave with one-of-a-kind specificities integral to the character of the particular institution. The highlighted elements lead toward both understanding and use. The composite account adds to the possibilities of contextual use, first in self-reflection and learning in the studied case, and then to inform other institutions in the same realm of possibilities they might consider amid the uniquenesses of their own heritage and setting.

The case-study approach then is a powerful vehicle for studying universities in some depth. As organized purposive institutions they determine much of the action taking place in their sector of society. As we move from cases to concepts in such research, we seek explanations of change that can be seen as use-inspired basic research. Working close to the efforts of practitioners immersed in interacting complexities, we can aim for serviceable concepts that offer local variability as they range across cases. This approach offers a practical sense of theoretical possibilities. It is an important form of research for 'social science that matters'.[3] One outstanding exemplar may be worth a thousand remote theories.

From cases to concepts

I use a narrative style in this book in which concluding results accumulate piecemeal as analysis moves through a set of institutions. This approach is the opposite of offering a quick-and-easy summary at the outset, which in its neatness and simplicity grossly understates complex realities. Better to unfold conclusions gradually, with new findings adding scope and depth to previous ones. This procedure also parallels the cumulative incrementalism so important in university change: we can mimic that phenomenon in a free-flowing analysis as it moves from case to case. We gain both in understanding and potential use by confronting concepts in successive realities where the common features we extract are still immersed in the swirling actions of individual institutions. Between the general and the particular, we strive to have it both ways. What follows are brief institutional summaries of the previous case studies. What did we learn that may have lasting value elsewhere?

Accumulative findings from cases

Warwick An entrepreneurial university second-to-none in Europe, Warwick has developed a capacity to generate resources for both support of new ventures and enrichment of basic traditional programs – excellent under-graduate teaching in history, economics and physics, for example – thereby beating traditional universities at their own game. In the university's ascent in the ratings and rankings of British higher education to near the top – just about as good as they come – the evidence is clear that an entrepreneurial university, carefully crafted, can do traditional things well.

To insure the sustainability of its transformation, Warwick defines 'generating significant resources ourselves in order to build for the future' as a core objective on par with providing excellent research and teaching today. An income growth rate of 10 per cent a year strongly supports this aim, allowing the institution to nourish both the present and the future. The university has engrained a willingness in its management structure and academic culture to seek out and develop new ways of strengthening its highly proactive stance: e.g. develop a full-blown graduate school; offer a special program to attract and support young scholars; define alumni as a key asset; tap resources of the health sector. The university's attitude is optimistic and enthusiastic, verging at times on exuberance. Not every university gets the Prime Minister of Great Britain and the President of the United States to jointly celebrate on its grounds and in its halls – in full view of the televised world – the end of one century and the beginning of another, a millennium occasion to boot.

Three features to which we later return make Warwick a paradigmatic case: it strongly exhibits a reinforcing interaction among transforming elements; it strongly exhibits changes built incrementally and accumulatively over time; and, most important, it exhibits intense willpower to decide for itself what kind of university it will be. It is decidedly self-led. In these persisting features, we find the beginning of a generalizable formula for sustainability.

Strathclyde As it grew considerably in scale and scope, Strathclyde exhibited the important value of a clearly stated and easily understood identity – a place of useful learning – that connects a desirable institutional future to its past and present. The identity helps to fuse continuity and change; it offers a focus that contains diffusion, e.g., we do not do classics, we do not do sociology for its own sake. The university is also a strong case of generating encompassing interests; its vaulted University Management Group mixes faculty and administrators in a useful central form of shared governance that dedicates itself to the interests of the whole. Collegial entrepreneurialism is embedded.

Like Warwick, Strathclyde had gradually moved from transforming effort to sustaining work. Now well interlocked, the initial pathways of transformation have become a new steady state of sustainable change. That steady state includes what I later discuss as 'a bureaucracy of change' – the substantial addition of non-faculty professionals whose tasks involve promoting change. The office of Research and Consultancy Services at Strathclyde is a particularly clear and illuminating case of how such professionals become a 'factor' of production (as well as another administrative cost), as they systematically interact with faculty groups in a highly proactive fashion. Sheer usefulness has moved this office from its initial minor location on the outreach periphery to the administrative-faculty heartland.

Strathclyde has also developed such transforming features as using an alumni base for financial and moral support, mining royalties from patented inventions and ideas, and actively forming alliances with other universities. It has worked steadily to reduce dependence on faltering state support by always widening the portfolio of income streams to include more public agencies as well as business firms and philanthropic foundations. It, too, scores high on internal will; it too has invested its history with sufficient emotion to turn its culture into a saga. It is now well positioned to connect its search for independence to the economy and identity of a more independent Scotland.

Twente Self-defined as an entrepreneurial university since the early 1980s, Twente has pursued, for two decades, the pathways of transformation highlighted in my earlier research, long enough to become deeply involved in problematic issues of sustainability. From its experience we see the need for change-minded universities to be involved in balancing contradictions newly brought to life. Long known for its outreach capabilities, Twente has found that many of its faculties, departments and centers, now more self-supporting, become group entrepreneurs; this presented in an unintended way a problem of balance between administrative center and base units. During the late 1990s officials at the center worked to build more encompassing frameworks and interests; e.g., a new major–minor scheme applied to all undergraduate students; centrally conceived efforts to back cross-disciplinary innovation; a strengthened central management group. Balancing the authority structure required an effort to reinvigorate collegiality at the all-university level.

Twente has also become self-conscious about two other balancing acts: between focus and comprehensiveness; and between regional, national and international postures. To focus while expanding, the university pushed beyond its established foci of technological sciences and social sciences to develop a group of fields in the health sciences. Like Warwick and Strathclyde, Twente can point also to a range of initiatives and programs that simultaneously orient it locally, nationally and internationally.

Such balancing acts, we begin to sense, are part of a steady state that promotes change. In practice the balance is never just right, never perfectly poised for the ages; from one half-decade to the next, it needs adjustment. Traditional self-satisfied universities, short on volition, simply let rooted imbalances continue: let sleeping dogs lie lest they rise up in angry conflict. Complex universities that strive to keep up with the times attend to their various imbalances. They work at ways to maximize initiative at multiple levels, maintain some focused control over diffusion of character, and strengthen capacity to serve diverse communities of interest.

Joensuu After developing university-type academic departments and opening the door to research in its first fifteen years of existence, Joensuu used modern pathways of transformation in the late 1980s and early 1990s to move toward, in its terms, greater 'self-realization'. Strong willpower was required to move sharply away from encrusted state lines of control, emphasizing decentralization of initiative to faculties and departments. Along the way, the university developed several points of distinction by focused investment in the sciences and forestry. Particularly in these fields, the university has been able to compete for funding that supported research activities and doctoral-level graduate programs.

As at Twente, Joensuu has had to cope with stirred-up contradictions: authority at the center versus the operating parts; selective focus amid generous comprehensiveness; and local, national and international orientations that do not readily coincide. With the government and the private sector insisting that the country's universities rapidly develop more strength in science and technology, the university has used its reputation for competitive excellence in selected fields to take up the national challenge. This would-be role is the basis for both international standing and regional relevance. It also provides the rationale for focus, spelled out in selective investment.

A combination of teachers'-college inheritance, rural location, and small size has been a heady set of constraints. But collegial entrepreneurship is possible in diverse settings, notably in ones characterized by heavily constraining conditions. Joensuu makes its way as a small but comprehensive public university (humanities, social sciences, sciences, forestry, education), in which a good deal of daily activity must be devoted to the preparation of local schoolteachers. Strain is unavoidable between this central feature and the effort to be a competitive, fast-adapting research enterprise. But the university committed itself anew at the beginning of the twenty-first century to build on its excellence in selected academic fields: the shape of a regional university here would follow from competency as a national and international university.

Chalmers This technological university has for some time exhibited close connection and intense interaction among the five transforming elements set forth in my earlier round of research. From 1980 onward, the university invested in infrastructure designed for the promotion of innovation. It gradually encircled the centers and programs thereby created on both the periphery and in the traditional departments with a strongly accented 'entrepreneurial spirit'. It backed the new cause with a strengthening of managerial leadership at the major organizational levels and a steady diversification of income that brought in new resources and slowly diminished dependence on state core allotment.

Increasingly eager to be more autonomous – 'to assert ourselves', 'to do things ourselves' – Chalmers took a major step in 1994 toward becoming freer for self-development by taking up the status of a foundation university, a hybrid form in which it could be a separately incorporated private entity but still receive some basic state allocations. Between 1995 and 2000, the university used its enhanced freedom to become a beehive of activity in generating 'places of initiative' and 'special places for innovative behavior'. As it did so, by encouraging individuals to exercise initiative in those many special places, it learned how to create context-specific leadership deeply committed to change. It learned how to be a 'networked university' and assemble networks of internal units in new 'systems'. It increasingly became a complicated 'company', with 'subsidiaries'; it became the direct owner of properties. As it became a federated structure of incorporated entities, the university further institutionalized autonomy from state control.

Like Warwick, but in a technological university form within a continental state system, Chalmers is a virtual prototype of how to become a self-reliant university by means of entrepreneurial actions. It has learned how to further and sustain change by granting the power, the right, the responsibility to initiate and to innovative in a spreading plurality of places. Its success in doing so has led it to be well-balanced as a regional, national and international university. All in all, Chalmers is a remarkable case of the workings of persistent institutional volition.

Pathways of transformation revisited

The five categories I developed in *Creating Entrepreneurial Universities* were somewhat broad. I wanted to be parsimonious in specifying explanatory concepts, utilizing no more than a half-dozen rather than naming ten or twenty or more categories that would diffuse explanation into a laundry list. The search was for a certain few things that were more important than others in the modern transformation of universities. I also wanted the named elements to apply across the examined cases, if in varying degree, and then potentially to many other unseen cases. In short, I was aiming for the middle range; I was generalizing at only one or two recognizable levels above the gritty, messy details of each university's complex reality, in a range that would shun grand explanations full of remote fogginess and lacking analytical bite relevant to application.

From the experience of the present study I recognize that the original pathways can pave the way for sustained change. Toward a conceptual swing from transformation to sustainability, I clarify further the diversified funding base, the strengthened steering core, the elaborated periphery, the mobilized heartland, and the embracing entrepreneurial culture.

The diversified funding base

When discussing the financial underpinnings of the entrepreneurial university, I have in past writings mainly referred to three streams of income: mainline support from a governmental ministry or department; funds from governmental research councils; and all other sources lumped together as 'third-stream income'. This threefold breakdown was useful in showing movement toward the second and third streams, a shift that raised more money and increased local discretion in how to spend it. Such financial diversification seems essential for increased self-reliance. A university can then move ahead on desired initiatives without waiting for system-wide enactments that come slowly and with standardizing rules attached. The university can better roll with the punches, replacing a loss in income here with a gain there. Provided new monies are raised by legally and educationally legitimate means – nothing from the Mafia, thank you – the general rule is simple: it is better to have more money than less.

The third-stream category lumped together a host of different sources. A few substreams point to different arrangements and possibilities.

Other organized government sources. Many government agencies, other than the core-support department, want to link up with universities and receive useful services in return. Increasingly common among nations, these include departments devoted to defense, health, transportation, agriculture and forestry, economic development, and technological development at the national level; similar departments in regional and city governments; and supranational public bodies such as the European Union (EU). Such public sources, particularly traditional ones, may grant long-term support for 'their' part of a university – or even their university, as has historically been true in the case of agriculture, nursing and schoolteaching. But the modern trend is toward grant making characterized by agency peer-review and competitive allocation.

Thus, as universities actively seek out additional supporters, their income portfolios prominently exhibit government departments. The multiplying possibilities are as broad as governments themselves. What alert agency does not want relevant university research? What department does not want a dedicated pathway trodden by well-educated graduates from the university to its door? University relations with such departments do not bother critics of entrepreneurial universities who worry about 'commercialization'. And income from other government sources may readily top the contribution from business firms, even at technological universities: at Chalmers in 2000, for example, income from 'other state grants', 'public foundation grants', and 'EU grants' totaled over 25 per cent of total income, compared to less than 10 per cent from private companies.[4]

Private organized sources. These sources include professional associations based on business specialties, accountancy for example, that promote continuing professional development for their members. A key private organized source, of course, is business firms, large and small, with whom the university becomes involved in contract research and contract education. Large industrial and commercial firms, short-term and long-term, want something for their money, sometimes even firm-specific research or training. Industry-university 'collaboration' may then entail tough bargaining over contractual arrangements and compromises over priority of interests. The operational meaning of 'partnership' has to be spelled out. Open publication of research results can be a key issue, as firms seek to guard results, at least in the short term, while faculty members want to tell the whole world. Small companies, especially those spun off from the university, are a different matter; they generally receive nurturance from a mother institution. Governments also look kindly upon university sponsorship of small and medium-size firms that are needed in high technology and require special support in their tender years.

Obtaining financial help from business firms in the short term – or later down the road from equity positions in start-ups – moves universities beyond interdisciplinary research and teaching to transdisciplinary outlooks brought in as industry-centered problems. Universities have to be on guard in a fundamental way about bridging this new relationship. For good or bad, results may bring basic change in its knowledge base. Here in this terrain is where academics worry most about the character of universities as they undergo change. Leaping over traditional boundaries, entrepreneurial universities have to worry about the leap too far. However ambiguous and porous, new boundaries have to be thrashed out, with academic criteria serving as guideposts.

Philanthropic foundations are a third, often major, private organized source. Local, national and international foundations have become important supporters of universities in many countries other than the Anglo-Saxon ones, pre-eminently the United States and Great Britain, in which they have for a long time played a shaping role.[5] A few huge foundations can provide income to universities for certain activities that equal or exceed government support: the Wellcome Trust in Britain for biomedical research infrastructure; the Soros Foundation for selective program support in Eastern and Central European universities; the Wallenburg Foundation in Sweden for buildings and expensive scientific equipment; the Rockefeller Foundation and World Bank for infrastructure subsidy in African universities. Philanthropic support even becomes a finely tuned business in which small foundations help to equip a specific room in a specific university building, provided the foundation's name is engraved in stone over the door. Between state agencies and market organizations, the foundations, becoming more numerous and diverse, are a self-constituted 'third sector' of support. These non-profit organizations can be key supporters for new initiatives. Universities alive with centers of initiative seek them out.

University generated income. For change-oriented universities, the most promising income providers are those the university itself can develop and directly control. Foremost is income from endowment. A strategic decision of the first order is to squirrel away some 'surplus' income as endowment, rather than to spend it all next year on immediate needs – a decision that mirrors the hard choice that individuals and families have to make between saving for the future and spending now. But this decision is more difficult to make in a bloated university family. Endowment income (properly managed!) offers compound income growth for years to come. It also offers the highest degree of discretionary expenditure. It is really 'money in the bank' – diversified according to choices located on the safe-to-risky investment continuum.

For the best reasons, building endowment has become a primary tool that universities transforming themselves use to move from state control to self-reliance. For them as much as for individuals, owning assets confers independence and autonomy. Endowment is groundwork for more freedom and less regulation – and less public spending for university support.

Similarly, income obtained from alumni fund-raising, earmarked to be spent contemporaneously, is a first-class source. When a well-oiled alumni and development office can dependably bring in an aggregate sum of relatively free money each year, money that is more likely to go up than down compared to previous years, and up faster than the inflation rate, soft money has indeed been turned into hard money. The trick of convincing graduates that they are alumni who willingly contribute to the education of later generations of students at their alma mater is more difficult in continental systems where free university education is still claimed as a birthright by qualifying students; as graduates they feel that they owe nothing to the university or future generations. But the alumni source is too valuable to continue to ignore in cash-strapped universities, especially when near-term poverty is coupled with ambition. Proactive public universities get to this option faster and more fully than do the institutions that simply want to do things the old-fashioned way.

Universities, nationally and internationally, can teach each other how to do it. Once alerted, a university can figure out (a) how to reach graduates at different levels of personal wealth by different means, (b) how to ask for backing of specific projects versus contributing to general funds, and (c) how to boost sustained results to new levels by occasional, well-timed fund-raising drives. Such alumni outreach can always be worth exploring: it can even be initiated and developed by hiring an experienced American as development officer.

A third source of self-generated income is, of course, student tuition and fees, if the institution is free to set and change student payments. In strictly state-led systems, universities have few, if any, such options. These systems set across-the-board rules that, for example, the charging of tuition fees is not permitted, or that it is possible only at a nationally defined level, or is not permitted for domestic undergraduates but can be applied to foreign and graduate students. Students generally contest the imposition and raising of tuition payments: they and their parents threaten revenge at the ballot box; student organizations march on various seats of power, sometimes gathering bricks and rocks on the way. Just ask French ministers!

But the advantages of tuition and student fees are too great to ignore. As the state retreats as a full-cost patron, this particular source of substantial income is widely seen around the globe as the natural substitute for diminished state aid.[6] Private universities that run the gamut from degree mills to the best universities in the world can be observed extracting large sums from students and their families. As the competitiveness of public universities increases within nations and internationally, they find they are disadvantaged if they ignore this source. Hence it sneaks in first through one door then another – for foreign students, certain graduate programs, adults in continuing professional development (sometimes paid for by firms), and continuing education generally, and then in increasing increments in undergraduate education. By 2000 the clear mark of a state-led national system of higher education was a continuing state prohibition on universities raising their own money in serious measure by assessing tuition and fees to cover at least part of the cost of students' education.

A fourth source within immediate university control is earned income from campus operations, a fascinating possibility modeled to the world by Warwick's development of an earned-income portfolio. The university's Earned Income Group has learned to closely monitor income from over fifty distinct operations, in such subgroups as: *academic-driven activities*, based in academic departments and focused on fee-paying teaching and research (accounting for 70 per cent or so of earned income at Warwick, with large sums obtained from research grants and contracts, the work of the business school, the manufacturing group in engineering, and overseas students); *spin-off activities*, sales of services arising incidentally from mainstream university activities, property leasing, printing and library services, for example;

stand-alone activities, operated both to provide services and to generate surpluses, e.g., conference centers, campus store, news agency; and *self-financing
activities*, which provide services but are expected only to break even, e.g.,
student residences, food services, photocopying. From all these amassed
sources, the amount of income over direct running expenses is totaled as
'gross surplus'. Some of this money is paid out to departments and to special
funds; the remainder is taken as net surplus available to the university for
reallocation to other purposes.

Total income thus raised annually can be major. At Warwick it totals
more than the combined income from the state core grant and domestic
student fees. In turn, the gross surplus is substantial year in and year out.
And with most of it taken as net surplus, the free money for all-university
reassignment greatly leverages initiatives and cross-subsidy of needy
departments. This well-developed portfolio puts in place the expectation
that 'we' can, by sustained attention and hard work, not only increase total
income but also develop substantial surpluses that can be divided up as
rewards for all and in the end be finally used as funds that are almost totally
discretionary.

A fifth source that can be brought under direct university determination
is royalty income from patented inventions and licensing of intellectual
property. This source can readily prove more difficult to construct than
first anticipated. The first thing a university has to do is to keep inventions
from going 'out the back door', or 'over the wall', as creative professors or
graduate students, seeking the chance to make a lot of money, take their
ideas to the outside and commercialize inventions themselves. To establish
minimal controls around such 'exit' behavior, the university has to move
into a new gray area to establish norms, rules and procedures on patent
ownership. Did the invention or new idea come from research done under
university-based sponsored grants? Were campus facilities used? Was the
assistance of staff and graduate students taken into account? How much of
the brain of the researcher, or teacher, or professor-consultant does the
university own?

The issues are many and keep shifting. But the point is to share the income
from exploited research at least between the university and the inventing
individual(s), and more commonly with involved research groups, departments and faculties. The aim is to both maintain incentives for use-inspired
research and to distribute monetary returns among the parties who made
the research possible, starting with the host university itself.

Determined but patient universities learn how to work out such relationships and develop another income stream of high potential. The lure on the
institutional side is the chance to be among the occasional big winners on
singularly successful patented items, a major useful drug for example; or to
build a reasonable likelihood of streams of patents that succeed one another
as older patents run out or as protected items lose their profitable place in
shifting markets. Even if difficult, the process is not Herculean, as long as
expectations are kept under control. Strathclyde's development of this

stream of income started more than twenty years ago, especially in drug research, and has been carefully nurtured by specialized administrative officers working with specialized research teams. We never rely on this royalty stream, an officer commented in 2002, 'but it is "free money" that the university can use with no strings attached'. Part of that income goes to the inventors: 'We have some wealthy professors in our departments – it's a great incentive.' And some side effects can be highly beneficial: 'The atracurium deal cemented the relationship between Glaxo Wellcome and the university and has brought in many research contracts over the years.'

Across Great Britain, the increasing number of universities pursuing this income stream – for example, University College London, Oxford, Nottingham, Aberdeen – have been kept on their toes by the realization that lurking in the background 'were the ghosts of the blockbusters that got away – penicillin and monoclonal antibodies – as reminders of what can happen if you do not seize opportunities'. A university could even 'be accused of negligence if it missed the chance to exploit some new technology simply because it had not been patented beforehand'.[7]

But filing patents is expensive, large additional legal costs may come into play vis-à-vis major business firms, and the specialist staffs who deal with such commercialization do not come cheap. Hence, this source requires time and skill – and modest expectations. But it is also too promising to let it slip by without careful examination. When it is worked out carefully, as at Strathclyde, with norms of sharing, it can even add to mutual staff respect and enhanced loyalty.

With non-core and non-research-council income possible from (a) other government agencies, (b) private organized entities, particularly business firms and philanthropic foundations, and (c) university-constructed streams of support, there is virtually no limit to the possibilities of 'all other sources'. Even in still heavily nationalized university systems, we find regional and city governments, as well as national economic and technological agencies, joining in. Income is generally obtained from them on competitive grounds and hence becomes differentiated among universities – not only among winners and losers in competitions but also among those who try hard and those who do not in seeking new sources. Heritage counts: technological universities are in a favorable position when government *and* industry *and* the general public want universities in the twenty-first century to be centers of science and technology relevant to economic progress.

Because they utilize many sources, entrepreneurial universities build and sustain virtuous circles of income generation; they overcome the now-common vicious circles of decline in unit-cost support occasioned by persistent state cuts that over decades change student–teacher ratios in universities of 10:1 to 20:1 or 30:1 or higher. In some non-laboratory fields in mega universities in Mediterranean Europe and Latin America, we can even find ratios of 100:1 and more. Such shameful stuffing of students into large lecture halls, along with allowing them to absent themselves after registering, makes a mockery of modern university education. Diversification of income is then not a luxury. It is a basic determinant of whether universities in such twisted settings will provide more than symbolic student participation.

A high degree of financial dependence on a single mainline source is a flawed way to develop modern universities, particularly proactive ones. The interests of national and regional governments multiply and change. University support, as repeatedly demonstrated in the late twentieth century, can readily slide down the government's list of priorities. Often higher on the scale are health, welfare, primary and secondary education, foreign affairs, defense, environment, and issues of the day which have large constituencies or interest groups more effective than the university lobby. Universities then learn about the enduring downside of single-source dependency. Why keep 'waiting for Godot', when experience has shown that the minister toting a sack of money will not appear? Why keep betting on an old horse when it has repeatedly come up lame? Why keep all your eggs in one basket? Enterprising universities know better: they learn how to shape, even control, their financial underpinnings by diversifying their sources of income.

To disentangle the many streams of diversified income now found in modern universities, and particularly to distinguish their usefulness, institutional case studies are a necessary research tool.

The strengthened steering core

The pathway of university transformation identified as the strengthened steering core – avoiding conceptions of overpersonalized leadership – covers many possible structures and relationships also best revealed in specific case studies. As they involve the basic authority structures of universities, the possibilities work out somewhat differently in one national context than in another, in Great Britain and The Netherlands, for example; and differently in diverse locations within nations, in a small university in a rural location than in a large university in a dominating city, as, for example, in Holland or Finland. But as seen in the five European cases, a few commonalities exist. A strengthened steering capacity embraces central management groups and academic departments: operationally it has to reconcile new managerial values with older academic orientations. How? The case studies exhibit three notable methods: first, pursue flat structure, eliminating intermediate units to minimize barriers between the center and base units; second, increase authority and responsibility at existing multiple levels, especially at center, faculty, and department; and third, professionalize administration all along the line and particularly at the center.

Warwick and Joensuu have made their way without the help of deans. Warwick, for example, has taken great pride in its flat structure. Its departments and research centers have direct contact with a center consisting of the vice-chancellor's office and a small set of interlocked committees. The university has managed to make this simplified vertical arrangement work well. It depends on effective departmental leadership, personal and collegial, and on a corps of highly competent administrators working in and around the central committees. A steadily expanding volume of 'business' in a growing university puts great strain on this simplified arrangement. But by 2000 Warwick was still stressing its effectiveness and the advantages of direct personal communication between center and base units. The flat structure helps to speed coordination. It also reduces greatly the we–they gap that so naturally develops in universities between faculty and administrators-managers.

The second more widespread pattern builds on the traditional university basic structure; a small central office headed by rector, president, or vice-chancellor; faculties headed by deans; and departments chaired by a head. Strathclyde, Twente and Chalmers exhibit this basic type; it pivots on a middle faculty level that relates both upward in an administrative hierarchy and downward to a set of departments. In all three cases and at all levels the institutions have developed stronger personal authority in line positions and simultaneously greater collegial authority in surrounding committees. At the center, the Strathclyde UMG (University Management Group) has emerged as a prototype, combining stronger individual authority with stronger collegial authority, along with much professionalization of central administration.

The distribution of authority in change-oriented universities turns out not to be a zero-sum game. More initiative is useful all along the line, as vividly revealed at Chalmers: you really cannot have too much of it and its frequent occurrence depends on the diffused power to act. With dual and triple personnel assignments located in cross-cutting matrixes, enterprising universities risk conflicting arrangements. They prefer disorder over order; they press the choices of liberty over those of equity.

The third pattern is used in both flat structures and three-level arrangements: hire and develop administrators expert in specialized administrative domains, especially finance but extending through such sprawling activities as student affairs and alumni relations. Sizeable chunks of university coordinating work are now too complicated to be handled well by amateurs retired from the professoriate or hired on the cheap off the street. In the cases at hand I found at Strathclyde central finance officers who, in comparison to personnel in other government agencies, were prize-winning experts. At Twente I also saw high levels of expertise in large faculties where the senior administrator headed a staff of fifty or more whose specialties recapitulated many of those found in the central administration.

Two ongoing problems were common as the studied universities went about strengthening their steering core. Managerial values, useful in running an evermore complex organization, have to be reconciled with traditional academic expectations, useful in tapping faculty base-unit expertise and sustaining common identity. The contradiction here is in part a clash between personal and group-based leadership, the 'I' and the 'we'. Extremely personalized forms of leadership – the dictator, the authoritarian figure, the commanding CEO – do not endure. They do not permanently fit.

More than in traditional business firms and government departments, collegial forms of governance are used to surround the more personal forms. Based on professional expertise and disciplinary competence in the basic task structure, the 'we' comes to dominate the 'I'. Enterprising universities, I stress repeatedly, are characterized by collegial entrepreneurialism.

A second never fully solved problem in the various arrangements for a strengthened steering capacity is the balancing of authority and responsibility across levels and among the many parts to both enhance initiative and maintain coherence. The balancing act is conditioned by the natural bottom-heaviness of universities, the simple fact that a university is fundamentally an assembly of many different fields of knowledge – disciplinary, interdisciplinary and now transdisciplinary; it is as different as chemistry from classics, biology from political science, medicine from the performing arts, law from physics, cultural studies from environmental pollution, continuing professional development for accountants from Shakespeare Studies for senior citizens. The departments, research centers, and special teaching programs that constitute the base where the work is done have the authority of the required professional expertise.

If we are asked simply how do universities think and act, we can but offer the accurate but limp answer that they think and act in increasingly diverse ways in increasingly diverse internal sites. Their authority structures, their steering cores, alone tell us that universities are the last place for simple managerial bromides and one-size-fits-all solutions. About the many conflicts and complications of university steerage, extended case-study analysis has many stories to tell that can have sensitizing effects elsewhere.

The elaborated developmental periphery

The new peripheries enterprising universities construct (to supplement traditional offices and departments and to stretch across old boundaries to link up with outside agencies and constituencies) take two primary forms: administrative offices and academic units.

Administrative offices. One compelling reason why the administrative structure of a university increasing becomes a rabbit warren of specific offices occupied by specialized administrators is that every new connection to the outside world requires an office, or a new part of one. The discussion above of the many sources of diversified income suggests a virtual catalog of necessary offices to relate to varied sources: to other national agencies, in health, defense, technological and economic development, *and* to agencies of regional and city governments, *and* to supranational bodies, all calling for in-house expertise; to widening sources of private funds, pre-eminently business firms in different economic sectors and professional associations clamoring for relevant continuing education and philanthropic foundations; to specific offices for all the hard work that goes into the incremental development of self-generated income, from alumni and other individual supporters, from different categories of students paying tuition and other fees, from an array of campus operations, from potential inventions, intellectual property rights, and equity positions in assisted firms. Just as there are seemingly no limits to the possibilities of extra sources of income, there is virtually no limit on the addition of bureaucratic units and hence on the constant need to reorder and concentrate them.

Thus, they multiply: the ever busy grants and contracts office; the office of industrial relations; the alumni segment of the multi-sided development office; the technology transfer office; the continuing education office; the retail services office; the conference and special events office, the capital projects office, and more, all make sense, all are needed. The bureaucracy grows in transforming universities but it is one based on a change orientation very different from the old rule-enforcing, state-mandated bureaucracy left behind in the jettisoned framework. Transformation is particularly a threat to the traditional civil servants located in universities who operate primarily as supervising arms of the state. They are gradually replaced or dominated by the new bureaucrats of change.[8]

Boundary-spanning new academic units. The part of the developmental periphery that makes the greatest difference in university character is the added array of boundary-spanning academic units and programs. Together they move a university toward a dual structure of basic units in which traditional, discipline-centered departments are supplemented by centers – generally multidisciplinary and even transdisciplinary – that link themselves to the outside world. These centers admit external definitions of research problems and needed training. The new groups cross old lines of authority and draw faculty from departments to compose project groups – a useful form of matrix structure for growing the service role of universities. They serve as exploratory operations and turn over more rapidly than disciplinary departments. They generate income that helps to diversity funding. Like multi-sponsored science parks, they can even operate as mediating institutions situated halfway between a host university and outside organizations, facing in both directions.

The concept of developmental periphery, then, insists that we stop thinking of modern universities simply as places composed of disciplinary departments and programs, topped by a central administration. Old core departments remain basic, but they are increasingly supplemented by other operational units that naturally trade with the outside world and thereby develop knowledge that is more applications-generated and problem-oriented.[9] Entrepreneurial universities cultivate lively peripheries in which they multiply alliances with outside organizations.

The increasing duality of basic units presents fundamental problems. At a minimum, some 'epistemic drift'[10] will take place as new definitions of knowledge are added in parts of the university. At a minimum, a broader, more distributed university is created around a combination of old and new approaches to knowledge. An adaptive university gives new modes of thinking a chance to stake a claim for internal support and space. The danger to be guarded against is that the center will not hold – that core academic values will no longer remain the touchstone for choices of lines of development.

Younger scholars are often more interested in participating in multidisciplinary clusters than serving only in a department. Jan-Eric Sundgren, President of Chalmers, says it clearly:

> young faculty will become increasingly more interested in projects in which the background of the project team members are diverse and complementary. The loyalty towards projects will most likely be higher compared to the loyalty toward the institution or the department. This tendency is already clearly seen in new start-up companies working in the IT [information technology] and biotechnology areas. Innovative universities need to stimulate formation of transdisciplinary projects and centers as a complement to the more traditional departments and institutions. *If this is not done the quality of the academic heartland will gradually decrease.* [emphasis added][11]

His point is most relevant for science and technology departments. But it also applies to the social sciences and humanities. A second, more multidisciplinary home perhaps more inviting and invigorating than the department of first appointment can readily be observed in campus area-study centers. Experts on Japan, for example, who are loners in their departments – literature, history, political science, economics – can find colleagueship and common interest in an interdisciplinary Center for Japanese Studies. Their spouses particularly perceive the center a hospitable place to share the language and to connect culturally. On summer vacation and research trips, they all meet again in Tokyo.

If the 'knowledge center' is to hold – no endless shopping mall here – then the university's central groups have to draw upon traditional departmental faculty in deciding which new activities are permissible and which are beyond the pale, even within wider boundaries. A gradual interpenetration, formal and informal, of heartland departments and peripheral units is helpful. When departments are expected to look to their own income-producing potential, they acquire a greater interest in external service. And when newly established peripheral centers have been successful for a few years they move into the zone of campus legitimacy in which, similar to departments, they become established interests and sunk costs. Our distinguishing concepts do not point to airtight compartments. Heartland and periphery overlap and fuse in gray combinations.

The stimulated heartland

In my 1998 book I pointed out that

since universities consist of widely divergent fields in their traditional departments, enterprising action typically spreads unevenly in the old heartland. Science and technology departments commonly become entrepreneurial first and most fully. Social science departments, aside from economics and business, find the shift more difficult and lag behind. Humanities departments have good reason to be resisting laggards: new money does not readily flow their way from either governmental or nongovernmental patrons. Deliberate effort on their part to go out and raise funds by offering new services may seem particularly out of place, even demeaning.[12]

Hence, uneven adoption of new ways should be expected. And we should expect such unevenness in heartland departments to be greater in comprehensive universities than in technological ones, in large universities than in small- to middle-size ones. Particularly tough nuts are large European-style universities composed of large stand-alone faculties or schools – geographically separated faculties of medicine, law, science and humanities are examples – that have long had their own direct lines of funding from a central governmental ministry. Schizophrenic character may develop along an entrepreneurial/traditional faultline, with minimal interaction and little or no cross-subsidy across major components. The entrepreneurial side, looking to new forms of outreach and knowledge production, depends on diversified income. The traditional side depends on mainline subsidy based on student enrollment and such other standardized bases of state allocation as faculty size and needed floor space.

The heartland departments in my study gradually bought into entrepreneurial change for the most part. More money overall is better than less money: it can be used to add faculty and support students. Income surpluses can be turned to helping poor departments maintain and develop themselves. Becoming educationally useful in meeting such new social demands as continuing education can also be seen as moral, not simply as a grab for money. Departments, then, instead of expecting full subsidy without special effort on their part, and drifting year by year from one configuration of demand to another, were encouraged to respond selectively to the demands made upon them, ranging from potential students, young and old, as well as from professional associations, business firms, and local and national government departments.

Thus, small size helped in seizing the entrepreneurial option, particularly at the outset of transformation. Generic focus helped, as in the science-and-technology grounding of Strathclyde, Twente and Chalmers. But such features of established character did not alone determine the acceptance of entrepreneurialism across the older segments of the university. Stimulated by the ambition to be a better university, in effective capacity as well as in reputation, the gradual build-up of a broad institutional will could be discerned. To better understand sustained change, we will focus in the concluding section of this chapter on how volition is organizationally constructed.

As stimulated heartland departments join the many units of the expanded periphery in promoting widely diverse entrepreneurial actions, a university becomes a very different place from the historic one seen by the public. It is no longer centered on young undergraduates. The educational program itself is extensively altered. The university attends to the development of graduate education (or 'postgraduate education'). When the first degree is normally reached in three or four years – the British bachelor's, for example – the graduate level, composed of both master's and doctoral degrees may rapidly become a second tier that rivals the lower tier in student size and outweighs it in financial resources. When the first degree has been taken traditionally after completion of a five- or six-year program – as in The Netherlands and Germany – it is seen as equal to the Anglo-American master's degree and as signifying achievement of a professional level of competence in a subject. How to go about producing PhDs in much greater numbers, appropriate to mass higher education, then becomes a new business. Commonly in the 1990s it took the form of discipline-based groupings of faculty and students across universities rather than a university-wide aggregation of many subjects in 'the graduate school'. In either case much more investment in doctoral students becomes a basic trend, one promoted by contract research done for industry that seeks the highest level of trained competence. Income from industry particularly becomes income for support of the most advanced work. 'Post-docs' are then also likely to appear on the scene in greater numbers.

Alongside this programmatic development upward in educational levels, a second trend of outward development exists – continuing education or life-long learning, especially in continuing professional development of adults already employed. Contract education soon accumulates various types of specific service programs for professional associations as well as business firms. Programmatically, the university is extended, becoming both more vertical in levels of educational preparation in old fields and more horizontal in its provision of additional service programs for previously unserved groups. Entrepreneurial universities work hard on both fronts to achieve competitive advantage.

The integrated entrepreneurial culture

'Culture' remains one of those generous concepts in the social sciences we can hardly do without but find difficult to pin down. If we are not careful, we are soon grasping at the fogginess of a symbolic phenomenon that seems to hover in a wispy way over daily life. Universities are particularly prone to discuss their institutional cultures in maudlin, even pious, abstractions. Their self-concepts can readily levitate and float grandly over the hard realities of day-to-day action. A certain amount of bloviation is virtually part of the job description laid down for the modern university rector or vice-chancellor or president, necessary for both improving public relations and uplifting staff morale.

But my studies point to two ways to deploy the concept of culture and still stay close to practical realities. One is to depict the development of a new culture over time, from an immature idea to a matured, grounded, and widely accepted bundle of beliefs. The second is to insist that the more symbolic side of the university is interwoven with its structural features and develops in interaction with them.

The development of an entrepreneurial culture can be viewed as movement from idea to belief to culture to saga. New organizational ideas – such as the tentative idea of earned income that Warwick tried out in the early 1980s – are but small symbolic probings in what is possible. For the idea to make headway, it has to be organizationally feasible, be somewhat successful, and then be spread among participants to blossom into a set of linked ideas, beliefs that stress distinctive ways. As these ideas spread to embrace much or even all of the institution, they become a new culture expressive of a will to change. The initial simple probe – it could have died at birth – becomes a self-asserting, shared view, offering a unifying identity. The institution is then prone to embellish its story of successful accomplishment: see how we have overcome all obstacles placed in our path, especially by the wicked government, look at what we have done through determination and hard work. The culture then acquires saga characteristics.[13]

This ideational transformation does not occur in isolation. However we conceive the road traveled by institutional ideas, we have to understand this pathway in interaction with concrete practices – the everyday ongoing realities of efforts to diversify income, to strengthen and balance a new steering capacity, to develop outreach by means of added non-traditional components, to convince old departments to act in new proactive ways. Ideas about what should be done are little more than musings until they are made to happen. They happen when they acquire a social base of believers; they happen when structures and procedures are put in place that turn them into practical expressions. All this takes place over time, over years and even decades of cooperative development; it nearly always takes place in staggered increments worked out in adaptive interaction, rather than in initial grand plans or stated ends. Culture is real when it is embodied. We understand what it means, beyond idle talk and wishful thinking, when we observe how it is grounded in such material elements as the other four pathways projected in this study.

Dynamics of sustainability

The five elements defined as pathways of transformation can also be used as elements to understand how transformed universities go about sustaining changes they have made and how they avoid regression to an earlier state. In successful cases of entrepreneurialism in universities, what is sustained is a capacity to go on changing.

My case-study European institutions, in the last half of the 1990s, revealed one hint after another about sustained change. We saw the spiraling advantages of continuous diversification of income: more money from more 'other sources' frees up discretion. The gain in self-reliant autonomy is a financial foundation for a host of initiatives. A stronger steering capacity works across the board to energize the search for income, develop multidisciplinary outreach capacity, build respect for entrepreneurial behavior in disciplinary departments, and make creditable the claim of distinctive culture. The steering apparatus itself is worked on steadily: new initiatives, new groups, and new criss-crossing relationships shake up the structure of authority and responsibility. Rebalancing is frequently called for in the all-important connections between central groups and the faculties and departments. The continuous reworking of the developmental periphery, producing a more hybrid university, feeds back upon income diversification and the distribution of authority – and contradicts the primacy of departments. We attempt to isolate one pathway, to study in greater detail its nature and effects, and we find ourselves involved in the others in what appears to be sustaining interaction.

The pathways of transformation, then, carried forward in time and seen as processes rather than as endpoints, offer a base for sustaining both initial transformation and further change. Sustainability depends on three dynamics that appear empirically in the studied institutions: the dynamic of re-enforcing interaction; the dynamic of accumulative momentum; and, most powerful of all, the dynamic of ambitious collegial volition.

The dynamic of re-enforcing interaction

In my 1998 report, I warned against the idealization of any one feature of university change as *the* change that would sweep everything before it, as, for example, a charismatic new CEO who could put the university on his or her back, overcome all obstacles if not part the waves, and carry the institution to the promised land:

> We have noted repeatedly throughout this study that the five elements of transformation become just that by means of their interaction. Each by itself can hardly make a significant difference. Those who see universities from the top-down might readily assume that the strengthened steering core is the leading element. But a newly constituted management group, for example, is soon without teeth if discretionary funds are not available, new units in the periphery cannot be constructed, heartland departments fall into opposition, and the group's idea of a transformed institution gains no footing.[14]

Concentrated on clarifying the build-up of the individual transforming capacities up to the mid-1990s, my previous account only briefly and tentatively stressed the importance of their interaction. But with additional tracking of the case-study institutions through the last half of the 1990s, and with the question of sustainability more directly confronted, we can assert a fundamental dynamic. Namely, that sustained change in universities is rooted in changes on a number of fronts that lead to a combined infrastructure in which the substantial alterations are mutually supportive. There is an emergent organizational foundation that we can appropriately understand as *the steady state of change*. Traditional universities have a steady state oriented toward inertia: the status quo has the upper hand. Universities that transform themselves on many fronts develop a steady state – full of vested interests, sunk costs, and standard operating procedures – oriented toward change: the new status quo is development oriented. Newly institutionalized elements, developed out of interaction with one another and now linked together, resist a sliding back to the old status quo: they first of all prevent a reversion to earlier character.

The new steady state contains both change-oriented segmental interests, e.g., departmental ones, and change-centered encompassing interests, e.g., those held by central groups. Ongoing primary tensions center on counterbalancing those different interests and on bringing together collegial and managerial styles in check-and-balance interaction.

Our first new principle, then, is that elements of transformation become elements of sustainability as they become interlocked in a new basic organizational character.

The dynamic of perpetual momentum

Change in universities needs to be understood in incremental terms. I earlier noted: 'As we have seen by reviewing development over 10 to 15 year periods, the building of structural capability and cultural climate takes time and is incrementally fashioned.' Change 'does not happen because a committee or a president asserts a new idea'. Rather, 'action taken at the center requires faculty involvement and approval. Change in new and old units in the periphery and in the heartland is piecemeal, experimental and adaptive. The operational units, departments and research centers, remain the sites where research, teaching, and service are performed: what they do and do not do becomes finally central.' Change comes 'when it happens in the trenches'.[15]

Further: 'Even in the business world . . . careful analysts who trace organizational change over many years observe that successful firms essentially engage in "cumulative incrementalism": they inch forward by making rapid partial changes. Firms choose to "spread and minimize risks by initiating many different projects," rather than try to engage in large-scale strategic change.' Capabilities grow 'through the behaviors of employees at all organizational levels'.[16] Such findings fit well our developmental studies of universities. An incrementalist view of organizational change points to cumulative results.[17]

The steady state of change, a creature of interlocking interaction, itself changes incrementally. As step-by-step adjustments are made to changing demands and newly-appearing opportunities, cumulative change propels a university forward. The institution thereby acquires a steady momentum that need not have a particular stopping point. Depending upon small incremental gains, fashioned essentially out of learning by experimenting, such forward movement does not depend on lucky throws of the dice in selecting one major investment. Rather, momentum is acquired from the cumulative thrust of small steps. It is not implausible to think of this process as leading to all but perpetual momentum. Chalmers, for example, has conceptualized its dependable momentum as *perpetuum mobile*, thereby offering its true believers an optimistic sense that in turn helps to generate momentum.

So, a second new principle warrants that elements of transformation become elements of sustainability as their cumulative incremental gains produce a perpetual momentum. Their interlocking interaction acquires a forward impetus. The university leans toward the future.

The dynamic of ambitious collegial volition

Is there any doubt that some universities try much harder than others to improve their performance, especially if that improvement means unsparing work to effect long-term change in character? The play of sheer will repeatedly comes to the surface. The studied European institutions clearly made decisions to seek major improvement. Behind the interlocking interaction and the perpetual momentum, something like institutional will played a basic role.

Volition, a concept here borrowed from political economy, helps to explain. In the framework developed by Charles E. Lindblom, democracy or 'polyarchy' – rule by many – not only follows from the will of the people but also induces and shapes that will. 'Polyarchy is a process that forms volitions as well as a process for making policy respond to them.'[18] A volition is '*an emergent act of will*', in the form of a decision to pursue a certain path of development. It is a judgment that produces commitment. It is a social act: a volition is made in the context of a social setting; what is decided is done in a network of existing impositions and facilitating structures. Especially within institutions – universities in our case – volitions and social conditions interact. And especially in such organized settings, volitions are collective decisions producing collective commitment. In this fascinating explanatory framework for understanding political democracy, people create rather than find their wants, needs and interests. The decision decides what the want is to be and what is needed; it creates the interest.

But how and why do certain volitions get made in universities, whatever their stressful situation? We have to turn back to ambition and to a self-generating stream of decisions that follow. When Warwick was faced with a severe reduction in state income back in the early 1980s, along with all other British universities, decisions to go backward or to stand paralyzed were seen as simply not acceptable. The institution decided on a new approach – the earned-income policy – originally in the form of save-half/raise-half to get the money needed to cover the government cut. The raising of additional income proved surprisingly successful. The initial volition – the decision to try out a certain new path of development – then became a determined commitment, one that in turn promoted the development of attitudes and practices that encouraged a variegated stream of ongoing decisions leading to much greater self-reliance. At Warwick, in the beginning and then onward, *ambitious volition* helped propel the institution forward to a trans-formed character.

Chalmers chose to become a 'foundation' university in the early 1990s because it actively sought the means to achieve greater autonomy. A hard, key decision was then made to adopt a constitutional order that designed greater autonomy. What we also find buried deep in the processes of trans-formation and sustainability here are a steady stream of socially shaped voli-tions – decisions – that actively steer the institution in one direction and not in another.

The will to take the risk of being highly proactive, even entrepreneurial, despite contrary even hostile academic questioning about the propriety of this choice was evident in all the institutions studied. Others decided it was not worth the effort; or that it was best to wait for government to come to its senses; or that as a matter of principle we should hang together and share equally the pangs of poverty; or that old ways would prove best over the long term. Inertia in traditional universities has many rationales, beginning with avoidance of hard choices.

Entrepreneurial universities, in contrast, accumulate small connected voli-tions – acts of will – that slowly adapt their character. Doing so as they feel their way from year to year, they are positioned to anticipate and adapt to the future, better than anyone can from a traditional passive posture or an initial grand design. Inescapably caught up in knowledge growth in old and new fields, universities will go on becoming more complex, widening and deep-ening their operational expertise. Their well-known 'chaos of production' across faculty members and departments will be more than a match for consciously controlled order. Then the stream of volitions rooted in ambi-tion to improve becomes the nearest thing to a silent guiding hand. The interaction rolls on: elements of transformation and sustainability are both the results of volitions *and* the institutional means of volition-building.

The newly-fashioned self-reliant university depicted in various forms and degrees in my European cases is built and sustained out of blocks of will reflecting assertive ambition. In the beginning of change there is volition; along the way are emergent acts of will; in the end the ambition to fashion an even better university remains. If there is a single tip-off in achieving signifi-cant ongoing university change, perhaps this is it. You start with volition, the willful decision to pursue a certain path of transforming action, and take it from there. Call it what you like, the point is to do it.

To put the matter in striking terms, the deliberate transformation of a university requires two miracles. One is to get started, facing down the fear of failure before beginning. Many universities will simply not try to start down the new road. It is risky: a hallowed institution may be laid low. The other miracle is sustaining a virtuous circle of successful accomplishments over a decade or more, facing down the multitude of conserving tendencies in organizations – especially universities – and among organized sponsors – especially ministries – that bring change to a halt. At the heart of each miracle lies willful agency. It is not the demands of the day in themselves that drive a university to change, we now know, but rather the many specific responses to those demands, in the form of emergent acts of will, that are summoned from within.

Part II

Amplifying Variations in University Entrepreneurialism: Africa, Latin America, Australia, North America

Part II extends a worldwide net in pursuit of proactive universities. Each case, in its own way, offers a fascinating story of entrepreneurial action as the institution attempts to transform historic character and keep up with a fast-changing world. We pursue changing realities, as we did in Part I, case by case; we first attend to the details and then use those facts to test and modify an explanatory framework. We dip into widely varying national settings in which transforming changes take place from different levels of modern academic competence. We find institutional will at work in contexts that vary from an almost hopeless societal setting to one in which university entrepreneurialism has evolved into a virtual genetic characteristic. They all show how determined universities turn their problems into self-guiding opportunities.

We begin in Africa with the stunning story of how during the 1990s the University of Makerere in Uganda raised itself from academic degradation. The results of the steps taken have turned the university into a model of what can be done in other African countries. We then turn to Latin America with an account of just how far down the entrepreneurial road a leading university, the Catholic University of Chile, progressed during the 1980s and 1990s as it negotiated a cutting-edge shift from state steerage to institutional self-development in the universities of that country. Third, we pursue Monash University, born in the 1960s, through several stages of rapid development as it became the leading entrepreneurial university in Australia. Monash avidly seized opportunities opened up under governmental insistence that the country's entire university system undergo far-reaching change.

The Chilean and Australian cases especially exemplify the increasing role played by institutional competition in generating and spreading entrepreneurial attitudes and practices. In Chapter 10, we examine the United States, a place where competition has long been inherently characteristic of the national university system. Brief accounts highlight the exercise of local initiative under inescapable competition in two private universities (Stanford and MIT), two flagship state universities (Michigan and UCLA), and two additional public universities (North Carolina State University and Georgia Institute of Technology) found experimenting at the turn of the millennium with new forms of university-business-state relationship.

As cases rotate before our eyes on a worldwide stage, the story is unending. From cases to concepts – to cases and concepts – we have to be quick on our feet to keep up with international developments. Lessons leap at us across national and continental boundaries. Rapid societal change, we note, establishes broad enabling conditions for much university change. But universities themselves have to go on to build the institutional capacity. How to do so becomes a widespread quest in the international world of learning. This study offers that quest fourteen cases that may be seen as amplifying variations of a new type of university – the entrepreneurial university.

7

Makerere University: entrepreneurial rebound from the academic pits in Uganda

Universities seeking an entrepreneurial evolution embark from different launching platforms established by inherited capacities and societal conditions. A reforming response is sometimes initiated as a reaction to deep crisis, even in the extreme to virtually unimaginable harsh constraints. The beginning point may be a university deep down in the pits of an academic hell, wracked by decades of steep decline to the point where it is barely able to hold itself together as a physical entity, let alone employ a core academic staff and generate some semblance of faculty morale and student service.

Such was the plight of the University of Makerere in Uganda, East Africa, in 1990. The 1970s and 1980s were Uganda's 'time of troubles' – a delicate phrase for horrible coups, atrocities and massacres – a period of brutal tyranny and backwardness under Idi Amin and Milton Obote. The impact on the country's main center of academic learning was devastating. Makerere began humbly as a government technical school in the 1920s; it had evolved under University of London supervision to become a university college (1950) with courses in arts and sciences. And then, after national independence (1962) it was upgraded to full university status – with a recognizable infrastructure, following British tradition, of vice-chancellor, secretary, registrar, faculties, departments and research institutes.[1] Two decades of appalling governmental suppression almost scrapped that sustaining infrastructure and left the entire university barely alive:[2]

> By 1990, Makerere exhibited in extreme form the resource constraints facing universities throughout Africa. No new physical structures had been built and no maintenance carried out in twenty years. Journal subscriptions had declined to zero, as had chemicals for science laboratories. Supplies of electricity and water were spasmodic, cooking and sewage facilities were stretched to their limit. Faculty members received the equivalent of $30 per month and were forced by this so-called 'leaving' wage to depart the country or seek any available paid employment for most of their day. Student numbers remained low, the government

subsidy small and research output minimal. A 'pillage' or survival culture prevailed which put at risk to private theft any saleable and removable item, from computers and telephones to electric wires and door fixtures – and sometimes the doors themselves! In a situation of limited transport, few if any working telephones and the absence of needed equipment and stationery, it is remarkable that the university managed to remain open throughout this period.

A second description of the depressing conditions stressed the effects of such conditions on the lives of students. Two local observers, Musisi and Muwanga, observed that, 'Makerere became a place of bare laboratories, empty library shelves, shortages of scholastic materials, and overcrowded halls of residence . . . Libraries and common rooms, toilets and washroom facilities were converted into additional student rooms, leaving students to make their own alternative toilet arrangements.'[3]

Teetering on its last legs, the university stumbled badly for another two years around efforts to supplement low government financing with some cost-sharing by students in the form of cash or work done for the university. Student demonstrations and boycotts shot down these efforts and even led to full closure for the first time in the university's history. The mentality that government should cover all costs and control all policy lingered. A new democratic government had come to power in 1986, but had little money with which to attack a host of overwhelming problems; it could only continue to provide a meager annual subsidy. The university needed to save and enhance itself by other means.

The mentality of full state dependency had to die or else the university would be barely able to function. Exercising its own internal will on top of more favorable societal conditions of political democracy and economic growth, the university initiated and then institutionalized between 1992 and the end of the century some transforming steps – 'a quiet revolution'. David Court has identified 'three key interrelated thrusts' in this institutional restructuring: implementing alternative financing strategies; introducing demand-driven courses; and installing new management structures.[4] His categories align well with transforming pathways set forth in my Europe-based study.

The first and most important way by which Makerere, in its wretched state, found additional financing was by 'encouraging privately sponsored students'. One exploring step after another by different faculties and institutes opened wide this door. In 1992 an institute of continuing education broke the ice with 'an external degree program exclusively for fee-paying students'. The following year law and commerce faculties initiated 'privately sponsored evening courses'. The governing University Council then sanctioned evening courses for all faculties and established the principle that 'faculties with places remaining after the prescribed government intake could fill them with private students'. 'Private' came to include students supported by parents, employers, local governments, churches and non-governmental

organizations (NGOs). From 1995–96 on, students admitted by this second
route exceeded those admitted under central government sponsorship – by
two to one for entering students in 1998–99. Total enrollment grew from
about 7,000 in 1992–93 to over 18,000 in 1998–99, a mere six years, on the
back of a huge growth in private enrollment from less than 500 to over
10,000, while government-supported enrollment grew modestly from about
6,500 to about 8,200.[5]

Behind those bald figures lies a story of change in faculty attitudes about
the nature of academic work, an alteration greatly helped along by a
decentralization of budget control in which those who raised income got to
keep a major share of it. M.K. Mayanja, Director of Planning, described it:[6]

> Initially, faculties were not enthusiastic about generating income. They
> wanted to stick to their traditional roles of teaching and research. To
> persuade faculties to venture into income generating, it was decided to
> give them a lot of say in how the income generated would be spent. The
> central administration took less than 40 per cent of the income and left
> the rest to the schools and under the control of the deans, directors, and
> heads of department and faculties.

Commercializing service units and enforcing user fees became a second new
source of income. By contracting out a set of campus operations to private
management, the university made extra money from the bookshop and the
campus bakery, the printing shop and the guesthouse. By strictly enforcing
user fees for diverse non-tuition users, additional funds were gained. A new
university framework around faculty consulting became another useful step.
Some faculty members had profited individually as consultants for businesses
and government agencies. The university formalized a Consultancy Bureau,
a 'limited liability company with 51% of shares owned by Makerere staff as
individuals and 49% by the university as an entity'. Now some of the profit of
outside consulting would go to 'the institution that houses the consultants
and provides their overheads'.[7]

As a result of such income-enhancing steps, particularly the revenue
gained from 'private' students, Makarere not only reduced its dependence
on government but also came up with much more total income that contained a steadily-increasing amount of disposable money. While the government subvention increased only marginally between 1995–96 and 1998–99,
from roughly 20 to 22 billion Uganda shillings, the income from 'internally
generated funds' rose from 4 to 10 billion, amounting in the latter year to
over 30 per cent of the total budget of 32+ billion. Court richly described the
outcomes:[8]

> The availability of funds which are not derived from government has
> enabled the university to move from a situation of hand-to-mouth
> dependency to one where autonomous initiative, planning and alloca-
> tion are possible. Funds gained from non-government sources have
> been allocated according to prescribed ratios to library enrichment,

faculty development, staff salary supplementation, and building maintenance, including some construction.

The most important impact of increased institutional income has been on staff salary structures and incentive schemes. Professors can now earn over $1,300 per month [compared to $30 ten years before] with the possibility of added supplementation on an hourly basis from evening classes. The consequence has been to staunch the exodus of academic staff and remove their need to undertake a range of activities outside the university ... At the same time the value-for-money demands of those who pay fees has raised standards of teaching as well as staff and student accountability. This, in turn, has boosted staff morale and improved the intellectual climate. Once again academics are being paid to do what they were trained for, in a place dedicated to this purpose.

More generally, the power of privatization engendered by fee-paying has spread an entrepreneurial ethos within and beyond the university. [The] willingness to provide services and take up trade to meet their costs has washed away the former hand-out, dependent mentality.

Thus, since the early 1990s, Makarere has made increasingly vigorous use of a diversified funding base. Here was the much needed financial footing for significant transformation, especially change that would be entrepreneurial in outlook.

That major thrust was closely interrelated with a second pathway that Court called 'demand-driven academic reforms', one that depended operationally on units that related more directly to the outside world than had traditional discipline-driven departments. By introducing courses 'for which individuals, families, and companies are willing to pay', offering new bachelors' degrees in 'business administration, nursing, tourism, urban planning, biomedical laboratory technology and many pursuits not previously available or contemplated' – and even going beyond the practical with specializations in drama, music, and dance – the curriculum was greatly expanded. More diverse course offerings were coupled with more flexible timing; courses were offered during evenings and weekends when working people could attend. Such curricular features have long been available in other countries, notably the United States, but 'for Uganda and old Oxbridge practice [the British legacy] they represent departures from tradition – departures that in an earlier era, and until very recently, seemed impossible'.[9] Makerere was remaking itself by organizationally asserting useful learning by means of new programs that stressed outreach. Here, in my terms, was a greatly enlarged developmental periphery in action.

The financial and curricular pathways were underpinned by a third reforming thrust, one defined by Court as 'decentralized and participatory management'. A new strategic plan in 1996 portrayed the key to revitalization as lying in a combination of 'improved funding and restructuring of governance to cultivate an innovative and entrepreneurial approach at all level'.[10] Traditionally the University Council had been composed primarily of appointees from government. Now it became a body that included representatives from business as well as administrators, senior faculty, and students from the university. Below the council, the university emphasized decentralization, propelling self-determination down the line to the faculties and institutes. Critically, 'exclusive financial authority' in the hands of a single central official responsible for a centrally planned budget was eliminated. Instead, faculties could now 'determine their own development through financial committees that receive a portion of earned income and decide on its allocation and distribution'.[11] The aim was to greatly strengthen management at the faculty and lower levels – better line management surrounded by collegial participation, more key people in positions of responsibility together with more participation from the general faculty. Faculty 'ownership' of change was enhanced.

The administrative center was also significantly strengthened. A new vigorous vice-chancellor – John Ssebuwufu – took office in 1993 and built a modern management team around such officials as the secretary and the development officer, a team that had overall authority 'to make structural decisions affecting the institution, including the ability to raise funds from private sources'. They sensed that many desirable changes 'could only take root through a consultative policy-making process and an inclusive and participatory system of governance'.[12] Despite the urgency, reforms could not be sprung as a mandate from above. The steady use of a consultative style over years of joint effort led to 'an almost palpable sense across all strata of the university' that the process affecting the whole community was 'owned and led by the institution itself' – neither the government nor the international donor agencies (from Norway to the United States they were offering a helping hand), but the university itself. With this growing sense, a popular vice-chancellor came to symbolize 'we' rather than 'I' – 'he is our man', rather than an agent of the government.

Much depended on up-and-down consultation and widespread transparency. To help keep the entire place on the same page, the bottom operating units reported their activities to 'consultative meetings of deans, directors and administrators'.[13] In turn, the Office of the University Secretary took to making 'regular fact-finding and information-sharing visits to faculties, schools and institutes' – visits that could give the administration a better appreciation of department-by-department operating realities, even the awareness of potentially explosive situations in time to defuse them. In addition, a bi-weekly newsletter, reporting on what was occurring throughout the university and available on and off campus, promoted 'a spirit of togetherness'. The new transparency 'killed rumour mongering'.[14]

In the interplay of Court's three institutional thrusts, we have seen three pathways in action that I previously identified: a strengthened steering core, with its intertwining of managerial and collegial authority; a diversified funding base, with its capacity to draw upon a widening plurality of patrons and its deepening of internal discretion; and an expanded developmental periphery, with its instinctive creativity in reaching across traditional university boundaries to link up with outside groups and to take on new problems. What of the remaining two of my five elements – the stimulated academic heartland and the integrated entrepreneurial culture? Do they show up in the Makarere transformation? If they do, what forms do they take?

In my European study, which depicted how rapidly and how much university traditional departments – the heartland – normally take up entrepreneurial practices and related attitudes, I stressed a progression from science and technology departments (the ones most ready and able to make changes), to some social science departments next able to cross the bridge, and finally the humanities and the arts departments as having the greatest difficulty in making proactive changes. At Makerere, however, the parade of disciplines had a different alignment. Court pointed to incomplete restructuring in 2000, in that 'privatization has not been uniform across faculties and departments. It has been most evident in Commerce, Law, Education, and the Humanities . . . and most difficult to effect in Medicine and the Sciences'. The first group of fields could most readily expand the base of limited staff and space by offering courses at night and at the weekends, and thereby lead the way in enhancing income and enjoying its benefits. The second set were more constrained by their need for laboratory space and expensive equipment and thereby were 'financially less productive'. In this context, if helpful cross-subsidization were to take place from fields able to raise additional income to those that could not, it would be from the humanities and soft social sciences to the sciences, and not the other way around. Here, in this context, it was medicine and the sciences 'which are no less important to the university and the nation but . . . constrained in their ability to produce revenue' are in need of cross-subsidy support.[15]

From American as well as European perspectives, this is a curious reversal of needed cross-subsidization across heartland departments and new outreach programs. But the point is clear: universities have to go with what tradition has dealt them. If the first handholds out of an undesired position – especially out of the pits – are not found in physics, chemistry, biology and computer science, for example, or any of the new technological sciences, then those handholds may be found in the relative ease of income-producing expansion in the humanities and the arts, law and business and education. Once first steps are taken on the ladder of recovery, possible successive stages lie where the rebuilding of research funding and research activity may receive deserved attention if not priority.

The Makarere case thus sharpens the element of a stimulated academic heartland. Instead of the tendency to change in the old heartland stretching from sciences to social sciences to the humanities, the line runs from departments that can most readily first enhance income, turning entrepreneurial in the bargain, to those that are most constrained in doing so by their particular operational base. Interests embedded in the material base of operations of individual departments are revealed to be more important than differences in general attitude, such as those that can be readily attributed – by me and others – to forward-looking scientists in comparison to backward-looking humanists and soggy social scientists. The take-up depends on who is best positioned operationally to turn problems into opportunities, especially during a first decade of climbing out of the pits.

My fifth conceptual element, an integrated entrepreneurial culture, also underwent year-by-year development in Makerere during the decade following 1992. Faculty first in one department, then in another, and then in the institution as a whole, acquired a sense of being key players in the production of change; they even become 'owners' of changes underway. The consultative efforts from bottom to top and from top to bottom, described above, helped to define an institutional ownership of change vis-à-vis state steerage and donor-agency influence. Efforts to deepen and widen transparency helped to develop a new mentality that we are in this effort together, that the V-C is 'our man'. After a decade of extremely challenging struggle in which reform had been 'gradual, phased and marked throughout by wide stakeholder participation', the effort was viewed as having had an 'enormous impact on the university'. This led to a set of pleasing results: an updated mission, less dependence on the state, professional management, awareness of market forces, and a capacity and willingness to invest in itself.[16]

Here we can see the stages of cultural development suggested in my earlier work: initial tentative ideas about what might be done – here the possible usefulness of privately sponsored courses and students – evolved into a set of successful beliefs, which then became a campus-spanning, embracing culture by 2000. It began to take on the emotional toning of an organizational saga – a place that had climbed, principally by its own efforts, out of a sorry state and could now claim again – or claim soon – that it was Uganda's flagship university for the twenty-first century, competent to compete against emerging private Ugandan universities and flagship institutions in nearby countries. It might even become a model for other universities in sub-Saharan Africa.

At the least, participant-observers could appropriately speak of the university as having undergone an 'embryonic transformation', a first stage of required development that established a platform for a second stage in the early decades of the new century.[17] That first stage had provided a forward-looking cultural thrust: 'The issue is no longer whether the changes embarked upon should continue, but how these changes can be harnessed, sustained, improved upon and consolidated . . . the reality is that reforms at Makerere have gained an almost independent momentum.'[18]

By 2000 a host of new concerns were pressing for priority in continuing reform. Rapid enrollment growth had greatly outstripped faculty growth, increased the overall student–teacher ratio, and led to more large lectures in place of the traditional British-style tutorial. Beneath the overall ratio of about 20:1 – not at all shocking by the standards of mass higher education in Europe and America – there were wide differences among the ten major faculties and schools: low ratios in medicine, science and technology (8:1 or less) to high ratios in education, business, and the humanities (40:1 and higher). Rapid 'massification' had exaggerated the student-load differences found elsewhere between clinical and laboratory-based fields on the one side and the humanities and social sciences and such 'non-science' professional fields as education, business and law on the other. Also, student housing had not kept up, leading to serious crowding in dormitories, and many students were turned over to the not-so-tender mercies of outside landlords. Consideration had to be given to 'slowing down' and to 'consolidation'.

Equity concerns became stronger on dimensions of gender, regional background, income and physical disability. With women making up to 40 per cent of undergraduate enrollment and climbing, gender equity was working out. But income differentials became the important issue, forcing the university to think about better subsidy for low-income students and students from poorer regions of the country.[19]

Foremost among the emerging concerns that followed upon Makerere's particular embryonic transformation was how to bolster research and the science and technological fields. Rapid student growth had caused teaching time to overwhelm research time. And the march of the disciplines in changing the heartland left the 'hard science' fields as institutional laggards, unable to muster the resources that expensive science requires:

in 1998–99, the Faculty of Medicine and Surgery generated less than a tenth of the income produced by the Faculty of Arts . . . Laboratory-based and faculty-intensive faculties such as Science and Medicine do not have the facilities to expand student enrolment or mount evening courses in order to increase income generation. At the same time, the higher tuition charged for science over art courses prevents some students from enroling in this area.

Beyond further appeal to donor agencies for grants earmarked for science and medicine, the university was clearly on the threshold of new internal mechanisms for investing more money in the support of research generally:

The university already has a precedent of providing funds to cover basic costs and upgrade facilities to departments that do not generate income themselves. It allocates five per cent of each fee-paying student's tuition to the library. A similar arrangement could be made for vital but low income-generating faculties . . . In 2000–2001 the University Council decided to charge both undergraduates and postgraduates the amount of US$7 and US$13 annually per student, respectively, to underwrite research.

At the beginning of a second decade of transformation, 'if Makerere University is to live up to its vision of becoming a centre of excellence in teaching and research, then research infrastructure and management need to be given centre stage in its short- and medium-term strategic plans as well as in funding considerations'.[20]

The development of information and communication technology (ICT) would also need to be part of a modernized structure. Donors were willing to assist: the African Development Bank and the US Agency for International Development would fund campus-wide networking, centered in the Institute for Computer Science; the Norwegian Agency for Development would support ICT activities generally, with an eye on improving instruction. Building an ICT infrastructure was a daunting problem – an expensive problem – but one full of possibilities for keeping apace with the cutting edge in the international flow of information and knowledge and becoming an active member of an international 'community' of universities.[21]

Court in 2000 suggested an almost inevitable slower-paced reform effort at Makerere; exhaustion had set in from the sheer pace of change and a need for consolidation was felt. New cohorts of students had little or no memory of how much worse conditions had been just a few years previously and would press new demands. After a decade of high national economic growth, the highest in Africa (6.5 per cent average annual increase in real GDP for 1990–2000),[22] similar growth was not guaranteed. Turndowns could affect all the sources of income, governmental and private. And governmental stability in at least a rudimentary democratic form remained an essential condition. But the university was positioned to move on to new problems; it possessed in its new culture a promising capacity to turn those problems into manageable opportunities. Better, far better, to be on the higher institutional plane of 2000 than to be down in the hopeless state of a decade before.

That new plane, as of 2001–2003, notably found the university embarking on a promising large outreach initiative to provide expertise and training for decentralizing Uganda's government. What a valuable thing to do: the university's contribution to the nation in this sustained effort could be major and lasting – and, again, a model for what could be done in other countries.

Decades of futile efforts to strengthen universities in Africa during the last half of the twentieth century had given rise, with good cause, to extremely pessimistic predictions of the impossibility of sustained reform. Trying to change an African university, it was claimed, was like trying to move a cathedral – or, with an undertone of academics dead before their time, like trying to move a cemetery! Such definitions encourage patrons to give up on university support. They encourage university staffs to hunker down in empty shells of academic life or to flee to any available alternative. All the more reason then for those who wish universities well to engage in the study of successful cases of effective adaptation, much as is done in the empirical literature on business firms.

The Makerere case is relevant for the universities of Africa generally. Court has stated it well:

The Makerere accomplishment has lessons for other universities in Africa that face similar resource constraints. It shows that expansion and the maintenance of quality (indeed, even the enhancement of quality) can be achieved simultaneously in a context of reduced state funding. It puts to rest the notion that the state must be the sole provider of higher education in Africa. It dramatizes the point that a supportive political and economic environment is a prerequisite for institutional reform. It also demonstrates the variety of institutional factors that go into the creation of a management structure suited to ensuring efficiency and effectiveness in the use of resources.

. . . changes long thought to be unattainable and even unmentionable in several African countries have been achieved in Uganda and a new mindset established . . . [T]he struggle continues, the accomplishment is incomplete and the outcome is unknown. However, in its own quiet revolution, one university has shown that it is possible to move the cathedral![23]

Conclusion

The two papers by David Court (2000) and Musisi and Muranga (2001) on which I have drawn heavily stem from a large initiative, backed primarily by four American foundations – Rockefeller, Ford, MacArthur and the Carnegie Corporation – 'to improve the ability of key universities [in Africa] to undertake reform and thus serve as models of successful transformation'. The effort 'also aims to show that relevant reform is possible and can be sustained'.[24] As of 2001, case reports had reviewed reform efforts not only at Makerere but also at the University of Dar es Salaam in Tanzania and in the entire higher education system in Mozambique.[25] In each, a study team sought to identify enabling conditions in the larger society: substantial economic growth, more stable and somewhat more democratic political structure, a more vigorous civil society, an expanding middle class – and the lessening of civil wars and border wars, corruption, grinding poverty in many regions, and, lately, the drain of HIV-Aids on human resources. But most of all the case studies aimed to find the 'substance', the 'ingredients', of the university reform process itself. Looking inside universities, as much from the bottom-up as top-down, the studies richly attended to university-led financial strategies, new access procedures, curricular changes, alterations in governance and management, ways of responding to market forces, conditions of student life, and much more.

My evolving conceptual framework, expressed in Chapter 6, suggests that the substance, the ingredients, of 'the university reform process itself' can be reasonably captured in five elements of transformation and three related dynamics of sustainability. We have seen the transforming elements develop at Makerere in a decade of hard work dedicated to getting the institution out of a deep hole and back on its feet, strongly augmented. Not to be missed are a diversifying of income, a strengthening of steering capacity, a developing of new border-crossing administrative and academic units, a taking up of proactive postures in heartland departments, and the emerging of a wrap-around entrepreneurial culture. Trial-and-error experimentation abounded. When early steps taken in 1990–92 failed at Makerere, entrepreneurial minds tried another, and another.

The newly conceived dynamics brought forward by the analysis of European cases in Part I, also seemed operative here in East Africa. The five elements grew up together in the Makerere self-led effort, incrementally bolstering each other in year-by-year interaction. That interaction produced some momentum grounded in a new bureaucracy of change and a larger steady state of change. More staff professionals as well as more academics acquired a vested interest in pushing change forward – in new fund-raising, in new capacity for planning and development, in new units and forms of outreach, in a culture of consultancy and wider service. All proceeding in a piecemeal, experimental, adaptive fashion.

Institutionalized volition can also be seen at work in steady build-up of change-minded initiative. Willfulness resulted in part from the assertiveness of a single individual but then became embedded in the university's changing character. The will to improve through group effort, thin in 1992, became ten years later a widely-institutionalized mindset. Makerere offers much evidence in its many behaviors that it tried harder than numerous other universities in a roughly similar situation to push for change – in the beginning, then along the way in the mid- and late-1990s – and will predictably go on pressing for improvement in university capability.

The growth of a strong institutionalized will to change, in some universities but not others, is a phenomenon about which we can hardly learn too much. Evidenced in dramatic clarity at this particular university in Uganda, it is near the heart of sustained transformation.

8

The Catholic University of Chile: lessons from South America

Academics, university administrators, and attentive outside observers generally see public and private universities as two distinct types. But in many countries today the two institutional types converge considerably: public universities raise money from private sources and relate to a host of non-governmental enterprises; private universities, in turn, seek income from public sources, provincial and national, and build ties to government agencies.

At the extreme of convergence, we find the unusual case of Chile, where public and private universities have intersected in two fundamental ways: historically, private institutions acted like public ones, producing a traditional statist homogeneity; in contemporary reform both types have undergone much privatization, moving from state control toward market involvements and self-reliance. The Catholic University of Chile – PUC (Pontificia Universidad Catolica de Chile) – has been at the forefront of both the historical homogeneity and the recent parallel transformation. In 2000 it stood as the country's leading private and entrepreneurial university, as it fashioned a transition to institutional self-direction. Andrés Bernasconi highlights in his research report, on which I have extensively drawn, that PUC is a case study in 'the privatization of a private university'. How this came about, and with what effects, is the story we need to unfold.[1]

PUC dates from 1888. For nearly a full century, it stood formally as an arm of the Catholic Church, with church-appointed priests as rectors. Because it was influenced by the Napoleonic model of a single all-embracing national university, the Chilean higher education system also placed PUC and other public and private universities and colleges under the tutelage of the University of Chile, the oldest central public university, dating from 1842. When the constitution of the country separated church and state in 1925, PUC became legally recognized as a 'collaborator in the educational mission of the state' and was given public subsidy. Ebbing and flowing during the next four decades, that subsidization stabilized in the 1960s and topped out in the early 1970s at 90 per cent of the university's income. PUC was an arm of *estado docente* – the teaching state. That state saw public education as a 'preferential activity', and only an arm of the state 'could provide liberal choices of values and professions, equity for those unable to purchase higher education, effectiveness for a progressive system, and freedom from religious dogma'.[2]

The Chilean universities, public and private, exhibited teaching and program practices that had a strong European heritage – particularly a Mediterranean flavor – in the mid-twentieth century. They centered on preparation for professional practice, notably medicine, law, engineering and agronomy, and the universities themselves granted professional certification along with the academic degree. For faculty they depended considerably on part-time employment of practising professionals committed to their outside work. Professors did not need a doctoral degree, or training beyond the first major degree (holders of the doctoral degree were only a quarter, 23 per cent, of the PUC faculty as late as 1985). Students were the main full-time occupants of the university sites; their governance rights were heightened by the continent-wide student political culture that had developed – although only mildly in Chile – after the Córdoba declaration of 1918.

The various faculties, European style, were considerably self-contained and admitted students to autonomous tracks of specialized study. In keeping with the principle of university autonomy proclaimed in Córdoba, the national ministry provided funds; faculty members and elected deans and rectors ran the university from the bottom-up. But the PUC was different: as a Catholic university, it had a 'centralistic tradition'. The single rector of the university from 1920 to 1953 combined church-delegated, personal authority with his own style. According to local lore, he carried the university's checkbook in the pocket of his cassock. In its over-all governance, PUC thus operated under the constraints of both state and church. Educationally, it was a 'professionalist teaching university', little committed to research.

Formally embedded in a state-supervised system, the universities of Chile became very politicized during the 1960s and 1970s; they experienced and participated in stormy swings of national politics from the strongly contested civilian administrations of Eduardo Frei and Salvador Allende (the latter who took office in 1970 was strongly state oriented, even Marxist in conviction), to the authoritarian military-led government of Augusto Pinochet (who took power in 1973 and was determined to bring about a minimalist state). 'Whereas Chile had long been a Latin American leader in state activism, it abruptly became *the* leader in a campaign to diminish the State role . . .' With Pinochet came *privatizacion* – an effort applied to social areas such as health, social security, and education as well as to such economic fields as industry and agriculture.[3] Universities that had been under pressure to play a role in state activism by emphasizing their common publicness now came under severe pressure to take the opposite path by developing independence from the state to become essentially private non-profit organizations.

The Pinochet government remained in power from 1973 to 1990. It enacted system-wide reform in 1981 that formally did away with the concept of the teaching state. It pushed creation of private universities and private non-university institutions, transformation of regional colleges into small independent public universities, and generally promoted growth in private enrollment.

If we view results in 2000–2002, we can identify broad outcomes of growth and transformation at PUC and then return to the historical detail of how extensive change occurred near the end of the Pinochet government, especially after it was voted out of office in a plebiscite. At the beginning of the twenty-first century we find a modernized fully comprehensive university composed of eighteen schools spread across the usual fields: medicine, science and engineering, humanities, social sciences, education and business. About 20,000 students were enrolled in forty-five undergraduate and over forty graduate programs. A faculty of about 2,200 (1,000 full-time and the rest half-time or part-time – 1,300 FTEs) had turned to research, placing the university second to only the historic University of Chile on such indicators as the number of externally funded research projects and publication of research-based articles in international journals. Over 80 per cent of full-time faculty had graduate degrees. Remarkably, the university had developed to the point where it conferred about 40 per cent of all PhDs awarded in Chile and enrolled close to 30 per cent of the 5,500 undergraduates who had the best scores in the country's standardized university entrance test. In short, the university had achieved a position of significant educational achievement and related high prestige. It attracted faculty and students alike and had become a national favorite.[4]

While this climb in academic capability and status was taking place, the university had seen its dependence on the public purse diminish year after year. The block-grant subvention received from the government, known as 'direct public funding', decreased by almost 40 per cent between 1982 and 2000. At the same time the university was greatly increasing its total income, doubling it in the 1990–2000 decade alone. These twin financial trends caused public funding as a share of total revenue to drop sharply from 90 per cent in 1973 to 70 per cent in the mid-1980s, to 17 per cent in 2000 and still declining. The remarkable improvement in academic performance and associated national prestige occurred in parallel with an enormously reduced dependence on public subsidies and a large increase in reliance on 'private', non-core, sources of funding.[5]

Using the categories of my conceptual scheme, a diversification of income had clearly taken place. A more important source than core support was tuition income at 29 per cent, which in turn was trumped by 48 per cent or more of revenues coming from what the university defined as 'sales of services'. This broad category of one-half of total income had many significant components that stemmed from: (a) a greatly strengthened steering capacity in which the central offices of the university retained considerable power of initiative at the same time much formal decentralization stimulated faculty and department initiative; (b) the development of new outreach units in the form of aggressive commercial operations and discipline-based consulting services; and (c) the spread of entrepreneurial attitudes and behaviors in the academic core composed of heartland departments. These infrastructure and cultural elements were highly interactive, producing cumulative momentum. We start with the steering core and proceed around the circle of interaction.

The strengthened steering core

A new secular rector, Dr. Juan de Dios Vial, who took over in 1985, faced a very difficult situation. Government support had fallen significantly in the previous four years and was just about half-way in a decline that was to reach a 40 per cent decrease by the time it was halted in 1991. Salaries were in such bad shape that the university's professors had gone public with their deep unhappiness. Student opposition to the political repression of the Pinochet regime, as in the country at large, had become more open, vocal and organized. Powerful student organizations opposed increases in tuition, the most obvious administrative answer to the decline in public funding. Some alternative ways of funding were badly needed.

The new rector saw the dire situation as an opportunity for the university to again emphasize its Catholic roots and thereby return to the financial independence and freedom from political power that had characterized its origin. Diversification of funding sources would now be an essential key for doing so. As put by Bernasconi, 'cutting costs and seeking additional funding became not simply a financial strategy, but a sort of crusade for the preservation of the identity and values of the University'.[6]

The new rector and his immediate staff decided, when they embarked on a host of transforming steps, to take the critical one of going against the flow of what other universities deemed appropriate:

> While in the mid-eighties Chilean university leaders everywhere were staking the development of their institutions to the hope that the end of the Pinochet regime would bring back the days of generous public funding and minimal competition – [a return to a status quo ante, we may note] – PUC was the only institution to plan for the opposite scenario, betting there was not going to be a reversal of the new funding and competitive environment brought about by the reforms of 1980–81, and starting to work in earnest within the new rules.[7]

The new path had even been conceptualized in a 1982 policy statement on 'fundamentals and objectives' – 'the Blue Book' – which looked toward a new university framework for administrative rationalization, extensive decentralization and general academic strengthening. The vision foresaw a university that would actively compete for the best students, superior faculty and greatly expanded resources.

The decision was made to continue to privatize as actively as possible. What was possible was a two-headed development: to turn the faculties loose, encouraged by incentives to come up with revenue-enhancing initiatives; and then also to exercise more initiative in the central administration to raise income and control costs for the entire university. Central agency would counterbalance strength of the faculties and serve to keep centrifugal forces on a short leash.

The central administration, to decentralize, moved from elected deans to those selected by search committees who in choosing stressed entrepreneurial ability. The new deans were granted the autonomy to manage their own budgets, hire and fire faculty, set salaries and define workloads. Deans had to discuss their budgets with central officials, but they were allowed to retain in their schools all revenues from their graduate programs, minus a 10 per cent overhead, and to keep any surpluses remaining at the end of the fiscal year. By such means, the university established strong incentives for deans and faculty members 'to go get the money' and use it for their own projects. When it turned out that deans, new and old, were not prepared technically to fulfill such encompassing major responsibilities, the central administrators gave them administrative assistants – in effect, a new bureaucracy of change – to round out their managerial competence.

Deans were strongly encouraged to get rid of unproductive faculty. The central administration even lent faculties the funds needed for severance payments. After the loans were repaid deans could use the monies freed-up from the salaries of those dismissed to hire new people or increase the salaries of those who remained. Here was a powerful form of decentralization, one that stimulated the faculties – by specific means detailed below – to the point where they not only doubled their combined revenues in the 1990–2000 decade but also, in many of the eighteen schools, rebuilt their academic staff. Reform was drastic, controversial and painful.

The central administration was equally hard on itself. Aggressively seeking to cut costs, it reduced the size of the administrative staff – the old bureaucracy – from 1,600 to 1,200, an unusual step in a growing enterprise. The pain induced by this move caused a twenty-day strike by workers' unions; resistance was overcome by a bargain in which one-half of the savings from vacated positions went to the remaining workers to improve their salaries. Supervisors had a powerful incentive 'to keep their most productive workers and fire the rest'.[8]

The central administration had funds at its disposal from the state core allotment, student tuition, and their own revenue-enhancing ventures. It could promote research and innovative teaching and manage cross-school and interdisciplinary projects. The central management team also oversaw the university planning and budgetary process, based on proposals of the deans. It attended to such campus-wide capabilities as the development of a computing network. It was responsible for the maintenance of common standards – in the awarding of degrees, for example.

The expanded developmental periphery

To raise income, deans and their faculties built new aggressively commercial operations. In the school of medicine, the university 'partnered' with a group of professors to build a private clinic, adjacent to the existing middle-class-oriented teaching hospital; it would be upscale and capture a larger, more affluent clientele. Proven successful, the clinic in 2000 had income equivalent to US $65 million. The school also built a network of community health centers throughout the city of Santiago. Medical services, in short, became a much extended 'ancillary enterprise'.

Beginning in the seventies and eighties, a Department of Scientific and Technological Research expanded its engineering services around consulting, certification, and professional development. This operation was then incorporated in 1994, with the university as 99 per cent owner. Its sales in 2000 totaled US $4.1 million. Serving as project supervisors, engineering professors earned significant supplements to their academic salaries. With research increasingly underway, and funds flowing in, the school embarked on a doctoral program for students, hired more professors, got 70 per cent of its full-time faculty of 100 up to the doctoral level of qualification, and invested in the faculty 'nursery' program (described below). During 2001 thirteen young faculty studied abroad for their PhDs and another seventeen were about to leave for this purpose. Engineering, in short, moved sharply and quickly to effect a major upgrading of its faculty. It was a model of how to steadily invest for the future.

The central leadership also developed new out-of-the-box operations devoted to markedly increasing university income. The most notable effort was a profitable television channel. The university set up a small TV station back in 1959. During the following four decades, it built this Channel 13 into the second largest commercial TV network in the country. No BBC or PBS, it was run as an independent business unit, headed by professional managers expected to maximize profits by capturing mass audiences. In short, it could be, it had to be, low-brow. With enough financial success, it could perhaps subsidize high-brow programming and satisfy critics. What it critically did for the university was to pay its bills: 'During the eighties and the first part of the nineties the TV station was the key financier of the operational deficit of the university. Only in the second half of the nineties, after debt had been eliminated, and the revenue base of the university had expanded through tuition hikes and the full-scale operation of the other ancillary enterprises, did the university achieve operational balance.' And even then, in 1999, the television operation remained a key source of income from the university's extra 'holdings': 33 per cent TV advertising, 30 per cent medical services, 20 per cent tuition, and 11 per cent government funds. Here was a large, bold step into an outside endeavor, one risky for academic reputation, but a step that did indeed measurably enhance income, which in turn could be used to build academic capabilities.[9]

Underpinning all the ancillary enterprises was their legal incorporation, a basic administrative step that took them out of reach of normal restrictive state and university regulations on finance and personnel and freed them to operate more quickly, and more adaptively. In a sense, they became 'businesses'. But for the most part they operated close to core university activities and provided developmental funds that otherwise would not have been available; they certainly offered useful services that otherwise would not have been performed. The separate incorporation of outreach endeavors, increasingly common among entrepreneurial universities around the world, became a primary means of change in this Chilean university.

The spread of entrepreneurial attitudes and behaviors in heartland departments

One by one, basic faculties and departments changed dramatically. In biology – a key field – over 100 professors were earning very low salaries as late as the 1980s. 'Perhaps 20 were doing genuine academic work and the rest were working outside, even in high schools.' The school took the harsh measure of firing unproductive staff and redistributing their salaries among those who remained. By 2000–2002, biology had 57 full-time academics, all with doctorates and post-doctoral training, and averaging two articles per year in research output. Junior faculty had just three years in which to show they could do independent research and publications. The department had pledged to work under 'first world standards' – up to what a good, not a top, American or European department would do.[10]

Similar severe action was taken in the business school. It moved from being an 'overstaffed teaching school where faculty were paid salaries not competitive with their outside income opportunities', to a much slimmed-down school of only twenty-five faculty in which research became an integral part of its output; two-thirds of the faculty had PhDs. Aware that they had to be paid more if the best ones were to be retained – they could be lured away by high salaries paid by private firms – the university and school moved to a 'fifth-day' scheme that paid faculty 60 per cent of average market salary of a business executive in a relevant industry for three days per week of teaching and research, another 20 per cent for other university work, for example, extra teaching in extension courses, and a fifth day free for personal business. By 2000, the school ranked among the five most prestigious in Latin America and was able to recruit the best students in the country for its MBA programs, the only ones in Chile accredited by the International Association to Advance Collegiate Schools of Business.

These examples of innovation in medicine, engineering, biology and business show how PUC pulled out the stops to transform itself by investing in research capability and related strengthening of faculty. Chile, during the 1980s, built a national research council to distribute funding to individual researchers on the basis of competitive, peer-reviewed proposals. As the council's funds increased, the university pushed its science departments to tap this source of external funding. Faculty as researchers were expected to initiate proposals and to win grants. To quote a university official, 'If a researcher does not have the initiative to seek outside funding, he is a bad investment.' Even graduate students were expected to try to raise funds; the reward, if successful, was additional resources from the university. To ease the replacement of research 'subsidies' with research 'incentives', the schools were not only granted 90 per cent of graduate programs' revenue, but the additional 10 per cent overhead was turned over to the specific academic units generating them. The stronger departments in the natural sciences were able to make the research council their source of regular research funding during the 1990s. The university was then able to shift its own internal research funding to fields that were not easily fundable via external grants – law, education, the social sciences, for example – a useful form of cross-subsidization from those who could get the money to those who could not.

Further undergirding the many incentives developed by the individual faculties and ancillary enterprises, the university developed broad incentive schemes that rewarded faculty for entrepreneurial activity. By 2000 this institution was reputed to pay the highest academic salaries in Chile. But salaries and overall income varied. Even base salaries had common and variable parts. The guaranteed part was intended to be a stable component sufficient to decently support a middle-class family; the variable component allowed professors in various ways to earn more and to obtain bonuses contingent upon performance. One way to increase one's salary was to compete *within* the university for a 'dedication allowance' – a 40 per cent bonus over base salary – assigned to some professors for a three-year period and held by about one half of the faculty at any one time. As a minimum requirement for this valuable allowance professors had to pledge not to teach in other universities: this held them to the campus full time, against the opportunities growing in Chile to make extra money by teaching in new private universities. The dedication generally also required unusual productivity in teaching or research and publication or 'services', or combinations thereof. Beyond the reward of the variable salary, specific additional bonuses could be obtained: for example, an extra salary increment for publication in internationally indexed journals – and a little more added if the 'impact index' of the journal was high. By such means, the university steadily benchmarked faculty against international standards, with immediate effects.

As a counterpoise for all the rewards, large and small, based largely on research activity, the central administrators also ran a special fund for the development of teaching, with extra honoraria available for working on the development of multimedia or web-based materials or textbooks. Additionally, especially through the ancillary enterprises, full-time faculty could extend their income by consulting and providing professional services.

All together, productive professors were likely to more than double their guaranteed salary.

Most interesting of all in the university's support of faculty was a 'nursery' approach toward the development of young faculty. New faculty in the sciences, with the doctorate and even post-doctoral training, could generally be found. But outside the hard sciences, in the professional schools, humanities and social sciences, such highly prepared people were not available in Chile. So the university decided to build its own cadres. Young scholars were selected to work first with a senior professor for a couple of years. They were then sent abroad for graduate education with an obligation to return to the faculty after completion. PUC paid for all this training, a major long-term investment.

The standard of 'objective selection', that is, selection of faculty based on demonstrable academic merit, was a principle stubbornly held by the institution. This was a major turn in the road from patterns of personal favoritism long practised in Latin American universities and Mediterranean European systems, and not unknown in even the most advanced national systems of higher education. Repeated assessments were effected: full and associate professors, although tenured, became subject to periodic review; even full professors were assessed every four years. Such assessments caused one or two professors to be dismissed each year, or assigned to part-time or adjunct tracks. To help them go, the university made use of its severance fund. This fund became 'a key enabler of PUC's strict enforcement of productivity standards and of its mandatory retirement policy'.[11]

The altered structures and incentives increasingly in place at PUC by 2000 led to the emergence of a new type of academic in Latin American: the entrepreneurial professor. These highly active academics are productive, dedicated researchers 'who run their professional activities as CEOs of their research lines: advising the government, writing consulting reports, and charging for conferences, all along managing, unlike professors 15 years ago, both to make good science and a good living'.[12] According to Bernasconi, such professors are found at the university in all fields. Still a minority, they shape the culture of the profession and cause a shift in academic mentality that parallels that of the university – from state dependence to self-reliance. They 'go get the money', and induce change, program by program, as they initiate and complete new projects. In terms developed in the Chalmers narrative (Chapter 5), they are centers of initiative, multiple and widely distributed within the university. They relate better than traditional professors to outside enterprises. They are willing to cooperate with Chilean business firms who have seen how foreign corporations work closely and in mutual benefit with scientists.

Entrepreneurial universities, like traditional universities, have lasting problems. But following from success, their problems are more attractive. For example: as observed in earlier analyses, PUC, after fifteen years of transformation, found research projects spread quite unevenly among its departments. They were strongly represented in medicine, science and engineering but much more weakly in the humanities, soft social sciences, law, education and the arts. However, a research mentality is clearly in the saddle; continuing pressure for change is made on the departments where it is weak. PUC also has developed relatively little interdisciplinary research. Organized around a large number of established discipline-centered schools, departments, and programs, its outreach strength has been discipline-based applied research.

What of the undergraduate realm? Major change there has been difficult to effect. Coursework is crowned by the 'Licenciado' – the first major degree based on a five-year program, a six-year one in engineering, and seven in medicine. Needing widespread faculty participation and a change in attitude, a two-year liberal education program was not introduced as a requirement for all students until 2000. Whatever the outcome of this long-delayed new program, there was a feeling of optimism: better faculty and better students are key ingredients in improving undergraduate learning, especially when the improved faculty can give undergraduates a superior introduction to the virtues of unfettered inquiry.

PUC's transformation, with its high tuition, has turned the university into a place for the affluent and has brought charges of 'elitization'. In the face of a close relationship between high tuition and high socio-economic status of students, the university has had to struggle continuously to provide scholarships and other forms of financial subsidy for middle- and lower-class students. One-third of the undergraduates were receiving financial aid in 2000. But a substantial upward tilt in the social background of students is likely to endure. As Bernasconi has sharply pointed out: 'for the most part, it is not tuition level which prevents more students from low-income families from entering PUC, but a highly stratified school system that punishes needy students with a low-quality education in public schools'.[13]

PUC also needs in the early twenty-first century to come up with funds for major physical plant investment. Its main campus was built in the early 1970s with an Inter-American Development Bank loan sponsored by the government. It is not clear from which source such capital investment will come. Help from some agency of government will no doubt be required.

Conclusion

The Catholic University of Chile underwent a rapid 'privatization of a private university' between 1985 and 2000. In so doing, it served as model for change in the Chilean higher education system from state-led to self-reliant. It achieved a high degree of active autonomy. Claudio Castro and Daniel Levy, in an assessment of higher education reform throughout the continent in 2000, stressed that change in Chile was exceptional. 'Over the last decade, Chile has implemented a relatively successful market-oriented reform of its national higher education system ... the reform efforts include several pathbreaking features. Institutional autonomy has played a role in innovative student and financial markets. State subsidization has yielded substantially to mixed private and public funding, while performance-based state funding has increased . . .'[14]

I can identify three levels of change pertinent to the larger implications of this case study. Chilean universities offer a front-running model in Latin American countries. For the Chilean system itself, the Catholic University has been a leader. And in that institution's transformation we have uncovered a host of internal initiatives that add up to a highly proactive organizational character. We have identified organizational details at the grass-roots level which lead the way for significant reform at the national and international levels. Perhaps significant change in university systems is much more bottom-up than top-down? Does it really surprise us that greater academic strength can be built by greater university self-reliance?

Chile stands high among nations of the world that favor privatization of higher education. In private expenditures as a percentage of total higher education spending (1998), Chile at 76 per cent was second only to the Republic of Korea (83 per cent), ahead of Thailand at 67 per cent; and four Asian countries – Japan, Indonesia, the Philippines, Vietnam – were located between 60 and 50 per cent. Other major countries ranged downward from the United States (53 per cent) to Australia and Canada (44 and 43 per cent), to United Kingdom (37 per cent), France (14 per cent), and Germany (8 per cent). Private funding and support, including tuition payments, that is now so prevalent in Latin American and particularly in Asia has occurred least in the traditional statist systems of Europe, including the Nordic countries of The Netherlands (12 per cent), Sweden (11 per cent), Norway (6 per cent) and Denmark (3 per cent).[15] Number of universities and their enrollments show similar high private levels for Chile: 75 per cent of all universities; 71 per cent of all higher education enrollment, 60 per cent in the university sector. In marked contrast to the European scene, Chile has joined the dynamic systems of Eastern and South-eastern Asia in building dominant private sectors and it has been more enthusiastic than even the USA in assembling a private–public duality tilted toward the private.

Behind the so-called privatization of Chilean universities, as exemplified at the PUC, we find the elements of my conceptual framework interacting strongly with one another. Income diversification has moved swiftly and sharply, with state core support moving down to low levels – the 10 to 20 per cent range – and a diverse set of other income-producing services, beyond tuition, totaling up to one-half or more of financial support. Those services have been vigorously developed by units located on the university's old periphery, operating as 'ancillary services' that reach to the outside world. Departments in the traditional academic heartland also vigorously asserted themselves to raise their income by developing new outreach programs. In turn, strengthening the university's steering core at macro, meso, and micro levels – the center, the faculty, the department – played a crucial role in making possible the elements of income diversification, extensive outreach, and new proactive attitudes and behaviors in traditional departments. And, hovering over all the material changes, a new entrepreneurial culture has spread throughout, pushed by individual faculty heading up academic specialties and providing leadership in entrepreneurial teams within both departments and organized research units.

Not to be overlooked in our instructive case from Chile is the tough willingness to rapidly upgrade faculty. At a time when money was extremely tight, and endless demands existed on expenditure of limited funds, the university financed severance funds that subsidized early retirement and outright firing of faculty deemed not appropriate for upgraded, first-world status. Getting rid of 'unproductive faculty' was thorough in basic parts of the institution.

The happier side of faculty upgrading was the university's subsidy of young promising scholars in an effort to grow its own faculty talent in fields where top, well-educated experts were not available. Substantial funds were required to identify talent, provide institutional pretraining, support graduate work abroad for several years, and then integrate young scholars into the faculty on their return. This 'nursery' approach signified long-term investment and serious institution building. As much as any other single feature, at least for a decade or two, it insured forward motion. Next year some desired new talent, already owned, is scheduled to appear at the faculty door, and then more the following year, and in the years after that.

At PUC, the primary interacting elements of change, always evolving as a new organizational framework, pushed each other along. Here, too, as in some previous cases, we observe the growth of a bureaucracy of change embedded in a larger steady state of change. PUC not only enacted the first miracle of major transformation in getting started on a new pathway, a courageous against-the-stream mid-eighties commitment, but also engaged fully in the second miracle of sustaining a transforming evolution over a decade or more, thereby generating near-perpetual momentum. And behind these dynamics of interaction and momentum lurked uncommon institutional will. The university moved into the new character of being aggressively entrepreneurial not because it was told to do so by the state, nor because it was driven to do so by 'demographic forces', 'the market', 'globalization', or any other unanalyzed abstraction that does not closely connect up the dots between external conditions and multi-sided internal response. It became an entrepreneurial university, with collegial connections common to universities, by willing it to happen and by working hard over many years to build the internal mechanisms that would implement strong volition.

As stressed throughout this study, and as we have just seen at the ancient Pontificia Universidad Católica de Chile, the truth of meaningful, sustainable change in universities lies in organizational details. Those details necessarily include idiosyncracies that individual universities possess. But they also can be usefully summed in a few common elements appearing internationally among proactive universities.

9

Monash University: seizing the revolutionary moment in Australia

Monash University was born amid a gross mismatch in Australia between new societal demands for a greatly expanded university system and the constrained capability and willingness of a small set of established universities, with historic ties to British academic culture, to move quickly from elite to mass higher education. The existing universities were 'small and comfortable enclaves of professional training and elite culture' that had 'defined themselves as one remove from government and industry and a place apart from the more plebeian society around them'.[1] Monash opened its doors in 1961 as a second comprehensive university in the greater Melbourne region of the state of Victoria, where the University of Melbourne, founded a century earlier in 1853, was the local model of the traditional style – a place apart. The national system at the time was small and relatively tidy: the new institution was just the tenth university.[2]

The Australian transition into mass higher education, guided by strong governmental interpretation of public need, was made in an explosive fashion in the 1960s and 1970s. Monash opened with just 360 students, then doubled each year in 1962, 1963 and 1964, doubled again in the next two years, and then doubled again in the next five years. At the end of its first decade (1971), 11,000 students were enrolled. The enrollment finally peaked in this initial fast-out-of-the-box stage at over 13,000 in 1976, a plateau that lasted another decade until the mid-1980s. Despite its high rate of growth, Monash found itself, like the University of Melbourne, soon establishing quota limits on some fields, typically medicine, laboratory-based sciences and engineering, the areas of greatest faculty strength. A third university in Victoria, La Trobe, was then established in the late 1960s, joined by rapid expansion in a 'non-university' sector of higher education known at the time in Australia as the 'advanced education sector'.[3] By the mid-1970s, the headlong rush into mass higher education had extensively differentiated sectors and institutions.

In this initial stage Monash took on the organizational shape of a traditional Australian comprehensive university, with major separate faculties in science, economics and politics (social science), the 'arts' (humanities), and medicine, engineering, law and Education (fields seen as professional schools in the US structure), with over one-third of students enrolled in the hard-science complex of science, engineering and medicine, and the rest in the softer knowledge domains of humanities and social sciences, law and education. In Marginson's depiction, 'fortress faculties' acquired strong separate identities backed by 'full-time, non-rotating deans', equipped 'with a relatively high level of financial and operational autonomy'. The powerful deanship – a feature with 'British forebears' – was to become a lasting feature, one that would hamper cross-disciplinary innovation.[4]

On the plus-side, Monash had the excitement of a new venture: young faculty and young full-time students could see a campus being built around them, backed by British-style staffing in which low student–teacher ratios permitted substantial tutorial teaching. Although the university 'found itself always looking over its institutional shoulder at Melbourne' – a 'habit that proved hard to break' – a 'distinct Monash style emerged, with a fair admixture of brashness . . . and the ability to respond quickly and effectively, solve problems and get things done'.[5] Compared to the much older university that seemed antiquated and complacent, needing extensive modernization that began in the late 1960s, it seemed exciting. Besides, Monash itself had taken on characteristics of the leisurely style of traditional Australian universities:[6]

> When I came here in 1972, people used to disappear to play tennis at lunchtime. That is fine – they still do – but in those days they didn't come back. People used to play bridge: you would see two tables of bridge in the staff club that would go all afternoon. People accepted that as the norm. Those who quaffed their coffee quickly and headed off to the library were OK, there were people like that in the University, but they didn't set the tone of the place.

But the easy life had little future. The burdens of mass higher education alone would virtually eliminate such niceties in another few years: faculty were pressed to change the patterns of how they used their time. Government officials were soon to insist on more work for all Australian academics, effecting incentives that could readily be turned into sanctions.

And Monash students, like counterparts elsewhere in Australia, Britain and the United States, had come to college not only to study but to learn how to drink and contemplate sex. The student culture became in part 'a culture of young people having fun'. It also had a wing engaged in radical politics, that could leave 'a radical past' as a fading memory. Here, too, no-nonsense seriousness was just down the institutional road.

The rapid-growth 'foundation stage' was followed by a steady-state decade of 'consolidation' (1977–87), especially when viewed from the perspective of later transforming years. By the early 1980s, just two decades old and after the enormous initial growth, Monash had stabilized as Australia's fifth largest university, with approximately 14,000 students (women nearing one-half), not much below the 16,000–18,000 size of Sydney, Queensland, New South

Wales and Melbourne.[7] It had become a major institution in a university system that had become increasingly centralized and nationalized. A transition from state government to national government support and control had been fully effected, with an official university sector now dominated by the Commonwealth government. Dominance was spelled out for Monash in having 98 per cent of its operating budget coming from Canberra, the national capital, and four-fifths of that money was tied up in staff costs. Unfortunately, the national government, short of cash, had begun to make cuts in recurrent funding, similar to what was happening in Britain at that time. The main trend in the affairs of the university 'was the slow accumulation of cost pressures in a tightening fiscal environment'.[8]

It hardly mattered which political party held the main seats of governmental power: Labor continued the pattern established by a Conservative government of 'funding at a constant level'. As a result, the 1986–87 allocation ended up below the allocation for ten years before.[9] The staff could hope that 'the old environment would return', but government support was badly stalled. And in the deeply rooted culture of the universities, it was difficult to imagine private funding on a large scale. People at Monash could begin to identify 'some of the solutions to its difficulties, such as more strategic leadership . . . more active relations with industry, greater private funding, and the fostering of an alumni', but the university 'had not even begun to acquire the capacity to carry those solutions through'.[10] Monash would have to transform itself if it were to help alter a university-government relationship that froze the status quo.

The late 1980s ushered in that major transformation, proceeding at first through institutional mergers that made Monash a much larger and more complicated institution. Australia at the time was economically backward, still heavily dependent on such primary industries as mining and agriculture; it was only lightly invested in manufacturing and hardly involved in the service sector. When a balance of payments crisis erupted because of declining value of primary-industry exports, government officials, sending up a cry that Australia was 'in danger of becoming a "banana republic" ', shifted sharply their thinking. Australia would need industry to move rapidly into producing technology-intensive goods. To do so, it would need universities devoted to strengthening human capital and committed to research for industrial use.

The right man in government to shape up the universities was at hand. John Dawkins had held several major ministerial posts in Finance and Trade; he had been around the track in education policy since student days; and now, in 1987, a 'potent reformer', he was given an expanded portfolio in a new Department of Employment, Education and Training (DEET) that placed all higher education programs under 'an economic department of the Commonwealth'. In a state-led, hard revolution from the top, reform was swift and deep:[11]

In half a decade Dawkins completely restructured higher education. 'Enrollments grew by 60 per cent, the binary distinction between universities and colleges of advanced education [CAEs] was abolished and the number of institutions was halved by mergers . . . The map of institutions was completely redrawn. In 1987 there were 19 universities and 46 CAEs in Australia, a total of 73 higher education institutions with an average size of 5312 students. By 1994, the CAEs had disappeared and there were 36 public universities, with an average size of 16,166 students' – all in a new Unified National System. In this system, all institutions were funded on a similar basis. With government specifying a higher minimum size, 'medium-sized and smaller CAEs were pressured to seek larger institutions as merger partners, while universities such as Monash were provided with a one-off chance to expand in size, role and geographical spread'.[12]

Further, the government encouraged institutions to maximize income from non-government sources. This opened the door to full-cost fees for international students and some graduate-level students, alumni donations, funds from consultancy and commercial research, and even to some tuition payments from domestic undergraduates. With state funding turning soft, the state would push the universities into 'the market', whatever that might be.

With 'unprecedented changes in the wind', the universities were now at 'the revolutionary moment'.[13]

Universities had to sink or swim in this new highly turbulent environment. Some fell on hard times; some mergers even had to be undone. But no university was quicker than Monash in turning the new problems into new opportunities. A vigorous management team assembled by a new vice-chancellor (Mal Logan, 1987–96) gave the university the strong professional management at the center that the government had sought, on top of the assembly of strong deans already in place. Actively involved in the government's reform planning, the university developed a relationship 'with Canberra' that was 'based on continued trust and friendly dealings'. Positioning itself 'high in the Commonwealth's favor, it could do well in submissions for capital funding, and in competitive bidding'.[14]

In six years (1990–96), Monash, serving as the dominant base, effected mergers with four other institutions that had significant identities of their own. To its initial location it added campuses in five other places, absorbing former colleges of advanced education (CAEs). By the mid-1990s, just about half (approximately 20,000) of all Monash students were enrolled on the original site. The remaining half were distributed at approximately 9,000, 8,000, 3,500, 450, and 425 students at the other sites, with the new multi-site Monash totaling over 41,000, compared to the one-site enrollment of 16,000 at the beginning of the burst of mergers. No wonder that the vigorous and forceful Vice-Chancellor, stepping down in 1996, claimed that 'without question the mergers were the toughest job of his time in office'.[15]

Mergers in higher education are almost always difficult to negotiate and are especially painful and prolonged in implementation. Entire institutional identities have to be swallowed up and quite different embedded cultures brought into alignment with one another. Harman and Meek reviewed the situation for all of Australia. They saw that the post-merger and integration phase was complex, far slower than anticipated, and was attended by high financial and emotional short-term costs; it exhausted everyone and took up to a decade for wounds to heal and for new realities to be accepted.[16] At Monash the process was still being completed in the late 1990s. Even though the government stood in the background holding a shotgun to make sure that institutional marriages came off, the Monash management team could feel the choice of partners had been largely 'consent-based'. What was certain was that the scale of change was vast. Much had been done in just a few years.

A crucial element in making mergers work at Monash was a decision to use faculties rather than campuses as the basic units. Integrating along faculty lines kept the merger-transformed university from falling into a weak federal structure lacking educational coherence. The university chose not to have 'locational and historical boundaries' as its main internal fault lines. Rather, the major faculties rooted in areas of knowledge and already in place would integrate across the half-dozen traditional institutional identities. Additionally, the doubling of size in a few years provided the university with a much expanded physical plant and a large increase in operating resources, giving it a greatly enlarged role within Victoria and the country as a whole.

However, multiple mergers carried out at a rapid rate were bound to lead to much unevenness. The combined business and economics faculties experienced the greatest growth: with over 12,000 students in 1996, the new single faculty was probably the largest in Australia, earning over $A17 million in non-governmental income. In contrast, in arts, science and engineering faculties, busy with the major structural change that mergers induced, some departments were deeply worried about their inability to keep up with changes in their own disciplines. For them, the effort to integrate a new institutional culture was weakening the local expression of all-important disciplinary cultures. Students, on the whole, profited. They had the choice of more courses, combinations of courses, modes of study and location. They could move midstream between many options. And all awarded degrees were now Monash degrees, not those of a CAE.[17]

If major transformation by means of such mergers was not enough, Monash also moved sharply to become an international university, in a very direct sense. From its earliest days the university had an interest in East and South-east Asia which became operationally expressed in two forms: in research centers and language programs that studied Asia as the 'other'; and in on-campus addition of students from countries in the Southern Asian region. When, in the late 1980s, 'the international dimension became more significant in every Australian university' – key was the deregulation of fee charging of international students – Monash, moving ahead from its early investment, leaped at the opportunity to become 'an international university' that would vie for leadership in this role. Its management team worked closely with government and business in a common effort to engage with the now dynamic countries in the region – Malaysia, Singapore, Hong

Kong, Taiwan, for example. Monash was positioned to be in the forefront of a wave of international university developments, on- and off-shore; research collaborations; staff and student exchanges; face-to-face courses for international students on-site at Monash; franchising and twinning arrangements whereby off-shore institutions provided part or all of a Monash degree; international distance education.[18]

Particularly important initially was the on-site welcoming of students from other countries whose education-eager families were happy to pay full-cost tuition for sons, and increasingly for daughters, to receive a modern education, in English, without going off to the United States or Great Britain to do so. With students from Malaysia, Singapore, Hong Kong, Thailand and Indonesia as the initial base, 'international marketing had the potential to both augment the university's income and drive its integration into the [Southeast Asia] region'. Because its growth in full-fee enrollment was moving faster than in the nation as a whole, by 1992, Monash had over 4,100 international students, the largest enrollment in Australia (the second largest, University of New South Wales, had a thousand less). And where mergers drew much fire from 'critics unhappy with the main entrepreneurial direction that the university was taking', the income from international students 'carried a force of argument of its own'. Deans and their faculties got 70 per cent of the income generated, with 30 per cent flowing back to the university center.[19]

The university went out of its way to be accommodating and appealing. From 1991 onward, it held offshore graduation ceremonies for international students so that families could attend. Leading officials of the university flew in and did the ceremonies 'in style'. Furthering the cause, the university quickly moved on to networking efforts among Southern Asia alumni and set up 'Monash societies' in Singapore and Indonesia and in other countries. It not only drew up defensive strategies to sustain enrollment from main source countries, against inroads from new eager competitors from other countries as well as Australia, but it also devised developmental strategies to apply to target countries where current demand was relatively low but potential demand was high, for example, in India; and on down the line to where long-term links with governments and other universities could be explored in a 'tiger economy' of the future, as in Vietnam.[20]

The university was roiling in near chaos for a few years, as 'different campuses, courses and individuals pursued their own interests, using the Monash brand name'. But order was imposed in 1994 in the form of a private corporation, Monash International, owned by the university. The Vice-Chancellor chaired both this new entity and the university's academic board, controlling relations between 'the commercial and educational drivers of decision-making'. When the cost of offshore graduation ceremonies vexed academic board members – and the Vice-Chancellor believed in the value of the ceremonies to connect Monash to home country families – he could remove the cost from the university budget by transferring it to Monash International. He could personally drive 'the Asian agenda', where if 'we had argued it through all the processes of the university, we might never have got it through'. In any event the pay-offs were generous and for all to see, in one faculty after another. Funds received from foreign students and families ran surpluses that could be kept by the faculties. As expected, business, economics and computing were much in demand. What was not antici-pated was that the enrollment of women had overtaken that of men in Monash's international student community by the mid-1990s.[21]

Beyond the on-site inclusion of foreign students, the university increas-ingly turned its 'Asian agenda' toward long-term sharing (twinning) arrangements with foreign universities, and the establishing of its own cam-puses abroad. In the Monash University Foundation Year program, students completed preparatory English-language studies to prepare them for degree programs. In twinning programs, students could enroll for the first year at a cooperating university in their own country – Malaysia, for example – and then transfer to Australia for the remainder. Twinning arrangements reached as far as Beijing and Shanghai in China, in business education, with the possibility of 'parallel streams in Mandarin and English, leading to Chinese and Australian qualifications respectively'. As other Asian edu-cational systems expanded their domestic capacity in higher education, Monash would seek to become 'a partner in their evolution'.[22]

After all the hard work of working through the sensitivities and oper-ational details of twinning came the more ultimate objective of developing fully-owned branch campuses outside Australia. Here, the political and cul-tural sensitivities of the countries of South-east Asia were major obstacles. For example: the creation of a Monash campus in Malaysia was seen as a high priority – a prospect that 'engaged Logan from the beginning of his term in office' in 1987. Seven years later he could be found in Kuala Lumpur talking up education as a factor in regional economies and pointing out that since Singapore had not yet become the educational hub of the region, a vacuum could be filled by Malaysia, especially if it built upon the twinning arrange-ments already established with Australian universities. The opportunity opened up for Monash when Malaysia entertained applications from inter-national universities to establish branch campuses. Two more years of nego-tiation and gradual governmental acceptance finally led to the establishing of a Monash branch campus in that key country. Consideration of other branches soon followed in Laos, Thailand, Indonesia and as far away as in South Africa,[23] the latter becoming a reality in 1998.

And then came sustained effort, only partly successful, in perhaps the deepest form of internationalization of a university: the inclusion of the perspectives and learning styles of other cultures – those of Asian societies, in this case – in the curricula of the departments and faculties, at least to make 'the inclusions of Asia as a "normal reference" in all disciplines'. Staff and student exchanges seemed the best way to effect such 'corresponding experiences' for more Australian students. Progress was slow, but by the mid-1990s the university had effected formal cooperative agreements with more than 50 overseas institutions, stretching from Indonesia and Thailand to a handful of universities in Canada and the United States and onward to universities in Britain and Germany – the latter especially difficult because of the 'hierarchical conservative structure of the German universities'.[24]

Australia's annual *Good University Guide* ran a contest in 1994 focused on internationalization, with an emphasis on the Asia-Pacific Region. Four criteria were spelled out: the number of international students and the quality of educational and other services provided them; offshore programs; programs enabling domestic students to study and work abroad; and the extent and quality of opportunities for undergraduates to develop a genuinely international and cosmopolitan perspective. Judged exceptional in all four areas, Monash won, in competition against such other leading exemplars of internationalization as the University of New South Wales and the Royal Melbourne Institute of Technology (RMIT). The Guide richly described 'the cosmopolitan character' of the Monash campuses: a student body speaking more than 80 languages; Asian, African, Mediterranean and Melanesian faces everywhere; students browsing the *South China Morning Post*, the *Singapore Straits Times*, the *Bangkok Post*; cross-cultural couples cuddling in the lounges; residence halls carefully assigned so that internationals and locals got rooms next to one another.[25]

In the effort 'to establish the University as a significant educational-corporate presence in the countries of Australia's geographical region', Monash was sensitive to the danger of placing too much emphasis on immediate commercial returns. True, by the mid-1990s it annually made over $A43 million in 'export income'. But to 'genuinely engage in the region' and 'to avoid a fragile relationship' built on trade alone and on the cult of 'short-termism', the Vice-Chancellor argued, trust was all important and trust is based on long-term relationships. There was no doubt, as Marginson concluded, that 'in the decade after 1986 Monash had gone global. It was probably the most important aspect of the remaking of the University. It was also an unequivocal "win-win" outcome for everyone, in contrast with the more two-sided experience of the mergers.'[26]

Internationalizing along so many fronts, Monash was at the leading edge of a general swing of the Australian university system from full state support to diversified income. 1998 figures for 'earned' or non-governmental income as a share of total income showed wide variation among the states and especially among the universities, around a national average of 32 per cent: from 28 per cent or less, in South Australia and the Capital Territory (for example), to over 36 per cent in Victoria and 38 per cent in Western Australia; and among universities, from as low as 20 per cent to over 40 per cent at the University of Western Australia (47 per cent), Monash (43 per cent), and RMIT (42 per cent).[27] At Monash, the trend away from Commonwealth core support to other sources of income continued in 2000 and beyond, and moved past the 50/50 half-way point and down to less than 40 per cent dependence on the core recurrent grant.[28]

'Fees and charges' and 'other income' became major items – about 40 per cent of total income – followed by monies from the Australian Higher

Education Contribution Scheme (the revolving fund from which students take out low interest loans and pay them off in whole or in part after graduation by additional income tax payments) at approximately 12–14 per cent. Donations, bequests, and investment income, and money from research grants and contracts, rounded the major contributing sources at roughly 6 per cent each. In short, diversified income was very evident on the financial ledger – a long way from the 98 per cent dependence on Commonwealth recurrent funding noted earlier for the pre-transformation days.[29]

The main tools of transformation at Monash, mergers and multi-sided internationalization, created an institutional 'soft underbelly' by weakening measured research performance. In a 1993 assessment by a new Commonwealth evaluation team for 'quality assurance', Monash was marked down to a second group of universities, below six others, because it 'lacked overarching principles on teaching and learning', and also lacked clear formal pathways of reporting, and a few other similar deadly sins. Using uniform criteria in preparing its rankings, the committee's approach emphasized one-size-fits-all. The two leading universities placed down in a B category (Monash and Sydney) had undergone substantial mergers, had brought in large groups of academics with weak research records, and caught (at Monash) some faculties deep in the problems of cross-campus integration and inclined to see the assessment as mainly a window-dressing exercise. The interrogation by the visiting committee was 'testy and sometimes hostile'. The rating shocked the university: the vice-chancellor was 'devastated'. His central staff immediately set to work to repair the damage and during the next two years worked up the statements and the structures the committee insisted upon in a paper trail meant to signify quality control – defined objectives for every course, evidence of clear reporting lines, for example. The committee was then duly impressed and gave the university top ratings. The Vice-Chancellor later remarked that the committee's system of quality assessment was 'grossly imperfect', but 'coming first beats the hell out of coming last'.[30]

Research assessments and ratings proved to be *the* ongoing problem that followed from all the local merging and all the international outreach. The mergers had been fashioned at the cost of research on the original campus; the international outreach meant a diffusion of the university in an uneven assembly of programs, alliances, and new campuses centered on teaching not closely related to research. Upon retiring in 1997, the Vice-Chancellor felt that the university still had not 'got it right' in research. Transformation had fashioned a new university prototype in Australia; it was characterized by diversity and responsiveness amid large size, which could function well in regional, national and international roles, much as was common in leading US public universities. What was needed in the next stage of achievement was 'absolutely front-rank research and teaching'. The remaking of the university was 'still a project in progress'. The remaining unmet priority was to strengthen the research foundations in the academic heartland.[31]

Conclusion

Monash adds to our understanding of the many varieties of proactive universities; it offers a type that Marginson has deemed 'the enterprise university'.[32] This variant did not undergo transformation primarily by contract research and research activity. Rather, as effected by mergers, the transformation was largely teaching-led: the university took on a much larger task in providing undergraduate education in the local region. The transformation was even more influenced by the extension of direct service to an international region – as effected in the many on-shore and off-shore structures that comprised its internationalization, with 'financial drivers' playing an important part. Monash became a new hybrid different in major degree, if not in kind, from the Australian traditional model.

But the educational values of the traditional model, widely upheld by academics in major industrialized nations, would not go away. There was still an international gold standard based on research-led teaching and learning that established the standing of universities. What I have elsewhere termed 'the research-teaching-study nexus',[33] was anchored in the values of the many basic departments in Monash's heartland and in the thinking of central administrators sensitive to the primacy of research activity and performance in university reputation. Australia is moving formally and informally toward a diversified system in which many universities will be teaching-led. In mid-2002, the government was promising more harsh treatment, with possible closures, forced elimination of courses duplicated within sets of neighboring universities or having very small enrollment, and the encouragement of 'teaching-only universities', even 'undergraduate-only universities'.[34] The few universities at the top of the reputational ladder, however, would be noted centers of research. For them, as in Europe, 'research university' would be an oxymoron. Post-2000, research capability would be the side of Monash's new hybrid nature that needed vigorous commitment.

In their excellent book *The Enterprise University* (2000), Marginson and Considine, in a concluding section on entrepreneurial universities, compared the five elements I set forth in my 1998 book with their own findings for Australian universities: 'his empirical findings largely accord with our own'; 'all Enterprise Universities in Australia display the first three Clark characteristics, strengthened steering core, expanded developmental periphery, and somewhat diversified funding base'; but my 'last two characteristics [stimulated academic heartland and integrated entrepreneurial culture] are weak or non-existent in Australia'. If 'some Enterprise Universities have created an institutional culture, none seems to be stimulating its academic heartland as Clark describes'.[35]

Monash, at the national cutting-edge, clearly exhibits an entrepreneurial culture in its central management team and in the orientations of the academic and non-academic professionals who staff and plot change in the places and programs of its international outreach. The concerns of Marginson and Considine center on the imbalance in the more enterprising universities in Australia between a new dominating, top-down managerialism and a subordinated academic culture, with a resulting lack of 'academic-managerial synergy'. Hence, the weaknesses of the Enterprise University, as they saw them, began with the detachment of leaders from 'that which they lead' and the tendency to work around and against academic cultures rather than through them. Looking toward further reform in the university system – 'beyond the Enterprise University' – they pointed to the importance of both stimulating the heartland departments to be more change-minded and developing a new overall institutional identity by 'generalising the culture'.

They conclude on the note that universities finally have to make their own way: 'The future of universities is affected by many factors, some beyond their own control. Nevertheless, in triggering the transition to something better, universities' own actions will be decisive. And their capacity for sustained and successful action will rest in their governance – especially the success of that governance in creating a healthy and productive synthesis of academic cultures and institutional identity'.[36]

The five elements of my conceptual scheme clearly interact with one another in the Monash case, with some weakness in the capacity of heartland departments – and administrators – to assert academic values as a frame for managerial concerns centered on 'financial drivers'. There is also good evidence of the dynamic of perpetual momentum in the continuing year-by-year development of self-reinforcing structures and processes. Most of all, Monash exhibits the dynamic of institutionalized willpower in an increasingly competitive setting. Throughout the critical decade of 1987–97 the then vice-chancellor emphasized the 'imperative of transformation', that universities could not stand still, that their real strength lay in their capacity to adapt, that it is better 'to create our own future than to have it forced upon us'.[37] Toward that future, Monash decided officially in 1990 'to stop benchmarking itself to the University of Melbourne'. It would 'get out and make its mark on its own, rather than trailing along in the stream of the old university'.[38]

In 2000, institutional will was expressed in *Leading the Way: Monash 2020*, which centered long-term vision on further becoming 'a broad-based, global, and self-reliant institution'. Second-tier planning documents centered on a plan for research and research training and on a framework for further global development. New openings included an on-site institute of public health and centers in South Africa, Italy and London. On the research front, the university was full of initiatives: it was in the first year of the Monash Research Graduate School; it was increasing the number of postgraduate [graduate level] scholarships and awards; it was expanding its commitment to Logan Research Fellowships 'to attract up to 30 world-class postdoctoral researchers to Monash over a six-year period'; and it was now financing a general research fund from its own resources.[39] The university had taken to heart the message that research could be, and should be, the integrating activity for a special kind of teaching and a special kind of student learning.

10

Genetic entrepreneurialism among American universities

The American system of higher education is markedly different from all the other national systems explored in previous chapters. It combines very large size, extreme decentralized control, great institutional diversity, sharp institutional competition and substantial status hierarchy.[1] Its most important feature is the radical disbursement of authority. It is a system composed both of major private sectors, in which over 2,000 private universities and colleges of all sizes operate under individual boards of control, devising their own viable niches, and of numerous public sectors in which another 1,600 institutions fall primarily under the 50 states rather than under the national government.[2]

This fundamental condition of decentralized public and private control in a large country set in motion, a long time ago, a restless proliferation of institutions. Long before the age of the college gave way to the age of the university, institutions were created in the first half of the nineteenth century in large numbers and at a rate unheard of elsewhere. At a time when England had two places of higher education – Oxford and Cambridge – the United States had developed hundreds of separate small colleges. But as academic scientists in the late-nineteenth century were to point out, what the United States had, by the standards of Europe, was a swarm of mosquitoes rather than a few soaring eagles. Numerous eagles began to soar in the 1870s, 1880s and 1890s. Some leading private colleges, pre-eminently Harvard, Yale and Princeton, transformed themselves into full-bodied universities, in competition with such new private institutions as Johns Hopkins (1876), Clark University (1889), Stanford University (1891) and the University of Chicago (1892), all constructed as universities from the outset.

At the same time, each of the proliferating number of states sought to have at least one public institution that could claim a substantial comprehensive character (for example, the University of Wisconsin and the University of Georgia). Stirred by the commitments of the land-grant tradition, one or more public universities in each state also prized their service to the state's general population, beginning with the admission of sons and daughters of farmers and workers. But private universities set the model of a quality research university. When the self-selecting club – the Association of Universities (AAU) – was formed in 1900 to jointly vouch for quality, it had eleven private and three public members. Many others of both types were soon lined up at the door, clamoring for admission. At the same time, in a setting where institutional initiative was unbounded and stimulated, both public and private non-university institutions continued to proliferate – numbers of small private colleges increased rather than died away and teachers' colleges grew everywhere, giving the United States at the turn of the century a census of accredited institutions that approached the unbelievable number of 1,000.[3]

The structure and diversity well in place by the turn of the century ensured a twentieth-century system characterized by sharp competition for faculty, students, resources and status. Comparatively, the US system became an open one – no inclusive official structure, no national ministry of education – in which competitive disorder and a competitive status hierarchy heavily conditioned the ways that institutions defined themselves, sought resources and arranged internal conditions for research, teaching and learning. Foreign observers, unaccustomed to the competitive mode, often saw these ways as decidedly unacademic, even brutish. Well they might. The habits of competition soon extended to the development of big-time sports – a benefit and an affliction that universities in other countries have managed to do without. Big-time competitive sports came with the territory; athletic prowess even sometimes arrived first, leaving some institutions for a time in the situation of building faculties that their football and basketball teams could be proud of. Institutions similarly placed can still be found in 2000, leaving university presidents with a headache second only to that produced by having to contend with a major medical school.[4]

Throughout the twentieth century, diffusion of control localized initiative. Private institutions had to survive and prosper largely on their own; public ones, considerably influenced by the independence and achievements of the leading private universities and four-year colleges, also sought self-constructed autonomy, over the mandates of state and federal government. The system's disorderly and competitive conditions encouraged a large number of institutions (but not all, of course) to build institutional willpower.

Since no one institution can represent the play of this widespread dynamic in many different sites, I turn briefly to six cases that, each in its own way, exhibit a high level of local initiative and self-determination: two leading private universities, Stanford in northern California and MIT in Massachusetts; two flagship level state universities, Michigan in the midwest and UCLA in southern California; and two public universities, North Carolina State University and Georgia Institute of Technology, not as well known at home and abroad as the first four, in which we find a determination, under current competitive conditions, to work out new forms of university enhancement. These latter cases also highlight the state-by-state competition that flourishes in a 50-state federal system of university sponsorship in which education officials do not get together across state lines to establish common rules and limit competition, as occurred in the German federal system, or surrender their control to national government, as happened in Australian federalism, but instead join together with universities and firms in their own state (or own region of the country) to compete more effectively against other states and regions.

Let us observe institution-building in action where ambition forms amidst competitive disorder.

Stanford University

Stanford University in Palo Alto, California, about forty miles south of San Francisco qualified during the last half of the twentieth century as the foremost entrepreneurial university in the world. The mother university of Silicon Valley, it remained the academic anchor during four to five decades of explosive growth in the network of firms that came to define this technological region. At the end of the century, Stanford remained a key player in 'the regional advantage' of the Valley, in comparison with the Route 128 combination of firms generated largely by MIT in the Boston–Cambridge area, and the science-and-technology parks that sprang up throughout the United States with an eye on what had been achieved in the Stanford-generated complex.[1]

For our pursuit of university transformation, Stanford's development can be divided into the 'prehistory' of its first half century and the later Silicon Valley decades of rapid change. The university was ambitious from the beginning. Its founding charter in 1885, prepared by the Stanford family, spoke of 'a University for both sexes, with the Colleges, Schools ... Museums, Galleries of Art, and all other things necessary and appropriate to a University of high degree'. High degree included not only 'the cultivation and enlargement of the mind', but also 'the study of agriculture' and 'mechanical training'. It ought to qualify its students for 'direct usefulness in life'.[2] Once a president and some faculty were on board, they were soon aiming to become the best private university on the West Coast, an institution that would in time step up to the status of a western version of the Ivy League.

From the 1890s to the 1930s Stanford's situation could be summarized as 'land rich, money poor'.[3] The university was blessed with more than 8,000 acres of farm land. The land was to be used for university purposes only, but only 800 acres, one-tenth of the whole was required for a campus. The value of the original monetary grant gradually attenuated: try as they might, successive administrators could not extract from alumni and business firms the sums appropriate for an expensive, costly private university; it had 'few active benefactors'. Its fifth president, J.E. Wallace Sterling, in 1958 felt that Stanford had had 'to adjust its physique to a kind of chronic malnutrition'. He saw the university as 'on a plateau from which it must either rise with the other research universities or be relegated to the status of a respected regional institution'.[4]

Stanford's rise from that plateau – the Silicon Valley take-off – began slowly in the 1930s. A legend tells the story of how Frederick Terman, an electrical engineering professor (later engineering dean and then university provost) talked two young Stanford graduates, William Hewlett and David Packard, into forming an electronics firm to be located in a new industrial park. 'Foreshadowing Stanford's active role in the Silicon Valley economy', Terman lent personal money, helped the two graduates to find work to finance their initial experiments, and then arranged the bank loan which allowed them to begin commercial production. The resulting Hewlett-Packard company (HP) is surely the classic successful university spin-off – along with Varian, a firm established about the same time, to which the university provided some materials and use of a physics laboratory, 'in exchange for a 50 per cent interest in any resulting patents for applications of the technology'.[5]

Stanford learned early in the Silicon Valley development that it could not only obtain year-by-year 'ground rents' from firms located on its property (working around restrictions placed by the founding charter) but could also take up equity positions in those firms that might have large pay-offs down the road. In any event the marriage between the university and the initial firms was close: ties of mentor and prized students, alma mater and assisted businesses, added emotional underpinnings that went beyond the straight business dealings of university–industry relationships. Ties between Stanford and local industry were to be collaborative in more than a narrow sense. When Varian Associates moved its administration and research and development operations closer to Stanford, it sought 'to bring the company closer to old friends, ease ongoing collaborations, and improve access to graduate students in physics and electrical engineering'.[6]

Annalee Saxenian, in her classic study of the Silicon Valley edge, noted three institutional innovations during the 1950s which 'reflect the relationships that Terman pioneered in the region'. First, Stanford established a major research institute of its own, 'to conduct defense-related research and to assist West Coast businesses'. Second, the university opened its classrooms to local companies, encouraging engineers in the firms 'to enroll in graduate courses directly or through a specialized televised instructional network which brought Stanford courses into company classrooms' – all this a half-century ago! By 1961 thirty-two companies and 400 employees were participating, and enrollment was destined to increase dramatically in subsequent decades. Stanford would be connected, even wired-in, throughout the Valley. Third, Terman promoted a Stanford industrial park located only a short walk from its classrooms, a park in which 'leases were granted only to technology companies that might benefit the university'. Between 1955 and 1961 the park grew from 220 to over 650 acres, to accommodate twenty-five companies employing 11,000 people. Beyond Hewlett-Packard and Varian Associates, such other present or future major firms as General Electric and Eastman Kodak were on board.[7]

The beat continued at a rapid, accelerating pace. To establish research laboratories or manufacturing facilities, in came Lockheed Aerospace, Westinghouse, Sylvania, Raytheon, IBM, Xerox, and others. Along the way, in the 1970s, the Santa Clara Valley then became known as Silicon Valley. Chains of successful spin-offs were central in the internal dynamics developed at the time. The new Fairchild Semiconductor firm alone spawned ten spin-offs in its first eight years. This process helped to establish a virtual regional monopoly; only 'five of the forty-five independent semiconductor firms started in the United States between 1959 and 1976 were located outside of Silicon Valley'. A key advantage gained by being there were 'open and reciprocal ties' with Stanford. When in the early 1970s more than 150 venture capital firms were active in the Valley, they replaced the military as the leading source of its financing. Stanford itself did not miss another opportunity to become cash rich instead of cash poor. It grew the habit of 'regularly investing a portion of its endowment in venture activities'.[8]

Through the 1970s, 80s and 90s, Stanford continued the substantial expansion of its financial base, moving up closer to Harvard, Yale and Princeton in endowment and alumni support along with its support from a wide range of federal agencies and an ever larger number of business firms. Its spin-off capability grew and grew: 'From 1973 through 1993, more than 300 companies were founded by Stanford faculty and students. This activity continues. In 1997, 1998, and 1999 Stanford reported 43 new start-up companies based on licensing of the university's technology.'[9] In the American context, where small start-ups need to grow much larger to survive the competition, spin-offs that start with two to three employees do not end up with a half-dozen or a dozen. Success hinged considerably in growing from small to medium-size to large – and possibly huge. The Stanford spin-offs have included Sun Microsystems, Netscape, Cisco Systems and Yahoo!

With the School of Engineering always available for 'core organizational and logistical support', the science-and-technology part of the Stanford campus became a hot-house of technology venture programs and entrepreneurial task forces developed as much bottom-up as top-down – and was open to participants from outside firms, including venture capitalists, attorneys, alumni entrepreneurs and 'returned faculty' who had worked in business. Openness and valleywide inclusiveness continued and became virtually a genetic characteristic. The campus was loaded with personal and organizational role models of entrepreneurial orientation and engagement. In the engineering school (stocked with one-fifth of all undergraduate enrollment!), a catchphrase had it that 'If you want to be an engineer, go to MIT; if you want to be an entrepreneur, come to Stanford'.[10]

But Stanford wanted to be much more than a leading technological university: it wanted also to be a top comprehensive private university, another Harvard. It took its expanding income and aimed for top national status in departments throughout the humanities, social sciences, physical sciences, life sciences, the performing arts, and in such major professional schools as medicine, law, business and education. Much impressed by

Harvard's toughness in guarding the tenure line in faculty recruitment and promotion, Stanford adopted a similar attitude to inch its way up in faculty (and student) quality, until in the 1990s it was ranked with Harvard and Berkeley as one of the top three universities. Geiger has shown that in national rankings of departments as early as 1957 and 1969 Stanford had in a dozen years moved classics from fifteenth to fourth, English from fifteenth to sixth, psychology from fifth to first, political science from thirteenth to sixth, Chemistry from fifteenth to third, and had four engineering departments ranked in the top four nationwide in their specialties. Academic achievement was remarkable – 'easily the best relative improvement of any research university'.[11]

Stanford also ran the circle of interaction in financial resources in a major way, utilizing substantial monies from private sources to build research capabilities that in turn attracted federal research dollars. Operating on a grand scale it cross-subsidized within the university from its flowing spigots on the interdisciplinary periphery and in a few core departments, to the many departments that needed subsidy far beyond their own income-generating capability. Driving it all was 'unquenchable ambition'.[12]

Thus, in 2000, Stanford lit up national numbers that mixed Harvard and MIT characteristics under one tent. Total student enrollment was 18,000, compared to Harvard's 24,000 and MIT's 10,000; all three had approximately 40 per cent undergraduate, 60 per cent graduate; students' doctorates awarded annually numbered approximately 600, similar to Harvard (one and two among private universities) and larger than MIT's mid-400; post-doctoral appointees had grown to over 1,200, running second to only Harvard's startling 3,300 and doubling MIT's 500. Harvard, Stanford and MIT appeared one, two, and three in national academy membership of their faculties; total research funding exceeded $US400 million at Stanford, compared to a similar amount at MIT and over $US300 million at Harvard. Income from annual private support now placed Stanford first at nearly $US600 million, compared to Harvard at nearly $US500 million, and MIT at $US240 million; and, after the stockmarket run-up of the 1980s and 1990s, endowment assets totaled $US8.6 billion at Stanford, placing it third nationally in the midst of the top five – Harvard, Yale, Stanford, Princeton and MIT.[13]

During the last half of the twentieth century, Stanford was both the university that initiated Silicon Valley and the university that built the internal organizational capability to capitalize academically on the riches it had gained. Its development provides another paradigmatic case of the elements and dynamics I developed originally from European proactive institutions. It highlights the critical importance, at a heightened level, of income diversification, strengthened steering capacity, highly developed new relationships that reach out beyond traditional university boundaries, disciplinary departments that unhooked themselves from the status quo and connected their collegial style to change, and the extensive spread of entrepreneurial beliefs and attitudes in administrative, faculty and student cultures. Stanford's overall entrepreneurial character provided new ground for autonomy, collegiality and achievement.

Massachusetts Institute of Technology

The Massachusetts Institute of Technology in Cambridge, Massachusetts began its assent to powerhouse status during World War II and the following decades known as the 'the Postwar Era'. Prior to the war, since its beginning in 1861 as a technical university, MIT had developed gradually to become the country's premier engineering school. In 1939 80 per cent of its students were still enrolled in engineering. From that base MIT pursued huge war-time research contracts that allowed it to give tremendous impetus to research, basic as well as applied, in fields other than engineering, in time stretching from physics and chemistry to economics and linguistics. Research became paramount: 'the other functions of training scientists and engineers, and of serving industry and government, were in a sense downstream from this central and overriding commitment . . . Research activity became the vehicle by which MIT exploited 'the potential of the postwar research economy more fully than any other university'[1] – an exploitation that depended on working closely with the federal government during World War II and the years of the Cold War. The MIT response contrasted sharply with that of many other universities; Yale, for example, strong in the humanities and social sciences, did not pick up on this science-and-technology option, leaving the development of applied science and engineering to a much later date.

For organizational instruments with which to develop great strength in research, MIT turned first to interdisciplinary research centers, the type of basic unit that became known as organized research units (ORUs) on the American scene; I have portrayed them in my cross-national framework as central parts of the developmental periphery built outside core disciplinary departments. By means of its ORUs, MIT quickly built research to the point where it measurably outweighed 'education'. In 1946–47, for example, the university's research budget of $US8.3 million was nearly double its academic budget of $US4.7 million. Research income became a mainstay of the institution's overall financing, paying for itself and much, much more. In 1947–48, research contracts exceeding $13 million gave the central administration more than $2 million for 'overhead'. That year, in addition, $1 million of the academic payroll of $3.8 million was charged to these contracts. Some departments expanded rapidly on this base: for example, the physics department from 1946 to 1956 was able to increase its annual salary budget from $400,000 to $600,000, and at the same time reduce its charge to the academic budget from $400,000 to $200,000. The department expanded from 34 to 48 regular appointments; *and* – a point not to be missed, especially in cross-national perspective – the majority of the additions were full professors. No tightly peaked rank structure here! No single Herr Professor in charge of everything in sight! As it lightened its financial burden on the university, the department in a short time became large and eminent.[2]

Research income raised faculty salaries to a competitive level with leading research universities in the Ivy League and among flagship state universities scattered across the country. It allowed the university to cross-subsidize from ORUs and emerging science departments to new departments in the humanities and social sciences. The ORUs also gave birth to disciplinary departments. Two major centers illustrate the institutional benefits that followed from center operations. First and foremost was the center that began during World War II as the MIT Radiation Laboratory, which became The Research Laboratory of Electronics (RLE) immediately after the war. It went on to soon spawn the Lincoln Laboratory (1951), hiving off weapons research as a federal contract laboratory administered by the university. The combination of RLE and Lincoln was to be fateful. Between them they soon spawn some 60 electronics firms. Students worked in both centers: in a dozen years, the Electronics Lab engendered almost 600 student theses.[3] The centers became places that generated branching, intertwining initiatives: 'Five distinct research groups existed at the [RLE] Lab in 1946, ten in 1951, twenty-two in 1956, and thirty in 1961. By the last date eighteen of those groups belonged to a separate Division of Communication Services and Engineering established in 1958 that had evolved from just one of the 1946 groups.'[4]

Here was the hothouse for the mathematician Norbert Wiener and his 1948 classic, *Cybernetics*; for applying ideas from new communication theory to the building of the university's pioneering digital computer; and – strangely – for spreading inquiries that took up the nature of speech and language and gave birth to a linquistics department joined by Noam Chomsky in the mid-1950s. That department launched a graduate program in the early 1960s, and acquired an international reputation – all from a research track cultivated in an applied interdisciplinary gathering of researchers.

Here was a prototype of the creative ORU that adds to the academic competence of a university, even to the point of giving birth to new disciplines and related departments, as it diversifies institutional income and directly links up with governmental mission agencies and private firms. The RLE's 'style, internal dynamics, and multifarious achievements epitomized postwar MIT. It was hardly accidental that two former directors became MIT presidents'.[5]

Similarly, another ORU at MIT, The Center for International Studies – set up to furnish knowledge to the federal government – became the mother of the Department of Political Science. And yet another large ORU, The Instrumentation Laboratory, became so massively involved in defense work and so dominating in the department of aeronautical engineering, it had to be spun off as an independent non-profit corporation, the Draper Laboratories.

MIT's budding relationships with defense-related government agencies and business firms were a constant challenge to established academic values.

Out of contentious relationships came a steady stream of internal reorganizations that sought to accommodate the academic and the heavily applied; the academic part often rotated into the structure of disciplinary departments and the applied part, particularly those programs related to the military, was spun off as loosely affiliated federal defense labs, non-profit labs, and profit-oriented business firms. Out of the science-and-technology focus of a technological university and an eager willingness to place research first among university commitments, came an exceedingly dynamic university willing to press the limits of involvement with military and industrial patrons.[6]

By the end of World War II, the greater Boston area already had a research row, 'composed of MIT, Harvard, and other local universities and a growing concentration of industrial laboratories [that] offered an intellectual and technological labor pool unsurpassed in the nation, if not in the world'. To an observant Frederick Terman, finishing his doctoral work and soon to be off to Stanford, there was 'an industry around Cambridge and Boston and MIT was right in the middle of it'. But despite its early pioneering role, MIT's relationship to what became known as Route 128 – a circumferential highway – was typified by a 'calculated distancing from the region's new technological enterprise'. It saw investing in start-up companies as 'too risky and not consistent with how "men of prudence, discretion, and intelligence manage their own affairs" '.[7] Thus, the university was not to build the intimate, involved relationship that Stanford later developed with Silicon Valley.

Still, during the 1950s and 1960s the region around Route 128 'established itself as the nation's leading center of innovation in electronics'. And MIT was *the* university that supplied scientists and engineers to the emerging firms and placed significant labs there. During the 1960s, for example, 'MIT engineering departments and research labs spawned at least 175 new enterprises, including 50 from Lincoln Lab and another 30 from the Instrumentation Lab'. By 1975, the Route 128 complex employed close to 100,000 workers and constituted an exceedingly robust combination of university and related industries. Even after it was superseded by California's Silicon Valley in the 1980s and 1990s as first in the nation, it remained the second most important complex, one that contributed to regional economic development – the Massachusetts Miracle – even though its federal base continued to predominate.[8]

What MIT gradually developed between World War II and the end of the twentieth century was a significantly productive model of how a university can combine a 'traditional academic department structure' that provides for continuity and quality with an aggregation of interdisciplinary laboratories and centers that 'provide mechanisms to support a dynamic research program'.[9] In 1995, the department structure consisted of just twenty-one academic departments grouped in five schools: engineering, science, humanities and social science, management, and architecture and planning. The department was seen as 'the stable core'; the overall department structure, organized by discipline, is 'the basic, building block'. These core units handle faculty appointments, student matriculation, teaching programs and degree certification. The second side of the university consisted of over fifty interdisciplinary laboratories and centers. They ranged from a Center for Space Research with funding of over $30 million per year and 135 employees to a center with $40,000 and one employee. This side of operations pursues 'a tradition of flexibility that tailors the organizational form to the task'. These ORUs are flexible organizations that can more readily come and go. They relate to the primary academic organization in different ways, some directly to the provost, some to the vice-president for research, some to the academic schools and their deans. 'All relate indirectly to one or more academic departments by virtue of faculty participation.' Very importantly, they are 'created on a need basis as new research missions and opportunities develop. They can be expanded, contracted, or redefined either internally or by MIT's administration. Their leadership is determined by the institution and their directors usually serve limited terms.'[10]

In 2000 MIT remained at the relatively small size of about 10,000 students, 40 per cent undergraduate and 60 per cent graduate, drawn from all fifty states and over 100 foreign countries. The tenure track faculty numbered nearly 1,000 (indicating a low 10:1 student–teacher ratio); and nearly 600 of the 1,000 were full professors, with another 100 associate professors also holding tenure. In contrast to so many universities in Europe and elsewhere around the world, MIT is an extreme case of the willingness of US universities to be top heavy in rank. It is a prime way to recruit and hold senior talent. The concentration of top academic talent at MIT is little less than awesome.[11]

Funding for this costly enterprise has become increasingly diversified. The university's research income of nearly $450 million was almost three quarters derived from the federal government. However, within that stream, funds came from five different major departments: Defense (18 per cent), Health and Human Services (18 per cent), Energy (15 per cent), National Aeronautical and Space Administration – NASA (9 per cent), National Science Foundation (12 per cent), and other federal agencies (3 per cent). Beyond these dispersed federal sources, another 19 per cent came from industry (topping defense as main source for the first time), with 2 to 3 per cent each from foundations, non-federal government agencies, and MIT itself.[12]

Beyond these research-funding sources, the university is able to charge top-of-the-line tuition fees that approximated $30,000 per year in 2002. It also could count on the large income-earning sums fully under its own control. Endowment zoomed from about a half-billion dollars in 1980 to approximately $7.5 billion in 2000, falling back to approximately $6.5 billion in 2002 after a major stockmarket downturn.

Blessed with strong central leadership, on top of vigorous faculty, departmental and interdisciplinary center leadership, MIT had become in 2000 an outstanding case of the entrepreneurial university. It had the will; it had the money; it had a distinguishing high academic reputation envied around the world. And it had adaptive capability on top of sturdy continuity. Given its competitive setting, and its ingrained sense of competitiveness, no slackening in its institution-building efforts seems likely. It is possible of course for an internationally renowned university to become frozen in thrall of its impressive self: sins of pride are widely distributed among American universities, nowhere more so than in the New England academic heartland. But the odds are high that there will be no settling for the status quo at aggressive MIT. Those who want to compete with this pacesetting university have to get up very early in the morning, 365 days a year.

University of Michigan

The University of Michigan in Ann Arbor, a small city about forty miles from Detroit, has long stood as flagship institution in its state's higher education system and as first (or second) among equals in a group of major public universities in the neighboring states of Wisconsin, Minnesota, Illinois, Indiana and Ohio, the American mid-continental academic heartland. Dating from a small college established in the late 1830s, when Michigan formed its state government, by 1900 the university acquired both the loyalty of a good share of the population of its home state – a place for our sons and daughters, with an exciting football team – and a substantial academic competence and status that earned it an invitation – it was one of three public universities along with Wisconsin and California – to sit at the table of the new Association of American Universities whose majority members consisted of private self-anointed pacesetters stretching from Harvard to Chicago to Stanford.

When Edwin E. Slosson wrote a major research-based assessment of *Great American Universities* (1910), he selected fourteen top universities defined by annual expenditure on instruction: nine private universities, Harvard, Yale, Princeton, Cornell, Columbia, Pennsylvania, Chicago, Johns Hopkins and Stanford; and five state universities, Michigan, Minnesota, Wisconsin, Illinois and Berkeley (California). Michigan was first among the public institutions, just behind three of the privates, Harvard, Columbia and Chicago, and above such notables as Yale, Cornell and Princeton. By that early date, Michigan had already stood 'for more than a half century as the typical and leading State university'.[1]

In transforming an existing college into a university, two strong presidents played a defining role during the last half of the nineteenth century. Henry P. Tappan and James B. Angell had each made the transatlantic pilgrimage to Germany before assuming office and had returned full of enthusiasm for a research-centered approach. They had seen the future. But enamored of 'Prussian ideals', Tappan (1852–63) was so much ahead of the times that he was 'summarily and ungratefully dismissed after 10 years'. A decade later Angell (1871–1909) then proved to be the right man at the right time to transform an undergraduate-centered college into a comprehensive research university, American-style. He organized a graduate school in 1893, *and* built faculty strength in medicine, law, and engineering, *and* by 1908 had more undergraduate students (over 4,400) than any other university in the country.[2] The college level served well in linking the university to the population of its state. The growing graduate realm reached to the nation and promoted specific streams of income: the law school, second largest in the country, drew nearly 70 per cent of its students from outside the state and they paid higher fees than Michigan students; in medicine, more than one half came from other states.[3]

Here were early steps, taken a century ago, toward a leading model of how US public universities could evolve into hybrid forms in which adaptive self-steerage would largely dictate the institution's path of development.

Two active decades highlight the trajectory of the Michigan phenomenon in the twentieth century. During the 1930s, under presidential leadership that was 'decidedly sympathetic toward faculty research', the university engaged in a 'general devolution of administrative authority away from presidents and regents toward the deans and departments', and appointed representative executive committees at these operating levels. With much influence exercised from the bottom-up, academic values of the faculty entered strongly into the determination of university policies.[4]

Equally important was a further major shift toward non-state revenue. The university actively sought private donors – but carefully. 'Not wanting their donors to appear to lessen the state's responsibility, they sought restricted [earmarked] gifts for purposes that the legislators would be unlikely to support.' By the end of the decade, the university had pulled in $44 million in gifts of various types. A good share of the new money went into lasting assets in the form of buildings and endowment. Increasingly, the voluntary support went to the improvement of research. The key donation by Horace Rackham went to the construction of a building for the graduate school and the endowment of research.[5]

A financial division of labor – a very early one in the history of modern higher education if viewed internationally – emerged in which state core support covered general operating expenses, while voluntary contributions went to support research activities, graduate education, enhancement of the quality and standing of such specific units as the law school, and a slow but sure build-up of endowment. The search for such support encouraged the university to be a leader among public universities in organizing alumni: their assistance first centered on the undergraduate realm, dormitories and student unions, for example, and then subsequently moved to research support and graduate program development. Diversification of income was well on its way; it positioned Michigan to compete against leading private universities across the nation, particularly for faculty, as well as against other flagship public universities from its midwestern backyard to the west coast.

Michigan became an extremely entrepreneurial university in the 1980s and 1990s, considering its age, size and solidity. Starting in the seventies, for a variety of economic, political and cultural reasons, its core support from the state became increasingly undependable. Between 1980 and 1983, for example, the state allocation rose by an average annual rate of 1 per cent and largely continued on this stagnating level throughout the eighties and nineties. This was not enough for growth, and was nowhere near what was needed to finance an outstanding university. The university responded strongly: it would 'privatize' heavily by greatly increasing income from non-state sources with which it was already familiar.

First, it had long developed a battery of tuition charges differentiated by level (graduate/undergraduate), discipline and residence (out-of-state/ home state). It now raised these lines prodigiously. In-state tuition was elevated to the top of the national range. The university became the first university to charge higher tuition to upper-classmen and graduate students, and these premiums were increased as well. With a huge demand from outside the state – its prestige drew students from such student-exporting states as New Jersey and New York – it became the only state university to set non-resident tuition at levels comparable to private universities. As a result, 'tuition revenues which were one-half the size of state appropriations in 1980 exceeded them by forty per cent in 2000'.[6]

Second, drawing on its strong tradition of voluntary support, the university in the 1990s vigorously expanded gift income from alumni and other willing supporters to build the largest endowment among single state universities. Only a handful of public universities derive significant revenue from endowments. Michigan's combined income in 2000 from tuition and endowment supported over one-half of a high per-student outlay.[7]

Third, Michigan grew its research base by investing in major research initiatives and in the parallel development of large ORUs (organized research units). It became in the 1990s the largest performer of academic R&D of all US universities, private or public – a stunning achievement, given the high level we observed in the leading cases of Stanford and MIT. Toward expansion of its research infrastructure, a $5 million 1986 grant from a private foundation was used to establish a permanent Presidential Initiative Fund. Successful in attracting faculty initiatives in high-risk/high-reward areas, it soon grew into a larger Strategic Research Initiatives program, under the Vice-president for research. It provided between $5 and $10 million *each year* to 'seed and stimulate innovative research' out of which came new research units, defined as 'hubs for collaborative work'. In 2000 the university had over 160 such units, more than one-half of them established in the 1990s.[8] The university then topped up its research infra-structure with a $200 million Life Sciences Institute as a massive investment in future biological and medical research; dual faculty appointments linked the huge medical school and the large basic College of Literature, Sciences and the Arts. Responsibility for new undergraduate courses was scrupulously written in. The institute was thereby 'structured to have an impact on the entire university'.[9]

Fourth, income from 'auxiliary services' became the largest sum of all, due to revenue brought in by a huge medical school-teaching hospital complex from third-party payments for patient care – an operation so complicated and expensive that it was spun off as a separate incorporation in the early 2000s.

Income diversification had arrived on a grand scale. All these major streams and their tributaries greatly enlarged the means for steady, substantial budgetary growth. The vigorous developments of the 1980s and 1990s put in place an income-snowballing effect clearly evident at the beginning of the twenty-first century. A twenty-year trend report for 1984–2003 indicated that an initially large budgetary base became colossal in the space of a few years. In 1984 the 'all funds budget' for the Ann Arbor campus was already four-fifths of a billion dollars ($824 million), certainly a solid base that reflected previous diversification of income. By 1991, a mere seven years later, the total budget had doubled to over a billion and a half ($1,690 million). At the end of the nineties decade, in 2000, income had doubled again, making it annually over three billion dollars ($3,200 million). Three years later – in the midst of a major national economic downturn! – annual increases in income had pulled the university up to over $3,800 million – approaching the $4 billion mark.

How were such staggering increases possible in a comprehensive public university? While income from traditional core support (state appropriations) went up from $161 to just $364 million, income from tuition and fees shot up from $130 to about $600 million. Federal dollars for research increased from $108 to over $530 million. And to add to the pot, hospital income (and expenditure!) had moved from $270 to over $1,700 million. Even 'other external' sources generated in fund-raising had become a significant item at over $200 million.[10]

In sum: the university's revenue in absolute dollars doubled during the 1980s, doubled again during the 1990s, and grew by another one-fifth between 2000 and 2003, even as state core support was falling to 10 per cent and less of the total. When 'hospital' revenues are put to one side, the state contribution to the rest of the university, other than the medical complex, still amounted to less than 20 per cent. This particular US 'state university' had clearly moved to become a 'state-assisted university' and then on to 'privately-financed public university'.[11] It had become, in my terms, a 'self-reliant public university' – a much more self-directed non-profit organization than a state agency or a business firm.

The large size of Michigan, similar to such other public universities as Wisconsin, Berkeley and UCLA, along with its demonstrated capacity to raise major resources from a multiplicity of public and private donors, gives it competitive strength. Out of a total enrollment of 37,000 in 2000, one-third of the students, 13,000, were at graduate school level. This large assembly of advanced students was greater than the overall student population of Yale (11,000), and three times the size of that institution's graduate student body; it was double the total size of Princeton (6,400). The result is a comparatively large number of doctorates awarded annually, 629 in 2000. This placed Michigan fourth among the public universities and fourth among all US universities. The highly selective private universities do extremely well in attracting post-doctoral appointees, but here, with 728 in 2000, Michigan was sixth among public universities and a respectable tenth nationally.[12]

Large size in US public universities starts with huge undergraduate enrollment. Michigan at the end of the nineties had 24,000 undergraduates. The university has long had the reputation of being student-friendly, part of its attractiveness for out-of-state as well as for in-state applicants who make it their first choice. In the reform efforts of the 1980s and 1990s, the university paid special attention to the undergraduate base. Beyond the resources of a huge library system, dispersed in myriad locations, the university created a Media Center to bring new technology directly to the students. It also created attractive special courses and programs that allowed some students to participate in 'research/creative projects', 'service learning', and even 'writing in the discipline'. National magazines and newspapers gave Michigan high marks for quality of undergraduate education – as high as third overall among public universities and fifth for 'best value' for the money in the public sector.[13]

Attention was further focused on undergraduates when Michigan intensely committed itself to 'affirmative action'. A 'diversity initiative', sustained over years of negotiation and adjustment, became known as *The Michigan Mandate: A Strategic Linking of Academic Excellence and Social Diversity*. The mandate insisted that 'diversity and excellence are complementary and compelling goals for the University . . .' The implementation of a succession of 'opportunity programs' let the university dramatically improve social diversity on campus. Over a decade, under-represented students, faculty and administrative staff more than doubled; the graduation rates of minority students rose to the highest among public universities; promotion and tenure success of minority faculty members became comparable to their majority colleagues; and a growing number of appointments of minorities were made to leadership positions.[14]

Specific actions taken under the diversity mandate on minority access were challenged in two court cases that simultaneously reached the US Supreme Court in 2003. The university interpreted new rulings to mean that race could indeed be considered in admission decisions, but could not be stated in quota-like numerical fashion. The case received enormous attention over many months preceding and following the decisions. Michigan, among all the universities of the country, was a standout for its forthright boldness. It became a heroic institution to many, but an institution that had gone a stage too far, for others. It certainly had not been a passive, heads-down observer of the struggle over a major national issue, one that involved social diversity in business corporations and the military as well as in universities.

For the undergraduates also there was always the great excitement of the nationally-ranked sports teams, particularly in football, where heritage stretched back over a century. Always a headache for university administrators and faculty to maintain some semblance of academic control over a domain that operates under deeply entrenched dynamics of its own, big-time sports led to embarrassing scandals. Heavily emphasized competitive sports attached to a university are a major drawing card for students, staff and alumni alike, at Michigan as much as anywhere. The price had to be paid institutionally for deeply undesirable effects on academic integrity. James Duderstadt, a former president, wrote after retirement a major volume on specific actions that universities needed to take to 'clean up' the sports realm while recognizing its continuing utility.[15]

Behind the diversification of income, constructing a huge developmental periphery, building a change orientation in heartland departments, and spreading an embracing entrepreneurial culture was a highly proactive steering core topped by successive able presidents and provosts that stretched during the eighties and nineties from Harold Shapiro (1980–87), who went on to become president of Princeton, to James Duderstadt (1988–96), who stayed on at the university, to Lee Bollinger (1997–2002), who went on to become president of Columbia University, to Mary Sue Coleman (2002–) after the turn of the century. Duderstadt played a particularly vigorous role in restructuring the university to enable adaptive change. A visionary about the open-ended possibilities of a massive self-determining university, Duderstadt drew a distinction between the traditional view of strategy which 'focuses on the fit between existing resources and current opportunities' and a *strategic intent* 'that cannot be achieved with current capabilities and resources'. The intent deliberately creates a misfit between resources and ambition: through this, 'we are able to challenge the institution to close the gap by building new capabilities'.

These new capabilities are not built, however, by grand leaps in design. Rather, they emerge out of *logical incrementalism*, 'a small-wins strategy, relying on a series of steps to move toward ambitious goals'. The planning process is evolutionary, and it 'moves from broad goals and simple strategic actions to increasingly complex tactics'. Experimentation should constantly be underway, and the organization ought to be prepared to take aggressive action on newly discovered fruitful pathways. Duderstadt was pleased he was known for a decision-making style of 'fire, ready, aim', as he launched 'yet another salvo of agendas and initiatives'. Anything to move the elephant! Anything to stay away from 'traditional planning approaches [that] were simply ineffective during times of great change'.[16]

'The University of Michigan had become a better, stronger, more diverse, and more exciting institution' as a result of the transforming efforts of the eighties and nineties, concluded Duderstadt. Organizationally, the university had institutionalized 'an exploratory approach to the future', one which took seriously 'our basic character as an inquiring institution' and depended on experimentation and discovery as 'the most realistic near-term approach'.[17] Pride of achievement had clearly deepened pride of place: stubborn continuity linked past and present to any emergent future. But, most important, step by step, this hugely complicated university had learned some secrets of perpetual change.

University of California, Los Angeles

UCLA was born reluctantly, fashioned out of small, tentative gestures as a second campus in the state's public university then identified with just the much older Berkeley campus. In his 1850–1960 history of California higher education, Douglas tells us that the birth of a 'southern branch' was difficult: 'Wheeler [the president] along with the regents, Berkeley faculty, and students proved extremely reluctant to "divide" the university into two potentially major campuses'.[1] But southern California would not stop growing. By 1910 Los Angeles had a population greater than San Francisco. Two years later, the newer sprawling city was sending more freshmen to the university (in Berkeley) than was San Francisco, the older long-established city – 'inconveniencing students, coming from 500 miles away, and taxing the physical capacity of the Berkeley campus'. As the situation became increasingly ridiculous, the university needed to establish an 'outpost of some kind in Los Angeles'.[2]

The outpost offered in 1915 was an extension office and a summer session. Local appetites for the higher learning were hardly satisfied. In 1919 the university took over the site of the Los Angeles Normal School in the downtown part of the city and called it the Southern California branch – a place that would educate schoolteachers but would offer only the first two years of liberal arts studies. So it went, at a slow pace. It took another eight years to redesignate the branch as the University of California at Los Angeles.[3] Two years later, after local boosters came up with a striking parcel of land in the western part of the city, the permanent Westwood campus opened with a small set of large buildings constructed in classical academic style and adorned with lofty sayings of Josiah Royce, the Harvard philosopher, carved in stone on the signature building. Trees and lawns and 5,000 students soon followed. UCLA was seriously underway, at least as a physical entity.

After the first bachelor-degree graduates issued forth on the new campus in 1933, the administration and faculty moved through the 1930s and early 1940s to further academize the undergraduate curriculum and introduce graduate and higher professional degrees. Some fields did not gain the right to give the doctoral degree until the 1950s: sociology and anthropology, for example, were two wings of an integrated department at the time, and the first doctorates on the sociology side were issued between 1952 and 1954.

Ten thousand students before World War II became 20,000 by the end of the 1950s, after the 'veterans' rush' to college under the GI Bill. Graduate students who had comprised one in eight became one in three. University-level professional schools were initiated or transformed from vocational predecessors. What was to become a huge medical complex was initiated in the late 1940s, built from the ground up by a strong dean with a background in radiological medicine and ties to the national Atomic Energy Commission (AEC). Cancer research became a major specialty and received abundant funding from the National Institutes of Health (NIH). And what was to become a significant graduate school of business had first to rid itself of a 'teachers' college legacy' – a college of commerce which as late as 1948 had in place 'typing and shorthand labs' for the preparation of schoolteachers who would later handle those practical subjects. From that vocational acorn came in the 1950s and 1960s a school of management organized to 'educate the business leaders of Southern California'. Such professional schools had 'comparatively little hindrance from Berkeley in their development': they could tie themselves to the professional communities of Los Angeles. 'The academic departments were far more affected by the overweening presence of Berkeley.' More than Berkeley, UCLA was to be dominated by strong professional schools, medicine in particular.[4]

Decidedly, the 1960s were a heady time at southern California's flagship public university. A new president of the entire university system, Clark Kerr, worked to decentralize budgetary and personnel decisions to the separate campuses: comprehensive ones in Los Angeles, San Diego, Irvine, Santa Barbara and Riverside in southern California; Davis, Berkeley and Santa Cruz further north; and a medically-focused one in San Francisco. Further, the president and regents officially accorded the same elite role to Berkeley and Los Angeles: to have all work 'grounded in research and in the intellectual disciplines'; to give primary emphasis to 'excellence in research and instruction'; and to restrict enrollment to the number of students that can be given 'high quality instruction'.[5] A strong new chancellor (Franklin Murphy, 1960–68) worked unrelentingly to stress UCLA autonomy and identity. A former oligarchy of deans in the letters and science college gave way to a more unified central management personified by the chancellor.

Income increased substantially from state, federal and private sources. New construction greatly altered the physical campus. Faculty positions expanded by one-third, with appointments made largely at the assistant professor level – an effort to build faculty from the bottom-up in many departments rather than pursue a focused 'steeples' approach.[6] Chemistry became the main steeple – an illustrious department that nurtured three of UCLA's five Nobel Prize winners (up to 2002).

As this public university expanded in a state and region of immense population growth, undergraduate enrollments continued to increase substantially rather than diminish; the demography of the state, rising aspirations for college education, and campus efforts 'to create traditional loyalties by means of alumni, athletics, and residential life' promoted the upsurge. The doctoral level, however, grew only marginally, representing 'a disappointment for UCLA's academic aspirations'. Still, by 1970 the campus had 'definitively entered the ranks of the major research universities': it was situated among the top ten recipients of federal research spending, with the life sciences (biomedical fields) leading the way.[7]

In the style of the leading public research universities of the midwest, preeminently Michigan and Wisconsin, the campus developed in the 1970s 'distinguished departments in a large number of fields, but few nationally leading ones'; it also featured a decidedly regional orientation expressed through vigorous professional schools, a large system of extension education, and ties to the local entertainment industry. Under Murphy's successor, Charles Young (1968–97) the university went on to solidify its standing as 'the most influential institution of higher education in southern California and, after Stanford and Berkeley, in all of California, and even in the entire western United States'. By the early 1990s, the campus had moved from fourteenth to tenth in the number of 'distinguished departments' in letters and science, and had even higher ratings in some professional schools. Medicine was ranked fifth to third in basic national peer evaluations and its hospital became known as the best in the west and the third nationally. Very high standing was given to the library; it was placed among the top two to three of all US university libraries.[8]

During the last half of the twentieth century, stirred by competitive ambition – and always with Berkeley in mind as a very high benchmark – UCLA claimed, on more than one occasion, a reach that was beyond its immediate grasp. The university would avow repeatedly that it was in the top ten universities of the country only to have new national ratings – based on traditional departments in letters and science – place it as, say, fourteenth or tied with four or five others for the often coveted number ten. The university would then lick its symbolic wounds, find temporary friendlier benchmarks, and go back to work on repairing weaknesses and enhancing strengths. Top Ten standing was always, for UCLA as well as for other second-tier ambitious universities, a constantly elevating target; seven and more private universities already occupied top spots and worked hard to increase their resources, especially from healthy endowments, and to provide attractive conditions for faculty and students. But the ambition at UCLA was ceaselessly elaborated in the institutional framework.

So, at the end of the century UCLA's income had become diversified at a very high level, similar to the picture we saw develop at the University of Michigan. State core support repeatedly turned soft, and fell to 20 per cent of all income. The university could report major annual increases in monies from 'extramural contracts and grants'. From $530 million in 1999–2000 to $655 million a year later, to $768 million in 2001–2002, the campus was placed in the top five universities for total research funding. For federal funding alone, UCLA could reliably claim it had risen in a few years from twelfth to third.[9]

Federal government sources contributed close to two-thirds of all research-award dollars, vastly outweighing state government (5 per cent), business (6 per cent) and charitable organizations (5 per cent), and a host of minor sources that still managed to contribute ten million here and twenty million there.[10] Financially, UCLA had become a 'federal-grant university' more than a state-supported university. And among the federal sponsors, the Department of Health and Human Services, which included the National Institutes of Health, became the main donor at a full two-thirds (over 66 per cent) subsidy, far in excess of the next two agencies (National Science Foundation at 10 per cent and the Department of Defense at 9 per cent). In research funding UCLA had become a biomedical campus centered on research and clinical departments of the medical school and the biological-science departments, with increasing reach to chemistry, astrophysics, and engineering.[11] Research funding broken down by major campus area showed 'health science' receiving two-thirds (67 per cent), compared to 17 per cent for the entire College of Letters and Science, and 8 per cent for engineering and applied science.[12]

In short, by early twenty-first century UCLA had become a campus characterized by research intensity on a grand scale. It had over 5,000 research awards on the books at any one time, garnered by over 2,400 'academic researchers'. In 2001–2002, records show, 1,663 new awards totaled over $300 million and 3,212 continuing awards amounted to over $466 million. Several hundred non-dollar agreements brought the total number of awards to 5,120. Stunningly, the university had doubled its funded research in eight years following 1995, from $363 to $786 million in 2003.[13]

Research traffic of this magnitude and density was generated by a spreading array of research units that had sprung up according to faculty research interests, in and alongside established schools and departments, in dizzying combinations of inside and outside, disciplinary and multidisciplinary. The campus inventory of 'research centers, labs, and institutes' continues on for six single-spaced pages. Major centers included: a $350 million California Nanosystems Institute headquartered at UCLA and secondarily on the Santa Barbara campus backed by California state government ($100 million), three agencies of the national government ($110 million), private donors and foundations ($90 million), and business firms ($50 million), which, intended to be a combination of basic research lab and business incubator, brings together faculty from chemistry, physics, biology and computer science with enormous amounts of equipment; an Institute for Cell Mimetic Space Exploration, jointly sponsored by the university and NASA (the federal National Aeronautical and Space Administration), to meld 'the molecular world with aerospace technology', headquartered at the engineering school; a reorganized International Institute serving as an umbrella for fifteen research centers and eight interdisciplinary degree programs, now expected to generate initiatives toward 'educating global citizens'; and the Jonsson Comprehensive Cancer Center in the medical complex newly focused on how to exploit the results of the human genome project – a center with a major board of its own and professionalized fundraisers who could list donors who have made gifts of up to '1 million and above'. Today the center has research networks focused on different types of cancer that stretch across dozens of locations in southern California and support young researchers whose nationality and ethnic backgrounds read like a United Nations assembly.[14]

Because so many centers, labs and institutes are in place, administrators no longer speak of all of them as formal ORUs. Beyond those that sought and received system-level official recognition, numerous 'small "c" centers' appeared among the more than 200 entities on the nearest thing to a master list. My element of developmental periphery is so enormous at UCLA that at any one time its many parts may not be fully known. Emergent units even include one-person groups banking on the value of a center name, on and off campus, in fashioning the real thing. The central enabling structure for research administration has undergone major reorganization, including great growth in the all-campus Contracts and Grants Office from about 6 officers in 1990 to 50 in 2002 specializing in different donor domains.

The high level of income-raising and the extensive development of non-department units increasingly had behind them a complex multilevel strengthened steering core. Authority expanded in a core academic structure of eleven professional schools (some containing departmental units), and the basic college of letters and science with over thirty departments. Some – chemistry, psychology, history and English, for example – had faculties of 50 to 100 and more, subdivided by major specialties. The authority of deans and department heads has steadily increased, and subheads and administrative support staff are created to assist them. Notably, in a highly decentralized fashion, full-time fund-raising officers have been assigned to different professional schools and clusters of letters-and-science departments.

An all-faculty academic senate takes seriously its role in 'shared governance'; it has primary control of courses and curricula and the choice and retention of faculty. In the critical faculty area, recommendations from departments and schools travel to senate offices when they go 'across campus'. From there, after due consideration and decision, they are sent on to administrators for approval, thus giving the campus two main intersecting lines of vertical authority. At the center – the top – the chancellor chosen by the system-wide board of regents selects a half-dozen to a dozen vice-chancellors to help supervise and develop major academic and administrative domains, including an executive vice-chancellor and an increasingly influential vice-chancellor for research, along with selecting the head of the very large college of letters and science that operates with at least four deans for major subject areas. This is nothing basically strange from other US universities, but very complicated.

The chancellor at the beginning of the twenty-first century, Albert Carnesale (1997–   ), former provost at Harvard, has taken a strong lead in voicing a three-sided but coherent 'vision' of what UCLA is and what it is yet to become: his first theme is to strengthen 'the foundations of a great university', in particular the College of Letters and Science, the library, and the IT infrastructure; a second, much emphasized, is to cross old academic boundaries in teaching, research and service, as exemplified in the multidisciplinary institutes set forth above and in an agglomeration of outreach activities flagged as 'UCLA in LA'; and a third of always concentrating on excellence in whatever the university does. This in practice means that the university, not able to do everything, must identify its 'comparative advantages' and determine how best to nurture them. For all three 'strategies', alternative sources of revenue beyond state core support – federal grants, tuition, annual private gift-giving, endowment income, returns from intellectual property – have been defined as absolutely necessary.

In a series of bi-weekly essays appearing prominently during 2002 in southern California's leading newspaper, the *Los Angeles Times*, the chancellor defined anew for a wide public the sheer complexity of the campus and what was taking place: the teaching hospital, the library and performing arts programs; the IT revolution, interdisciplinary programs (such as Genetics and Society), and the centrality of research; efforts to improve the public schools, lifetime learning through extension, and an expanding 'partnership' between the university and the city. The many highlighting statements were compiled into an accessible pamphlet, 'Perspectives on the Modern Research University', in which the concluding essay stressed the axiom that as state core support decreases, especially in comparison to what an expensive university requires, private gift-giving is 'an essential component of continued success'.[15]

That essential component grew to over $250 million annually, topping up to over $500 million in 2001–2002 bolstered by a 'landmark gift' of $200 million from an entertainment executive and philanthropist to the endowment of the medical school. A fund-raising campaign that started out in 1997 with a target of $1.2 billion had virtually doubled that amount ($2.3 billion) by 2002–2003. Total annual operating revenue had reached the very high level of $3 billion, mirroring the development of income at the University of Michigan.[16]

Similar to Michigan, UCLA exhibits how the growing scope and intensity of faculty research can be used to reshape both graduate and undergraduate education. The graduate school has increasingly stressed border-crossing: inquiry now requires 'a wholly new kind of scientist, one who is trained to work and communicate across the boundaries of divergent disciplines ...' We intend to produce 'hybrid scientists ... who can think beyond the boundaries of their own training'.

The National Science Foundation has sponsored new graduate interdisciplinary training programs at over fifty US universities; UCLA was one of five schools to receive backing for three such traineeships – in neuroengineering, bioinformatics, and materials creation. Claiming that these efforts fit well its 'institutional profile', the university has sought the means to establish additional traineeships of this type, including some in the social sciences. Thus, the university sees itself staffed to promote crossdisciplinary graduate education that will produce 'the new scientist'.[17] Assisting this aim is the erection of a large complex of new graduate student housing close to the campus, designed for the crossing of cultural as well as disciplinary boundaries.

UCLA has also paid considerable attention to the improvement of undergraduate education and the quality of life for beginning students. It has focused on three elements: curricular reform, residence on campus and undergraduate involvement in research. The general education requirements (40 per cent of course credit toward the bachelor degree) have been strengthened with year-long, interdisciplinary, team-taught 'cluster courses', in such subjects as the history of modern thought and globalization. In addition, over a hundred freshman seminars of fewer than fifteen students taught by senior faculty, including professors from the professional schools, have been created. Examples include one on Sexual Orientation and Health, taught by an epidemiologist, and a special post-9/11 short course on Rethinking National Security taught by the chancellor, an area well within his expertise.

A long-term shift from commuter school to residential university, begun in the 1960s with four major high-rise dormitories was measurably advanced in the late 1990s and in 2000–2003 by the addition of a new student village that doubled the living space on campus; and, with faculty and classes inserted, all housing was given a more academic tone. Entering students could now be guaranteed one year, possibly two, of campus residence. And last, but perhaps most important, the university has sought to increase the involvement of undergraduates in research. Two undergraduate research centers – Life and Physical Sciences, and Humanities and Social Sciences – anchor programs which help undergraduate students to get started in research projects and provide for more advanced linkage of students with individual professors. The ideal here, of course, now sought by many US universities, is to have research-based teaching and learning become more characteristic of undergraduate study as well as its taking place in graduate schools, where it is firmly ingrained. Even in seemingly 'mass' US public universities, willing undergraduates, too, can participate in the early training of 'the new scientist'. At a minimum, they can become better acquainted with rational inquiry that connects large ideas to empirical realities.

UCLA, by 2000, had acquired the habits of institutional change on a large and complex scale. It has become a grand case of multiplying centers of initiative throughout its administrative structure. It has a very wide base of initiative-generating faculty interests. It stands as an exemplar of chaotic multiplication and redesign of research centers, institutes, labs and groups propelled by insertion of multidisciplinary and transdisciplinary perspectives alongside traditional disciplinary ones. And the university is a model of ingrained competitive assertiveness. UCLA was born with attitude – a competitive attitude. There is little or no chance in the early twenty-first century that it will now settle for the status quo or hanker for the status quo ante. If it errs it will err on the side of optimism about future possibilities. Yesterday and today have been noteworthy. Tomorrow will be even better.

North Carolina State University

North Carolina State University (NC State) in Raleigh, North Carolina is an ambitious public university. By the early 1990s it had joined the top fifty US public research universities and was aiming for the top twenty-five by the end of the decade. Two universities, the Chapel Hill campus of the University of North Carolina – the flagship public university of the state – and Duke University – private with considerable status and wealth – were nearby. Together with these high ranking institutions, NC State comprised the three-university base of the North Carolina Research Triangle. There was no question that NC State was different from the others; its intent was not to model itself on either one. Its land-grant heritage and culture emphasized practical knowledge from which strong programs in engineering, food and veterinary science, and computer science had evolved.[1] Its home state considered it to be a second flagship institution.

How then to maintain and advance this status in the twenty-first century? How could the institution prove it was making progress in the very competitive American system? A partial answer was to turn to a scheme of strong benchmarking within a defined group of peer institutions. That set stretched from Georgia Tech and Virginia Tech in the South, to Purdue and Iowa State in the midwest, and to University of California campuses in Davis and San Diego in the west. In making comparisons, the university used the annually published criteria and ratings of the Lombardi Center for Measuring University Performance at the University of Florida (a non-governmental assessment): 'a top 25 ranking requires excellence in research studies, in private support, in faculty reputation, and in quality of undergraduates' – with research quality seen as 'the most important factor in defining the best institutions' and the faculty providing 'the most critical resource'. NC State thus established its current position and measurable targets: e.g., in total research expenditures, the university already ranked seventeenth among the top twenty-five public universities; however, its current endowment (raised largely from private support) ranked only forty-first – but then the university had neither a medical school or law school to help part the waves in fund-raising. Doctoral degrees annually awarded reached over 300, a ranking of twenty-sixth. Targets could be set; twelve graduate programs in the top twenty-five on faculty quality, with 'notably improvement already noted in departments of mathematics, physics, and chemistry, as well as chemical, electrical, and mechanical engineering'.[2]

Benchmarking has its uses, but much more important are new programs and structures that build institutional capacity for change and enhance autonomous strength. Beginning in the late 1990s, NC State committed itself to building a new framework, the Centennial Campus, which would offer a new model of how to go beyond technology transfer and the normal output of trained graduates toward a more thorough integration of academia and industry. The university generated the idea of a joint-use campus and pushed it through its embryonic stage at a time when industry lacked enthusiasm for the project. State government helped greatly by donating 1,300 acres of adjacent land. NC State used state money to put up the first buildings, brought in federal funds from the National Science Foundation for three University/Industry Research Centers, and floated self-financing bonds. A threshold was passed when three major corporations – the Swedish firm

ABB, Lucent Technologies, and Red Hat – seeking close interaction with faculty and students decided to construct buildings for research and administration. When Lucent, falling on hard times, had to retreat, Red Hat took over the vacated building. Smaller enterprises then came in and the university gradually relocated more academic units, and engineering was planned to be fully in the new location by 2005. Quite unusual among research parks, the university's school of education helped design a public magnet middle school and planned to build a high-tech professional development facility to open in 2005. Development has been rapid. In 2002 the campus contained 65 corporate and government entities and 70 research and departmental university units. The projected 'build-out' is very large: 12,500 corporate and governmental employees; a similar number of university faculty, staff, post-docs and students; 7,000 housing residents; 600 middle-school students; and 2,400 support services personnel.[3]

NC State's Centennial Campus stresses equivalent status and close interaction; industrial tenants are given the same campus privileges as faculty and students. Entry negotiations aim to establish complementary relationships, and a Partnership Office and individual partnership developers were assigned to follow through. University classrooms are interspersed with industrial offices and labs in four R&D 'neighborhoods': biological sciences/ biotechnology; advanced materials; information and communication technologies; and education. Industry researchers can readily continue their education, formally and informally. Students, including undergraduates, can be employed, now and later.[4]

The university announced the creation of a Centennial Biomedical Campus in 2003 as an extension of the original Centennial Campus concept. Focused on biomedical applications to both humans and animals, it too will emphasize partnerships and work 'to bring academia, government, and industry together'. Seeing itself as a national leader in 'the development of nanotechnologies, biosensors, and imaging modalities', the university intends to use the new unit to apply these new developments to 'animal systems', particularly research that uses animals as models for cures of human diseases. The biomedical unit will be highly interdisciplinary, drawing upon faculty in Physical and Mathematical Sciences, Engineering, Agriculture and Life Sciences, as well as the main host, the College of Veterinary Medicine. Planned financing for this campus start-up will focus on monies from private investment, selling university bonds, borrowing capital to build facilities, and leasing space to repay the loans. Early on, such major firms as Bayer, Pfizer, Merck and GlaxoSmithKline were on board, even signing up for five-year commitments on collaborative research. With human health benefits as a central aim, the university expected to double in five years its current $5.5 million in research support from the National Institutes of Health.[5]

The Centennial campuses immediately heightened NC State's local and regional impact because construction and new employers contributed to economic activity in and around the city of Raleigh. But the university aspires to larger goals, as Geiger has stressed, namely 'to stimulate a creative infrastructure with an entrepreneurial culture that would generate sustained growth . . . It has deliberately sought to create a critical mass of interactive scientists and to provide the appropriate conduits for their creative energies.' Centennial has 'established a working model for university–industry collaboration that generates more technological innovation and technology transfer than piecemeal efforts existing elsewhere . . .'[6]

And what of the widespread notion that close relations with industry compromise academic integrity, even threaten the soul of the university? Does it apply here? To the contrary:

> The university deals with industry from a position of strength: the only viable policy is to uphold academic standards consistently and uniformly . . . This model could not possibly succeed without the cooperation and support of the faculty who appreciate that the campus is not an real estate development reflecting the values of business. It is a true campus where academic mores predominate. Industry too seems to want it that way. All indications are that firms value the academic atmosphere and above all the enhancements benefits that they derive from the richness of the academic surroundings.[7]

The biggest problem is that the new collaboration calls for hard work and a large input of faculty time and effort. For some the new involvements are stimulating and worthwhile. But for others who are most centered in their own disciplines it may be otherwise. The model may, therefore, not be easily replicated at other universities (as of 2003, three other universities were closely studying the Centennial format). At the least, however, NC State 'has blazed a path for both university and economic development'. Early in the twenty-first century, it represents 'one extreme on a spectrum'.[8]

Georgia Institute of Technology

'Georgia Tech' started out in the late 1880s as a small engineering school of 130 students whose curriculum was heavily influenced by 'hands-on' shop experience. Growing slowly over the next half-century, it added a school of aeronautics and an engineering experimental station (later to become a research institute) and formally changed its self-concept and public definition from 'School' to 'Institute'. It developed a high level of competence in applied science and engineering during the last half of the twentieth century and became a nationally recognized public regional university, with 15,000 undergraduate and graduate students on its main campus in Atlanta in the 1990s. Having accumulated over fifty interdisciplinary research centers along the way, the institution was able to annually secure research funds totaling over $250 million, ranking on this score thirtieth among all US universities and eighteenth among public ones – a long way from its humble origins. The build-up of able faculty and graduate students positively affected undergraduates and gave Georgia Tech high marks on such indicators of undergraduate quality as high average test scores of entering students, number of National Merit Scholars, and notable recruitment and education of women and African-Americans in engineering.[1]

Georgia Tech, like North Carolina State, sought to develop university–industry collaboration aimed at economic growth in its home state. Georgia, like many other states, adopted measures in the 1980s to boost university research. This goal was spurred by long-standing local and national observations that Georgia and other southern states lagged behind other regions of the country in this crucial activity and needed to catch up. The governor established a research consortium that supported several specialized centers at the state's universities. When this project expired in the nineties, the state's six principal public and private universities together with important business corporations created the Georgia Research Alliance, directed by the university presidents and the heads of twelve Georgia corporations. With the state making additional appropriations to strengthen the research capacity of the member universities – a third partner, so to speak – over $300 million went into creating chairs for eminent scholars and research infrastructure support.[2]

In 1999 this coalition of state, university and industry announced a more ambitious undertaking – code name 'Yamacraw' – as a focused development of high-tech industry and employment. Yamacraw would concentrate on the critical technology of broadband telecommunications – systems, devices and chips – where the state of Georgia, and the city of Atlanta in particular, might gain a comparative advantage and international leadership. The universities would be the key element in a scheme to develop and fill high-tech jobs. The committed state funds, $100 million over five to seven years, were largely aimed at the creation of an additional eighty faculty chairs at eight participating universities, focused 'steeples' designed to attract lead researchers and associated students and staff. Yamacraw firms, to gain access to new technology, would pay annual fees and promise to create a specified number of jobs for the program's graduates. The universities added Yamacraw-inspired courses to their curriculum – 'a step that goes well beyond most economic development projects' – and aimed to increase graduates trained in this field from 400 to 1,000 per year. After the first two years, 1,000 new jobs had been filled and another 2,000 pledged, against the original objective of creating 2,000 additional positions for design professionals.[3]

Georgia Tech was ready for Yamacraw. It had strong departments of electrical engineering and computer science well-suited for this opportunity and was accustomed to outreach through its numerous interdisciplinary research centers; for example, its Manufacturing Research Center, its Advanced Technology Development Center, its bioengineering alliance with the medical school part of Emory University, a private university. With its extensive developmental periphery, it soon became the main location for the Yamacraw project. It acquired one-half of the new faculty positions, and a new building on campus – the Yamacraw Design Center – served as headquarters. For the university, a place whose self-defined mission had 'always encompassed a commitment to economic development', Yamacraw was seen as 'another building block toward becoming the country's foremost public technological university'. This venture helped take the university beyond the core support provided to a set of universities by the Georgia University System, where standardized funding on a student-credit-hour basis worked against the interests of high-cost research universities. Now the state invested selectively via the Yamacraw channel to allow Georgia Tech to add centers of academic excellence which base funding could never cover.

The undergraduate realm also moved up-market. The university was able to win more than its proportionate share of new state scholarships – 'Hope Scholarships' – which awarded free tuition to high-ability students in an effort to keep them in the home state. In short, with its high reputation in research and graduate education enhanced by Yamacraw funds and favorable publicity, the university has increasingly taken on the character of a selective public institution; it attracts talented undergraduate applicants from throughout its home state, the southern region, and even nationally.[4]

Aspiring to 'define the technological university of the 21st century', Georgia Tech had developed a vigorous entrepreneurial culture within its faculty, and its firm steering core stretched from central management to departments and organized research units. Income has become extensively diversified: in 2002 state core appropriations were down to 35 per cent of total income, tuition and fees amounted to 11 per cent, sales and services another 12 per cent, and 'gifts, grants, and contracts' had become the main growing funding base at 42 per cent. That base included various non-governmental sources as well as diverse local, state and federal public agencies.[5]

Through Yamacraw outreach, the university became an experimental paradigm for interaction with industry that transcended earlier models. Like the Centennial model at North Carolina State, Yamacraw at Georgia Tech expands the opportunities for technology development. As stressed by Geiger, both models 'deliberately aim to generate the effects of agglomeration where a heightened level of interaction between researchers and engineers in universities and industry will significantly magnify both the scale of university research and the amount of technological innovation conveyed to industry'. Embedded in this experimental model is a new academic role in which technology transfer is continual rather than sporadic, providing a steady state for supporting and speeding its transmission.[6]

Georgia Tech and North Carolina State highlight the important role played by competition among the fifty states in producing a certain genetic entrepreneurialism among US universities. The competitive spirit of public universities, already spurred on by comparison to leading private universities, is inescapably deepened by the competitive instincts of the states. Universities join with their immediate state to jointly square off against other state-based pairs, a systemic process across the country in which at least one-half of the fifty states are vigorously involved.

One study focused on case-by-case analysis of 'new university roles in a knowledge economy' has pointed to developments in ten public universities which involve close university–home state relationships: North Carolina State, Georgia Tech, Virginia Tech and Texas A&M in the south; Ohio State, Pennsylvania State, Purdue (Indiana) and University of Wisconsin in the midwest; University of Utah in the Rocky Mountains region; and the University of California at San Diego on the west coast.[7] A second analysis, focusing on 'science-based economic development' has noted university–state collaborations that stretched from Maine to Louisiana to Kansas to Montana to Oregon.[8] And what do we find? Three cases typify:

In Ohio, a major industrial state, the large, well-settled flagship public university, Ohio State University, 'has gone through something of a renaissance over the past four years', involving 'an exciting rethinking of mission, goals, and investment – particularly as they pertain to contributing to the knowledge economy of the state'. The university now 'aspires to be Ohio's leading asset in growing a knowledge-based economy'. This entails developing higher national stature in selected areas of research and scholarship, with such specific targets for 2010 as having '10 programs in the top 10, and 20 in the top 20'. In short, to become Ohio's leading asset in the new age, Ohio State has to develop additional organized capabilities that will place it higher in national standing, in competition with other major universities, public and private, located in all the other states.[9]

Since other universities in other states are similarly engaged in national benchmarking – top-100, top-50, top-20, top-10 – the aimed-for status is a moving target, forced upward by the achievements of others. The higher the aim the tougher the competition, because such deeply-entrenched institutions as Harvard and Stanford, Berkeley and Michigan, are already sitting on the commanding heights. And the problems of focus and niche development become acute, requiring sharp internal assessment of possible match-ups between organizational capabilities and changing external possibilities. Greater differentiation, rather than simple imitation, becomes a virtual requirement. And standing still becomes a means of falling behind.

The University of California, San Diego (UCSD), is a powerhouse west coast university that has risen rapidly in national and international stature to give the UC system a third flagship that rivals Berkeley and UCLA. Started late (in 1960), UCSD has used the high-quality base of the UC system as a launching pad for both investing heavily in a relatively few areas of science (instead of trying to be all things to all people), and opening itself to external partnerships with industry and the community. After just four decades of existence, it ranked tenth at the end of the century in faculty quality and sixth in total research funds, among all the private and public universities of the country. Its research funds exceeded Berkeley's, in major part because it has a medical school and Berkeley does not.

At the same time, the university has seen itself 'as very much a corporate citizen of San Diego, with an associated responsibility to build the economy and well-being of the region'. It has explored 'new modes of university–

industry cooperation and new approaches to economic development strategy': as early as 1985 it had underway a major 'connect program' as an economic development organization focused on technology-based entrepreneurship. The university has played a critical role in the transformation of San Diego into 'an entrepreneurial, technology-based economy'.[10] With 1,000 firms and more developing and locating in the region, the San Diego area has become California's second silicon valley, and UCSD serves as the anchor university.

My final example of successful state–university partnering is the University of Utah, the most prominent higher education institution in Utah, which has increasingly become recognized internationally as a distinguished American university. With enrollment exceeding 25,000 in 2001, its students came from 'every Utah county, every state in the nation, and 102 foreign countries'. The university stresses that it has 'a long tradition of service and outreach to the state and the mountain region'. Much of its research program is organized in more than forty centers and institutes, eleven of which are 'state-supported centers of excellence . . . explicitly designed to maximize industry partnering and technology commercialization'. Historically, the state has not been a national center for industry or finance. But in recent years university and state have worked together to develop a 'burgeoning Utah technology economy', where university spin-offs have turned into successful small and middle-size companies. Considerably aided by 'a robust and customer-friendly set of policies and procedures coupled with an enabling organizational culture' at the university, Salt Lake City has been viewed increasingly as a technology-oriented metropolitan area, and has been ranked in one national magazine 1997 report as sixth in the world on an indicator of new technology development.[11] In short, in a 'Utah culture' of entrepreneurially led economic change, the university and the state, especially the major city, have been mutually supportive and closely linked.

Conclusion

The Center for Science and Technology Studies (CEST) in Berne, Switzerland constructed in 2002 a census, 'The Worldwide Champions League of Research Institutions'. It was based on a bibliometric analysis of nearly 1,000 institutions that had significant quantities of research papers published in indexed international journals, as reported by the Institute for Scientfic Information (ISI). The researchers wanted to assess the performance of Swiss research on an international scale and then additionally to benchmark the famed Swiss Federal Institute of Technology Zurich (ETHZ) against the American MIT. The results were startling. At the system level: 'there appears to exist a performance gradient which separates US research universities from those of the rest of the world . . . Only 6 out of the top 50 most influential universities are non-US universities . . . ETHZ is the only university in these top 50 not based in an Anglo-Saxon country and the only one located in continental Europe (the other 5 non-US universities being located in the United Kingdom and in Canada).'[1]

Bibliometric analysis has well-known defects. It crudely replaces institutional and system complexities with simple numbers that obscure more than they reveal. It places a premium on the use of English and downgrades work done in other languages. It does not capture applied research as completely as basic research. Still, the crude measures of publication and citation offered by this form of analysis are readily understood and widely used. And if we take them as approximations, they can be justified as useful analytically. Thus, the world share of any country in research literature output can be studied field by field and aggregated for such major groupings as life and physical sciences. Output can be broken down by university, department, research group and individual researcher.

The great build-up of the American research base, primarily located in over 200 'Doctoral/Research Universities', was captured in ISI data that showed the US share of world scientific literature in the 1980s was between one-third and two-fifths (about 37 per cent), a share greater than that of Britain (9 per cent), Germany (6 per cent), France (5 per cent), and Japan (7 per cent) combined. The US share in life sciences was about 40 per cent in sheer volume and over 50 per cent in frequency of citations; in physical sciences, about 35 and 50 per cent, respectively.[2]

The American framework of academic research has clearly helped to position a large number of universities (and departments) to become world leaders. By the mid-1980s, citation analysis in four subfields of chemistry found 18–20 of the top 25 universities internationally and 8–9 of the top 10 to be American; in electrical engineering, 20 of the top 25, with 4 in Britain and 1 in Japan.[3] A special inquiry mounted by a British economist for his own discipline, using a set of indicators of research productivity, showed that among the top 25 departments in the world, 21 were American, 2 were British, and 2 were Israeli.[4] A knowledgeable American observer, Henry Rosovsky, former Dean of Arts and Sciences at Harvard University, was considerably justified in stating in the late 1980s 'between two-thirds and three-fourths' of the leading universities in the world were in the American system.[5] The 2002 Swiss data on research output indicated that this long-standing story still exists a decade later. It is deeply systemic.

When ETHZ was benchmarked directly to MIT, the results were again startling. Although this Swiss university was the best of the best on the European continent – Nobel Prize winners and all – when compared to MIT, an institution of similar size, 'the total number of publications in the fields qualifying for the Champions League differs in favour of MIT by a factor of almost 3'.[6] Of the 25 major fields assessed, MIT outperformed ETHZ in 19. 'In those fields where MIT had higher publication counts than ETHZ, MIT normally dominates ETHZ by factors of 2 to 10.' At a given output level, 'MIT sustains roughly 35% to 140% more fields . . .'. If 'we look at citations, MIT's position vis-à-vis ETHZ is even stronger than in the case of publications'.[7]

The Swiss study stressed that any comparisons of much smaller European university systems and the huge US system should not be made between gross system averages, share of publications per inhabitant for example, but should first grasp the vast differences that exist among over 250 universities in the US system, where universities in the top quarter doctoral programs greatly outperform those in the bottom quarter, on publication and citation counts, on number of doctorates produced. The top fifty US universities are much higher on a wide range of benchmarks than those in the bottom half and especially the bottom quarter. Comparing four universities that ranged from 'the very prominent to the nearly invisible', Gumport found in the late 1980s such huge differences as $200 million in federal research contracts at the high extreme and $3 million at the low end; in fact, the low-ranked university had less research funding than many departments in universities in the first and second quartiles.[8] And MIT is very high in the top cohort. Clearly it is not the average US performance that

> should be a benchmark for a small European nation of ambition, but the performance of 'peer regions' within the US, e.g., California, Massachusetts, the Research Triangle in North Carolina, regions in Georgia and Texas ... Better yet, we should concentrate on comparing individual institutions, a path pursued now by CEST ... if the average US program is the benchmark for Swiss universities, the wrong targets have been chosen.[9]

The university label has been widely distributed among – even freely assumed by – institutions in the US that do little or no research. Their hope to change that condition may be a motivator, but it is not synonymous with reality.

Bearing in on the ETHZ-MIT comparison, the Swiss researchers raised the question of the 'morphology' of universities and went on to speculate about a morphology of leading US universities that could account for their greater strength and specifically a morphology of MIT compared to that of ETHZ. The researchers judged that the critical differences were neither simply a matter of size and mass, nor of greater publish-or-perish pressures in the US. One quantitative item they picked up was a lower student–teacher ratio at MIT than in the European counterpart. But leading public universities in the US, such as the four reviewed here, normally have higher ratios than their private counterparts, closer to 20:1 than 10:1, and they still manage to come out very high on national and international scales. More revealing in the Swiss data was the number of senior faculty: 910 at MIT compared to 340 at ETHZ, a difference approximating three to one.[10]

No simple morphological differences will go very far in explaining the American outcomes. Institutional differences are complex, built up in the character of individual universities over long periods of time. As seen in this study, complexity necessitates case studies that can describe the play of idiosyncratic features perched on top of the role of common elements found in classes of institutions. In total morphology, there is only one MIT and one ETHZ.

But there are indeed some widely-shared features among the better universities in the American system. From among the six universities reviewed here we can extract some of these:

Deliberate construction of university self-reliance

Whether at Stanford or MIT, Michigan or UCLA, North Carolina State or Georgia Tech we find: diversification of income, with a wide range of private and public contributors; strengthened steering capacity, from top to basic units; extended outreach capability, a collaboration with a wide range of business firms and public agencies; strong willingness in heartland departments to develop adaptive outlooks, including teaching and service for older populations (especially professional development); and a widespread broadening of interests in the academic culture to include the interdisciplinary and transdisciplinary alongside the disciplinary. In short, we find a strong version of the elements of transformation and sustainable change that I developed originally from studying proactive universities in Europe and now seen at work at different levels of academic achievement in change-minded universities in Africa, Latin America and Asia.

Deliberate build-up of research intensity

The universities exhibit an almost exuberant push to develop a wide range of research groups and clusters. Large numbers of senior faculty, rather than just one or two, direct research areas. Junior faculty are relatively free to initiate and carry out projects and explore new lines of inquiry. Young non-tenured faculty participate as voting members of departments, rather than serve only as assistants to a head professor. Department organization mixes junior and senior faculty with graduate students, post-docs, and some undergraduates in a modernized version of a research-teaching-study nexus.[11] The research capacity of a university is greatly enhanced – intensified – when more faculty, varying in rank, are added and left free to innovate. A rapid build-up of research intensity particularly stood out in the UCLA story, indexed by high number of academic researchers, funded research grants, and total research income. This feature stands out in US-continental Europe comparisons.

Ingrained willingness to compete actively for institutional prestige

Constantly at work to protect and increase their standing in a competitive system where to stand still is to fall behind, highly proactive US universities seek to attract better faculty, better graduate students, better undergraduates, better administrators – and even better trustees! As stressed at the outset of this chapter, a competitive status hierarchy has been operative as the key system characteristic throughout the twentieth century. It has steadily included more institutions, enlarging the pool within which rugged competition has stimulated greater self-reliance and increased research intensity. More public universities have slipped away from the traditional posture of being fully state-led and have moved closer to private universities in a large, growing non-profit sector. MIT and ETHZ differ first of all, we can add, in that MIT, past and present, is fully a private university, free to select its own students and is thoroughly embedded in the national system as an exemplar of successful non-state institutions; while ETHZ has been and remains a major public university operating within a state-defined 'open admission policy',[12] and embedded as an exemplar in Europe of a particularly successful state institution.

It is hard to exaggerate the importance of competitively striving for prestige in the American system of higher education. Players include bordering community colleges, small private liberal arts colleges known nationally and locally, Catholic universities, Lutheran colleges, women's colleges, historically black institutions, masters' level universities, and doctoral-granting research universities. The universities in particular are indeed what economists would call 'prestige maximizers': their bottom line is prestige rather than monetary profit.

Accumulated prestige is central in that it allows a university to exert some control over a variety of markets it encounters. Prestige critically shapes interactions between universities and would-be students in consumer markets. It enters, often decisively, into mutual adjustment between universities and prospective faculty in academic labor markets. It weighs upon the minds of possible employers of graduates entering the general labor market. It conditions agreements between universities and such external institutions as banks in financial markets. Most of all, it is the coinage in how universities and colleges place one another in higher education's reputation markets. In 'the third way' of university development pursued in the concluding chapter – third between state and market – a determined bid for performance-based high prestige is an essential part of the character of the proactive, self-reliant university.

Part III

The Self-reliant University

11
The entrepreneurial road to university self-reliance

I have been searching, in this study, for the typical character of entrepreneurial universities. I have examined some clear prototypes and strong examples across nations and continents. I have also noted that when universities move only part way into assuming entrepreneurial habits they become hybrid forms in which problems of commitment and balance – between old and new educational programs, centralized and decentralized control, new and traditional sources of support – become paramount. Beyond such hybrid complexities, my case-study narratives have also given due respect to institutional uniqueness. My intent was to remain close to practice, risking a minutiae of detail. Now it is time to clarify, as much as possible, how modern universities go about transforming themselves and sustaining change.

I begin by observing that many traditional universities will operate in an old-style mode as long as they can; they hesitate to take on the entrepreneurial option. Why? Reasons for their inertia throw new light on the willpower that some universities exercise and sustain when they attempt to seriously transform themselves. A second section highlights the features that ought not be forgotten when examining the framework and dynamics of entrepreneurial change. Here I debunk certain stereotypes and myths about what highly proactive universities do and do not do; I find value in the metaphor of a steady state of institutional change. The concluding argument centers on the contest in national systems of higher education between state-led and institution-led change. Each of these major forms of directed change makes heavy use of markets. We note that universities are indeed prestige-maximizers and use prestige to control both state and market influences. With institutional steering increasingly advantaged over state determination, in the emerging realities of the twenty-first century, the entrepreneurial university offers a dynamic model of how greater university self-reliance can be realized in our time.

Why many universities will not become entrepreneurial

At the end of Chapter 6, I noted briefly that many universities will not attempt to transform themselves into a highly proactive form. They find one or another rationale for inertia: traditional ways will certainly prove best over the long term; if the university is hobbled by a lack of money, government officials and other patrons will surely come to their senses and realize, for the good of the nation, that universities must be funded as a first priority and at a much higher level; if our institution is going to remain cash poor after twenty years of cutting to the bone we should hang together, do our ennobling work, and share equally the pangs of poverty. Embarking on a new path seems difficult and risky. If a few reforming steps are taken, established interests resist and bring change to a halt. For a host of reasons, the risks of adhering to the status quo become preferable to the risks of change.

But the judgmental ground shifts in a way that alters the balance of risks. Outside groups conscious of rapid change in their own arenas and environments deepen their expectations that universities should also change and at a quickened pace. Increasing competition among universities regionally, nationally and internationally defines some universities as self-satisfied laggards. Entrepreneurial universities at home and abroad dramatize what can be done when institutional will builds adaptive character. As others move forward, a university may find itself standing still on a down escalator.[1] Examining the tangled underbrush of inhibiting conditions and attitudes also sheds some light on whether clear prototypes of entrepreneurial universities will come to dominate the university world nationally and internationally or whether proactive features will mesh with traditional forms in hybrid combinations strung along a vast spectrum between the fully traditional and the extremely entrepreneurial.

Michael Shattock offered some acute observations in 2002 of specific sets of 'inhibitors' in four English universities that help us grasp resistance to change.[2] One had been a non-university up to 1992 when the government did away with an official binary line and allowed fifty or so institutions, mainly polytechnics, to acquire the university label. Ten years later this university was 90 per cent dependent on state funding based entirely on student numbers. It had become an 'access university', with unfortunately low retention rates, opening the university to the risk of not making its student targets and therefore of having the national funding council 'claw back' some support. This university badly needed to find additional means of income as well as to meet its enrollment targets.

But the overall management structure was clogged with inhibitors. The university was quite hierarchical, with a senior management team separated from the academic staff. New policies could only be launched from the center, but a bureaucratic culture virtually prohibited such policies from being considered and the top team, concentrating first of all on survival, was locked into a defensive mode of thinking. Crucial inhibiting characteristics were evident: high dependence on state core support that could turn soft at any time; a hierarchical division that cut the academic staff out of the loop and left all power in the hands of management; and a management-dominated bureaucratic culture resistant to change. There was little or no organizational space in which a will-to-change could be assembled and perpetuated.[3] Instead, conditions were ripe for the deadening gravitational pull of routine.

A second university examined closely by Shattock was also a new one with the legacy of pre-1992 non-university status. It also was heavily dependent on the state: teaching-based funding centered on student numbers. But this institution had engaged in devolved budgeting, with power centered in the hands of faculty deans who in turn heavily dominated their subordinate departments. The university wanted to develop a research strategy and some entrepreneurial activity, but simultaneously it wished always to balance the books. The first commandment for a dean was to juggle incomes and expenditures across departments to stay within an overall faculty budget. Shattock puts it clearly:[4]

> Research success in one department was treated as a cash cow to pay the debts incurred by shortfalls in student numbers in another. Since departments were at the bottom of a long chain of command through deans, to a deputy vice-chancellor to a senior management group in which financial rather than academic priorities represented the dominant concern, it was not surprising that the drive to improve the university's research standing was stalled and that innovation and new initiatives were frustrated ... At the top level the intention was to grow research and make the university entrepreneurial but the structures designed to keep the university out of deficit in the difficult post-1992 years combined to stifle the initiatives required at the bottom to bring this about.

Here basic inhibitors were: again, high dependence on state core support, with rigid allocations based on student numbers; an unbalanced authority structure in which faculty deans had excessive control, compared to departments and central staff; a triumph of financial criteria which, at all costs, mandated sufficiency within budgets over academic judgment and initiative; and an extended vertical structure of command that frustrated new initiatives to the point where they were 'strangled at birth'.

A third Shattock case was an old-line major university in England that was slipping in status, noticeably sliding down the 'league tables' of rankings that evolved in the UK system during the 1980s and 1990s. It had over time become a complicated place with both a large central bureaucracy and an 'overlarge' structure of academic departments – a common combination in old-line universities in many countries. Much authority was devolved to faculties and departments by fixed financial formulae which allowed few incentives to reward innovation. To get things moving, a vice-chancellor who had been more concerned with maintaining the status quo than with competing was replaced by a new one 'with a remit to push the university up into the top 10'. The new head was able to cut back somewhat on the old central bureaucracy, reduce the number of faculties, and bring the remaining faculty deans into a strengthened steering core. But still formula funding remained, limiting 'judgmental decisions', and 'no one wanted or was able' to challenge the many departments to improve their income generation. And, shortly, administrative costs began to build again around the reorganized faculties.

Shattock noted that 'cultural change is extraordinarily difficult to achieve' in a large, complex public university where many years of effort are needed to eradicate the traditional structure: 'when any issue comes up the first solution is the old solution'. The university 'may admire the entrepreneurial model, and even concede its success, but may not be convinced it could work in its own [case]'. This particular university, slipping back toward the old status quo, then tended to settle for comfortable comparisons. It had

> previously benchmarked itself with its traditional comparators, other civic universities, against whom it performed moderately well. When compared, however, with the [new] league tables, in which many newer institutions had shot past it, it was shown to have performed much less well. Nevertheless the instinct deep down remained that these new institutions were not fair comparators, and that the university should continue to compare itself with its 'family' even though such comparisons would never provide the stimulation to get it into the Top 10.[5]

When push comes to shove, universities can always find friendly benchmarks that provide soft landings in self-esteem and public reputation. In the comfortable old family – other places like us – the will to change slackens. Lowered expectations become self-fulfilling.

Shattock's fascinating fourth case was old, wealthy, inordinately complex Cambridge, where he had been called in to see if he could help untangle a situation in which the university was 'unable to move funds around flexibly' and where 'the operating budget was forecasting a deficit due to mismanagement'. All this in the larger institutional context of a 'convoluted system which maximized the opportunity for stopping anything that the centre of the University wanted' and 'where relationships between academics and administrators at the formal level of university management are the worst that can be imagined'. At the same time, the university continues to attract the best qualified students, leads every league table, and, notably, has the country's most successful science park. Via technology transfer, it has affected the regional economy to the tune of 8 per cent or so of the UK total, making Cambridge along with Stanford 'probably the only universities that can actually claimed to have changed their national economy'.[6]

What Cambridge has beyond its heritage and wealth and related self-confidence is 'highly independent, dynamic academic departments which with minimal administrative underpinning maintain an extraordinary entrepreneurial culture'. This is 'par excellence an academically run University'. It represents 'an extreme example of self-directed autonomy –

indeed a visit to Cambridge is almost like a visit to an independent state . . .'
It is 'the living embodiment of the Matthew effect where high calibre academics attract other high calibre academics to create a spiraling effect . . .'
In the end, such characteristics 'outweigh or counteract the University's
weakness in developing an effective steering core'.[7]

But in the early twenty-first century, Shattock warns, Cambridge increasingly must compete with other genuinely world-class institutions – the fifty or
more noted here in the US chapter – and to do so it will need the help of an
internationally minded leadership group that can only be assembled if
there is some effective central decision-making machinery.[8] Internal chaos
at Cambridge will at least need to be better organized anarchy. A funded,
heads-up and outward-looking center could complement collegially
organized heartland departments as well as aggressive outreach units.

Shattock's review of the inside of four English universities reveals inhibiting conditions that vary with differences in institutional context – new and
old, small and large, teaching-led and research-led. Appearing frequently are
state-established blockages involving efforts to steer all universities in a system by enforced performance budgeting and other top-down oversight in
which no good deed goes unpunished: incentives turn into punishments for
three out of four institutions. Miss the targets that ministers can tick off from
performance 'agreements', and warnings will be made and funds cut, a sure
way to depress initiative. To be entrepreneurial, public universities need first
of all a very light touch by the state that, among operational advantages,
signifies increasing rather than decreasing trust.

My five elements of transformation have explanatory power in these cases.
Shattock noted that only Cambridge (and a very few other elite universities)
could get away with having a pitiful central steering capacity. Diversified
income is absolutely essential, with some monies from various sources kept at
the center for all-university initiatives. A holistic approach is needed in which
academic criteria dominate financial matters: finance should follow academic
efforts, not vice versa. Most of all, faculty members and administrators have to
be combined at two, or three, or four levels of organization, particularly at the
center. Entrepreneurialism works when it is significantly collegial. Management teams cannot do the job alone, old academic senates cannot dominate,
new forms of academic-administrative relations have to be worked out.

Key features of entrepreneurial organization in universities

With so many reasons to stay in the traditional box, with steady-state inertia
to wed the institution to the status quo, it seems likely that a large number of
universities, even a majority, will not venture very far down the entrepreneurial road. All the more impressive are the feats of universities that not
only overcome their fear of failure before setting out on a transforming

journey – the first miracle set forth in Chapter 6 – but also accomplish to a significant degree the second miracle of maintaining the will to change for a full decade and beyond. These are the places that then evolve onward into a new steady state oriented toward future change. They sustain the transformation – and more.

An institutional capacity to be highly proactive must be, I stress, rooted in altered organizational foundations. For a university to be entrepreneurial, it needs to acquire the right kind of organization, one that allows the institution to go on changing itself and adapting effectively to a changing society, one that allows its groups and individuals to become more effective than previously. The traditional box needs to be replaced by an organizational framework that encourages fluid action and change-oriented attitudes. Structures are inescapable, but they can be made into ones that liberate, that tutor groups and individuals in how to be smart about change.

Key features of the required organization can be briefly summed in three parts: transforming elements, newly clarified; sustaining dynamics; and a resulting steady state of change.

Transforming elements revisited

The many possible sources of support My first element, a diversified funding base, can be more fully understood when we breakdown funding sources into: (a) *other government sources* (other than the core-support department); (b) *private organized sources*, particularly business firms, philanthropic foundations and professional associations; and (c) *university-generated income*, for example, alumni fund-raising, garnered research contracts, profits from patents. Within each sub-category are numerous possibilities, and the three together point to virtually no limit to possible streams of support.

Some transforming universities turn heavily to student tuition, but not all, and we learn from international cases that tuition is not the only large alternative to state support; it may be the fourth or fifth item in magnitude. Some proactive universities turn significantly to business firms, but then many show industry sources only as a minor item in their pie-cuts of income sources. Entrepreneurialism in universities should not be seen as synonymous with commercialization. Industry is repeatedly outweighed by income from other government departments when research monies are won competitively from national departments of science, health, economic development, energy and defense; it often contributes less than the monies gained annually from alumni and endowment; and it can readily be exceeded by income from 'auxiliary services', especially when this category includes the presence of a large medical complex with substantial income from patient care.

Financially, self-reliance lies in a broad portfolio of income sources. The legitimacy of the portfolio depends on educational values guiding monetary decisions. There must be things that the university will not do no matter has much money is offered. Conversely, there must be 'useless' things it insists upon doing, for example, cross-subsidizing the teaching of classics and philosophy because it is an institution committed to cultivation and transmission of a cultural heritage as well as to economic progress.

For those who want to explore possible new income sources, a simplified inventory of a baker's dozen may help:

- public core-support: national and/or provincial ministries
- support from other national agencies: in any national setting ten to twenty and more may readily come to mind
- support from public agencies at other government levels, for example, provincial, state, county, city
- support from large business firms
- engagement with small and medium-size firms, particularly spin-offs
- philanthropic foundations, large and small
- professional associations (for professional development education)
- university endowment income
- university fund-raising from alumni and willing supporters
- student tuition and fees, applied to foreign students, graduate students, continuing education students
- student tuition and fees, domestic undergraduate students
- earned income from campus operations, a varied array of academically-driven activities plus spun-off, stand-alone and self-financing activities (categories derived from Warwick)
- royalty income from patented and licensed invention and intellectual property

Non-core sources often feed and encourage one another. National and provincial government departments may offer joint support for particular programs; business firms and professional associations may share costs of certain courses; wealthy private supporters may contribute funds to build endowment; tuition fees gained from foreign students and graduate students may be used to reduce costs for domestic undergraduate students. The greatest gain in independence comes from tilting the resource base toward university-generated and directly controlled sources.

Aligning the strengthened steering core My second element is an administrative backbone stretching from central bodies to major faculties to baseline departments and institutes. Balancing influence across multiple levels is an almost constant problem in entrepreneurial universities. New ventures embed new interest groups; aggressive departments seek more autonomy so they can race ahead; central bodies worry about integration of the whole and how to support weak departments and functions. In the steady reinvention of a productive balance, faculty participation in central councils is a critical component: improved steering capacity depends considerably on collegial connections in daily operations between academics and administrators. Both become responsible for the legitimacy of the funding portfolio. Absent the new class of change-oriented administrators, faculty can readily find comfort in old niches. Absent the faculty, administrators bent on efficiency and effectiveness can become forgetful about educational values. Shared governance is more than ever required, but in new or adapted forms.

Effective entrepreneurial universities are neither extremely centralized nor decentralized; they are administratively strong at the top, the middle and the bottom. At all levels they introduce professionalized clusters of change-oriented administrators – development officers, technology-transfer experts, finance officials, sophisticated staff managers – to help raise income and establish better internal cost control. Maturing entrepreneurial universities develop a bureaucracy of change as a key new component of their character. Such agents are clearly a cost of production. As much as faculty, they are also a valuable means of production.

Basic forms of an extended developmental periphery. My third element was devised as a way to sum the presence of an increasing number of operating units that are clearly not traditional, discipline-centered departments. They particularly take the form of interdisciplinary and transdisciplinary research centers focused on a wide range of societal problems, from global warming to improvement of public administration, from third world development to urban renewal. The extended periphery is also dotted with units of teaching outreach, proliferating under such labels as continuing education, lifelong education, distance education, and professional development. As part of their daily efforts, these research and teaching instruments move across old university boundaries to bring in populations, general and specific, not previously in the picture.

Such base units have natural allies in the bureaucracy of change built up in the steering core. Just as each new source of funding requires a university office, so do the new units of the developmental periphery require specialized offices to develop and process their activities, the office of continuing education, for example. Numerous administrative units paralleling the many research and teaching units of outreach are part of what makes the entrepreneurial university a proactive place. Awareness of their importance is one more step in eradicating old impressions that the university remains a place where only disciplinary departments provide research and teaching, and only young people are taught. New assemblies of subjects – cognitive territories varying in content, time and place – require supporting tribes in both operating units and the administration, resulting in greater organizational density.

Entrepreneurialism in heartland departments. My fourth element recognizes that strong universities are built on strong departments. Entrepreneurial universities become based on entrepreneurial departments – dynamic places attractive to faculty, students and resource providers. Heartland departments do not fade away. As knowledge expands and intensifies, they become more important. What they are willing to do gets done; what they set their face against is slowed down or eliminated along the way. The most frequent mistake made in attempts to transform universities is for a management team to proceed on its own without involving faculty and their departments from the outset.

As we have seen throughout these case studies, some departments can and will move faster than others in understanding the benefits of entrepreneurial actions – their own as well as those located elsewhere in the university. Generally, science and technology departments lead the charge, enabled by sources of support directly available to them and prepared by their experience in administrating costly projects, labs and equipment. But not always. We observed at the University of Makerere in Uganda that the first stage of recovery from depressed academic conditions was led by social science and humanities departments and 'soft' professional fields positioned to readily pick up on new ways of increasing 'private' sources of support. As they did in the teaching of law, they could readily become 'customer friendly' by adding new courses sought by potential students and scheduling them at convenient times. When external funding for science and technology becomes available, departments in these fields – in a higher stage of institutional development – will readily become more entrepreneurial.

Altered heartland departments, then, are a necessary part of the bargain of transformation. As they work harder to acquire the habits of change for themselves, they become part of the sustaining foundation of the entrepreneurial university. Minimally, departments positioned to raise income should be encouraged by other departments to do so, and thereby contribute to the welfare of the entire university as well as their own. It is then a second order problem to work out (fight over!) who decides who gets what shares of the enhanced resources.

Institution-wide entrepreneurial culture. Organizational 'culture' is the realm of ideas, beliefs and asserted values, the symbolic side of the material components featured in my first four elements. Always ephemeral, often wispy to the touch, it escapes easy empirical identification. But it is there: modern participants in universities are even schooled to conceive of culture and point to its appearance in concrete practices and particular beliefs.

Central in the drama of this fifth element is its relative intensity. High intensity was frequently exhibited among our cases. Warwick remains an entrepreneurial prototype in part because of its aggressive idealization of 'the Warwick Way'. With its foundation character, Chalmers intensely believes it is distinctly capable of enacting change in the Swedish setting. The Catholic University of Chile proudly asserts its character as a leading case of a new 'exceptionalism' in Latin America. And Monash in Australia 'knows' very well it is the leading entrepreneurial university in all of south-east Asia, or at least one of the top two or three. Brief characterizations of six US universities – two private, four public – revealed repeated vigorous assertion of institutional identities built around a forward-looking capacity to change. Here, competitive striving for prestige among peers, with no slackening, intensifies entrepreneurial culture.

As competitive striving heats up, nationally and internationally, more universities are encouraged to move toward an entrepreneurial state of mind. If they reach high cultural intensity, they acquire confident self-images and strong public reputations that enable institutional advance. True believers are affronted to even think of sliding back into a traditional box. Rather, their historical account, their saga, points to the volition they have assembled and used. They believe their special place has the willpower to continue to move forward.

Sustaining dynamics and the steady state of change

In Chapter 6 I conceived three dynamics of university change that propel transformation into a lasting entrepreneurial character: interlocking and supporting interaction among new elements; a resulting perpetual momentum; and – the crux – embedded institutional volition. These conceptions bring together how transformation and sustainability interrelate. Further, in Chapter 10 I reported the development of some powerful research universities in the United States and concluded with three shared features in their poorly understood 'morphology': their deliberate sustained construction of the means of self-reliance; their build-up of high research intensity; and their ingrained willingness, spurred by competition, to compete vigorously for institutional prestige.

These derived, tentative generalizations help fill in what I claim to be the steady state in entrepreneurially-transformed universities: a condition that inclines them to go on changing. That new mode, defined in juxtaposition to the commonly known organizational steadiness of traditional universities, is difficult to achieve. But it is well worth the effort. It is less of a risk than the risk of inertia. It positions universities, beyond survival, to achieve a consequential effectiveness in the twenty-first century.

Many US universities acquired a steady state of change in the last half of the twentieth century. The flywheel of forward motion was their competitive effort to develop and maintain high prestige. Competition ruled out any stopping point. Even the involved universities with the highest status had to be on guard against accumulating comparative weaknesses, and they had to look to necessary repairs. Some administrators and faculty at the University of California, Berkeley, for example, noted in the mid-1980s that their set of biology departments, somewhat in disarray, had slipped in national and international standing. Urgent institutional repairs were soon undertaken – reconstituting departments, regrouping research teams, constructing expensive new physical plant, investing in new promising faculty – and the desired level of observable effectiveness was restored.[9] Another example: in facing down increased competition, Harvard by adjusting its long-standing prohibition against awarding tenure to young academics – no matter how outstanding their promise – broke old rules by granting a tenured, full professorship in the humanities to a 32-year-old woman who was on the edge of moving to the west coast. Competition is very favorable to talented individuals.

When universities search for prestige they parallel and build upon the 'natural' striving of academics to acquire reputation and to be in the company of productive teams and departments.[10] High-reputation departments and research groups act like magnets in attracting able faculty and students. The high research intensity I noted in Stanford, MIT, Michigan and UCLA was the result. That intensity has become increasingly characteristic of the top fifty or so US universities. It is a stunning, self-sustaining phenomenon, a very peculiar steady state. It is a competitive advantage of the first order for a system at large as well as for individual universities.

The modern pathway to university self-reliance

Two decades ago when I compared national systems of higher education (*The Higher Education System*, 1983), I constructed a triangle of major forms of coordination by placing 'state' authority in one corner (with the USSR located nearby), 'market' in a second (with the US as nearest case), and 'academic oligarchy' in the third (with Italy in mind).[11] Despite its crudeness, this triangle of coordination became a useful heuristic. Readers could attempt to place national systems in a three-dimensional space by weighing their comparative combinations of state control, market-type influence and institutional self-control; they could then pursue sub-categories of political-bureaucratic, professional, and market forms of system integration. Under market coordination, for example, I pointed to basic types of markets appearing in higher education, consumer markets, academic job markets, and institutional markets, and concluded by stressing that (a) these markets were often shaped by state-sanctioned authority, and (b) privileged institutions, possessing the most desired parts of the markets, exerted even more influence than state authorities in determining continuities and changes in system capabilities.

The triangle can be usefully updated by insisting on a qualitative difference between market coordination and coordination effected by state officials and universities themselves. Lindblom, in his exacting analysis of 'the market system', reminds us that markets are 'mindless and purposeless'. Although each kind of market in itself provides 'coordination without a coordinator', abstract 'market forces' do not decide anything. They may push and constrain, but outcomes are 'proximately decided by human beings often in tough negotiations with each other'.[12] In short, people and organizations pursue purposes; markets do not. Those who pursue purposes attempt to carve out slices of markets – a specific consumer market, a specific labor market, a specific financial market, a specific reputational market – favorable to their cause. In higher education state agencies and universities themselves are deliberate designers of mutual adjustment. Both seek to define and use mindless markets.

Most interesting is the institutional market in which mutual adjustment among universities takes place (and between a given university and active proximate organizations and populations), the market in which reputation becomes the main commodity of exchange and turns universities into prestige-maximizing institutions. Reputation is so crucial because it guides the attraction (and retention) of administrators, faculty, students and resources. When a prestigious university, public or private, annually receives 30,000 applications from qualified students for 5,000 openings in the next entering class, it has extensive control of its 'consumer market'. It is not bothered by the wandering vagaries of large, sprawling arenas of inter-action – regional, national and international – between universities and would-be students. While competing at the margin with other highly selective institutions, it can largely select whom it wants and console the rest.

Without doubt, Lindblom is also correct when he stresses that 'all real-world coordinating systems are hybrids in which centrality [central control] and mutual adjustment depend on each other . . .'.[13] Two hybrids now count most in the university world: one where centrality consists of state agencies and a second in which universities themselves assume primary command and make a wide range of mutual adjustments in related markets.

Thus, in sharp contrast to the widespread use of anthropomorphic depic-tions of markets as actors who are elated or disappointed, who run and jump and otherwise act up, let us understand markets not as steering forces but as conditioning arenas of interaction. Steering takes place in how purposive organizations make use of those arenas. As long as they have existed, uni-versities have had consumer markets in which they find students, labor mar-kets in which they find faculty, and institutional markets in which they amass reputation. What has changed is that ever more complex universities have become enmeshed in many more market-type relationships than in the past, and have become greatly differentiated by the amount of self-control they are able to exercise. In this modern context we grasp collegial entrepreneur-ialism as a road to a keenly desired high degree of market control.

If we put markets in their proper place, we then come down to two main pathways of guided development. The first is not only state-led but also sys-tem-centered and top-down in viewpoint. The second is not only university-led but institution-centered and bottom-up in understanding and advocacy.

A modern example of the pursuit of the state-led pathway, a 2002 consult-ing report for the Scottish Higher Education Funding Council, entitled 'Higher Education in Scotland: Orchestrating an Adaptive Knowledge-Based System', is instructive. It recommends a search for a 'unified Scottish vision', one to be enunciated in an 'authoritative and long-term statement of Ministerial policy' and 'endorsed by the sector and other key stakeholders'. The document implies that all participants ought to agree on one blueprint; reform can then proceed by means of 'strategic management at the system level'.[14]

Down this well-worn path, UK universities have had to accept identical measurement scales placed on all eighteen Scottish universities (and over

100 UK universities) – to assess their research performance (research assessment exercises (RAEs) and their teaching quality (in separate assessments). This system generated simplified quantitative ratings with direct effects on both the reputation and financing of individual universities. Such system-level assessments mean that national subject-based review committees bypass the central offices and overall integration of universities and slice right down to individual subject departments to rate them quantitatively against their peer departments in other universities. The ratings follow a would-be standardized format in which over sixty different subject panels of judges (in the UK and Scottish cases) – from chemistry to economics, law to social work – are assumed to grade with equal severity. Anyone familiar with the subject-matter composition of universities knows this is impossible and close follow-up research has shown that the panels necessarily have to think and act in different ways.[15] Consistency across subjects is not even remotely possible. But never mind. The funding councils, working on behalf of government, want simple numbers to which they can attach financial rewards and punishments. The outcome has been a bitter adversarial relationship between government and universities in which universities (and some subject panels) seek to 'game' the assessments to get high scores, and funding bodies reciprocate by announcing belatedly that they will not pay for all that grade inflation and change the rules after the game is played.

Along this pathway, the dirigiste tendency in an officially integrated system comes strongly into play. That tendency produces a homogenizing effect in molding universities, even if differential sums magnifying differences between 'haves' and 'have-nots' are parceled out. What the favored few possess and practise becomes the model. With all institutions rolled up into one system, extended coercive comparisons up and down the line are inescapable: what they get, we should get.

Scottish academic critics of the 2002 consulting report highlighted the dangers of its government-centered approach:

- the focus becomes too much centered on universities as an economic good, losing the 'social and cultural dimensions of our work.'
- the report did not 'face the funding realities': if 'growth in public funding for higher education is going to dry up even further, we need an honest debate about alternative means of funding future development ... Universities are likely to spend even more time than they do now searching out new income streams.'
- Scottish universities need to be enabled 'to compete successfully with their counterparts in the rest of the UK and overseas'. More needs 'to be done to create the right environment for change at institutional level . . . a positive environment for change'.
- 'the trappings of central management control – stricter planning guidelines, performance targets and reporting systems – all in the name of public accountability . . . will drain energy and purpose from the sector and stifle initiative and enterprise – the very qualities that Ministers are

trying to promote in other parts of the economy'. Above all, one should 'avoid a dirigiste approach'.[16]

The state-led pathway is clearly not one appropriate for change in complex universities in the fast-moving environments of the twenty-first century. System-wide changes are notoriously slow in formation and blunt in application. And where is the positive environment for change, the promotion of initiative and enterprise, the rewards for universities finding their own configurations of new income streams, the stimulation of leadership in the operating units where all the activities of research, teaching and learning are located? In an IT world, how can the many parts of universities experiment with, differentiate, and alter their use of information technology according to its constantly changing fit with diverse subjects and forms of teaching?

A modern juxtaposing example of the pursuit of the institution-led pathway of change is a 'Kerr-Carnegie model' of reform that developed from a twelve-year effort (1967–80) by two successive study groups, supported by the Carnegie Foundation and led by Clark Kerr, to analyze the US system of higher education.[17] In this sustained effort, over 100 books and technical reports examined such institutional sectors as private liberal arts colleges and community colleges; such curricular and disciplinary slices as the undergraduate curriculum and legal education; and such organization and governance components as state policymaking and the college presidency. Ever concerned about year-by-year crises, the Kerr groups issued recommendations along the way, for example, on such matters as financing and equity in access. But although the groups were loaded with intellectual firepower and public stature, they did not sit down to write, from their collective wisdom, an integrated document on the strengths and weaknesses of the country's system of higher education, the shaping trends of the time, and what needs to be done. No government money was involved, no political white papers were prepared to make the case for certain system-backed changes. The study group clearly obeyed the dictum to do no harm: no institution, no segment of the system, was held up for ridicule; no college or university was tarnished or punished financially by low or middling scores on crude measures.

The final report of the Kerr-Carnegie assessment looked to the future under the curious title of *Three Thousand Futures: The Next Twenty Years for Higher Education*. Why 3,000? Why not 'the future of the system'? Because:

> At least 95 percent of all campuses underwent some significant change in the 1970s: they gained or lost enrollment, or opened or closed, or merged, or shifted to public control, or changed from one institutional category to another. Alteration of condition or status was almost universal: continuation of the status quo, almost non-existent. Each campus has had its own individual recent history and is likely to have its own individual future. Institutions of higher education have been riding off in all directions and will probably continue to do so: 3,000 different institutions face 3,000 different futures.[18]

The Kerr groups did not pretend that all are of a piece, that a particular liberal arts college is like a particular research university, that even two top research universities are carbon copies of each other or should be. The specific institutions are the ones that matter – their different heritages, their different geographic locations and regional environments, and their different embedded configurations of academic subjects and programs. And this is the way it should be when the values of institutional diversity and initiative are placed front and center. Then the 'advice to state governments', in 1980, was to 'prepare financing formulas that will encourage diversity and new initiatives'. States should stop pre-audit controls over expenditures, ease the possibility of transfer of funds within institutions, provide for portability of state financial aid to students, and allow institutions to keep the private funds they raise.[19]

The Kerr-Carnegie model offers a transferable logic in how to think about reform and change in higher education: begin by shifting attention to the institutional level, focus on development from past to present to possible futures, and then take it from there. So, if Scotland has eighteen institutions in its designated higher education system, there are eighteen stories of past, present and possible future development. Reformers can drop all pretences that St Andrews, Edinburgh, Strathclyde, and the Royal Scottish Academy of Music and Drama are cut from the same cloth and should somehow undergo a common system evolution. These institutions are diverse, and their valuable identities and competencies will only be harmed by homogenizing pressures.

The mantra for reform becomes: complex universities operating in complex environments require complex differentiated solutions. One hundred universities require 100 solutions.

On the university-led pathway, reform avoids at all costs a one-size-fits-all mentality. It encourages institutions to freely carve out their own solutions, in combinations of the traditional and the new. These new measures reflect their particular possibilities as well as their particular constraints – and especially their particular acts of will. Movers and shakers insists on system actions that enable differentiation and competition; they are aware that these broad conditions are necessary for future institutional competence at home *and* for the growing international competition generated by ambitious universities in Europe, Australia, Singapore and China, for example; and in the United States, in North Carolina and Georgia as well as in California, Michigan and Massachusetts. The home system needs to turn universities loose so they can develop capacities to adapt rapidly to change, and thereby to compete. The state has to find a new platform for trust, perhaps verifying in a general way every five to ten years just how well various universities are doing. As legislators, ministers and state planners grow increasingly remote from the thickening realities of universities, their best hope is to enable those in the institutions to do the job.

On the institution-led pathway at the cutting edge, the extremely proactive place will be hard at work early Monday morning to turn problems into solutions that compose a stronger capacity for adaptive change. Pursuing such institutional cases around the world, we have sought answers to the two simple questions of how they transformed their character and how they sustain a capacity to go on changing. In their common answers, we find the necessity of collegial forms if entrepreneurialism is to work well in universities. Above all, we find institutional will that reflects assertive ambition. Facing the same external forces, some universities change extensively, some change moderately, and some hardly change at all. The demands of the day clearly do not produce change. What counts are the responses summoned from within by diverse universities.

This side of the calamities of war, fire and earthquake – and repressive governmental tyranny – the future of universities rests in their self-reliance. The study of modern academic entrepreneurialism teaches, and teaches well, that, one by one, as the twenty-first century unfolds, universities will largely get what they deserve. The lucky ones will have built the institutional habits of change.

Notes and references

Introduction

Notes

1 Clark (1998).
2 OECD (2000) Beyond the Entrepreneurial University? Global Challenges and Institutional Responses, The 15th IMHE General Conference Paris, Sept. 11–13. Selected papers from the conference were published in the IMHE journal, *Higher Education Management*, 13(2), 2001. See Clark, 2001.
3 China Conference (2001) International Conference on Higher Education Reform and Development. University of Zhejiang, Hangzhou, China, October.
4 'Soul talk' so often comes shrouded in hoary mists and even a whiff of incense; it is best left to theologians and artists. Those who summon souls for 'the university' need to consider undesirable essences that should be eliminated. They might also see adaptive universities as engaged in useful soul-making.
5 See Clark (2000, 2001, 2002 and 2003).

References

Clark, Burton R. (1998) *Creating Entrepreneurial Universities: Organizational Pathways of Transformation*. Oxford: Pergamon/Elsevier Science.

Clark, Burton R. (2000) Collegial Entrepreneurialism in Proactive Universities: Lessons From Europe. *Change*, 2: 19 (January/February).

Clark, Burton R. (2001) The Entrepreneurial University: New Foundations for Collegiality, Autonomy, and Achievement. *Higher Education Management* (Journal of the Programme on Institutional Management in Higher Education, OECD), Vol. 13 (2): 9–24.

Clark, Burton R. (2002) University Transformation: Primary Pathways to University Autonomy and Achievement, in Steven Brint (ed.) *The Future of the City of Intellect: The Changing American University*, pp. 322–42. Stanford: Stanford University Press.

Clark, Burton R. (2003) Sustaining Change in Universities: Continuities in Case Studies and Concepts. *Tertiary Education and Management*, 9: 99–116.

Chapter 1

Notes

1 Shattock (1989): 5, quoted in Clark (1998): 38.
2 Clark (1998): 38.
3 Follett (2000): 2.
4 Follett (2000): 3.
5 Follett (2000): 3.
6 Follett (2000): 3–4.
7 Shattock (1989): 5.
8 Rushton (2001).
9 University of Warwick (1996).
10 Shattock (2000): 5.
11 *Times Higher* (1997) January 3: 18.
12 University of Warwick (1998): 8.
13 Clark (1995): 147–52.
14 University of Warwick (1998): 14–15.
15 University of Warwick (1999): passim.
16 *Times Higher* (1999) June, 14: 3.
17 Warner and Palfreyman (2001): passim.
18 University of Warwick (2000): passim.
19 *Times Higher* (1999) November 26.
20 University of Warwick (2000): passim.
21 University of Warwick (2000): 8.

References

Clark, Burton R. (1995) *Places of Inquiry: Research and Advanced Education in Modern Universities.* Berkeley: University of California Press.
Clark, Burton R. (1998) *Creating Entrepreneurial Universities: Organizational Pathways of Transformation.* Oxford: Pergamon/Elsevier Science.
Follett, Sir Brian K. (2000) Financing a research university: the diversified funding base. Paris: OECD-IMHE General Conference, September, 11–13.
Rushton, Jim (2001) Managing transformation, in David Warner and David Palfreyman (eds) *The State of UK Higher Education: Managing Change and Diversity*, pp. 169–77. Buckingham: The Society for Research into Higher Education & Open University Press.
Shattock, Michael L. (1989) Elements of a university constitution: management, academic self-government, and university policy making in a competitive environment (Statement submitted by Warwick to The Bertelsmann Foundation before receiving the Bertelsmann Prize for exemplary achievement).
Shattock, Michael L. (2000) Regenerating the University's Economy: Replacing Shortfalls in the State's Contribution. Bonn: CHE Conference, Centrum fur Hochschulentwicklung.
Times Higher (1997) Warwick Bares All on Air. January, 3: 18.
Times Higher (1999) Medical Schools Win Go-Ahead. June, 14: 3.
Warner, David and Palfreyman, David (eds) (2001) *The State of UK Higher Education:*

Managing Change and Diversity. Buckingham: The Society for Research into Higher Education & Open University Press.
University of Warwick.
(1996) *Annual Report.*
(1998) *Annual Report.*
(1999) *Annual Report.*
(2000) *Annual Review.*

Chapter 2

Notes

1 University of Strathclyde Annual Review (1999): 2.
2 Arbuthnott (2000).
3 Clark (1998): 137.
4 University of Strathclyde Strategic Plan, 2001–2005 (2001): 6, 9, 19.
5 Clark (1998): 74.
6 University of Strathclyde Annual Review (1998): 7, 4.
7 University of Strathclyde Annual Review (2000): 4.
8 University of Strathclyde Annual Review (2000): 4.
9 University of Strathclyde Annual Review (1999): 10.
10 West (2001): 4.
11 West (2001): 4.
12 University of Strathclyde Strategic Plan (1997): 13.
13 University of Strathclyde Strategic Plan (1997): 13.
14 'Between 1994 and 2002, UK departments offering physics degrees declined from 79 to 53 – a loss of 26 or one-third.' This large decline created 'deserts' among the geographical regions of the nation in the availability of study in physics, worsening, among other negative effects, an acute shortage of secondary school physics teachers. *Times Higher* (2002b) September 6: 6–7. Such are the backward steps induced by the strongly dysfunctional government-university relationship epitomized by the RAE.
15 University of Strathclyde Annual Review (1999): 18–20.
16 University of Strathclyde Strategic Plan 2001–2005 (2001): 6–10.
17 University of Strathclyde Strategic Plan 2001–2005 (2001): 16–18, 11.
18 Newall (2003): 14–2.
19 *Times Higher* (2002a) August 9: 2.

References

Arbuthnott, Sir John P. (2000) Towards a Strengthened Steering Core: University Management and Governance for the 21st Century. Paris: OECD-IMHE General Conference, 11–13 September.
Clark, Burton R. (1998) *Creating Entrepreneurial Universities: Organizational Pathways of Transformation.* Oxford: Pergamon/Elsevier Science.
Newall, David (2003) Scottish Higher Education Policy and Funding, in T.G.K Bryce

and W.M. Humes (eds) *Scottish Education*, 2nd edn, pp. 141–51. Edinburgh: Edinburgh University Press.

Times Higher (2002a) Scottish Watchdog Puts Its Faith in Trust, August 9: 2.

Times Higher (2002b) September 6: 6–7.

University of Strathclyde
   (1997) Annual Review.
   (1997) Strategic Plan, 1997–2001.
   (1998) Annual Review.
   (1999) Annual Review.
   (2000) Annual Review.
   (2001) Strategic Plan, 2001–2005.

West, Peter (2001) Paper presented to the Deans' European Academic Network, Annual Conference, 8–10 October.

Chapter 3

Notes

1 Clark (1998): 39–60.
2 Goedegebuure and van Vught (2000): 3.
3 Goedegebuure and van Vught (2000): 3.
4 Goedegebuure and van Vught (2000): 4–5.
5 Daalder (1982):174; quoted in Clark (1998): 42.
6 De Boer and Goedegebuure (2001): 173–8.
7 De Boer and Goedegebuure (2001): 176.
8 De Boer and Goedegebuure (2001): 176–8.
9 Goedegebuure and van Vught (2000): 5–6.
10 Neave (2002): 181.
11 Goedegebuure and van Vught (2000): 6.
12 Goedegebuure and van Vught (2000): 6.
13 Goedegebuure and van Vught (2000): 6–7.
14 Clark (2000): 10–19.
15 University of Twente Annual Report (1998): 9.
16 University of Twente Annual Report (1998): 14.
17 University of Twente Annual Report (1998): 19.
18 Goedegebuure (2001): 7.
19 University of Twente Annual Report (1998): 33.
20 University of Twente Annual Report (1998): 9–10.

References

Clark, Burton R. (1998) *Creating Entrepreneurial Universities: Organizational Pathways of Transformation*. Oxford: Pergamon/Elsevier Science.

Clark, Burton R. (2000) Collegial Entrepreneurialism in Proactive Universities: Lessons From Europe. *Change*, January–February: 10–19.

Daalder, H. (1982) The Netherlands: Universities Between the 'New Democracy' and the 'New Management', in H. Daalder and E. Shils (eds) *Universities, Politicians* and Bureaucrats: Europe and the United States, pp. 173–231. Cambridge: Cambridge University Press.

De Boer, Harry and Goedegebuure, Leo (2001) On Limitations and Consequences of Change: Dutch University Governance in Transition. *Tertiary Education and Management*, 7: 163–80.

Goedegebuure, Leo and van Vught, Frans (2000) The Entrepreneurial University Revisited: Integrating Academia and Entrepreneurship. OECD-IMHE General Conference 2000. Paris: 11–13 September.

Goedegebuure, Leo (2001) The Rise of the Entrepreneurial University: A Perspective From Europe. Paper prepared for the International Conference on Higher Education Reform and Development, Zhejiang University, Hangzhou, PR China, 24–27 October.

Neave, Guy (2002) Anything Goes: Or, How the Accommodation of Europe's Universities to European Integration Integrates an Inspiring Number of Contradictions. *Tertiary Education and Management*, 8: 181–97.

University of Twente Annual Report (1998).

Chapter 4

Notes

1 Clark (1998): 104–6.
2 University of Joensuu Annual Report (1998): 6.
3 University of Joensuu Annual Report (1998): 7.
4 University of Joensuu Annual Report (1999): 5.
5 Dahllöf *et al.* (1998): 10.
6 Dahllöf *et al.* (1998): 46, 49.
7 Dahllöf *et al.* (1998): 55.
8 Dahllöf *et al.* (1998): 64.
9 Dahllöf *et al.* (1998): 65, 66, 68.
10 Dahllöf *et al.* (1998): 69–70.
11 Höltta (2000): 88.
12 Höltta (2000): 90.
13 Höltta (2000): 89–90.
14 Höltta (2000): 90.
15 Clark (1998): 119.
16 University of Joensuu Annual Report (2001): 24.
17 University of Joensuu Performance Agreement (2001): passim.
18 Based on research in four other Finnish universities, Kari Kuoppala acutely observed that in the Finnish version of 'management by results' – performance based funding in the core grant – the negotiation process between ministry and university is 'heavy theatre' in which doctrine withers away to a 2 per cent level of funding. What counts for the university departments is the growth of funding from non-core sources. Kuoppala (2003): 11–13.
19 Vartiainen (2000): 3.
20 Vartiainen and Viiri (2002): 83.

References

Clark, Burton R. (1998) *Creating Entrepreneurial Universities: Organizational Pathways of Transformation.* Oxford: Pergamon/Elsevier Science.

Dahllöf, U., Goddard, J., Huttunen, J., O'Brien, C., Roman, O. and Virtanen, I. (1998) *Towards the Responsive University; The Regional Role of Eastern Finland Universities.* Helsinki: Publications of Higher Education Evaluation Council, 8.

Hölttä, Seppo (2000) From Regional Teacher Training College to Research University: The University of Joensuu and its Role in Regional Development, in F. Schutte and P.C. van der Sijde (eds) *The University and Its Region: Examples of Regional Development from the European Consortium of Innovative Universities,* pp. 83–90. Enschede: Twente University Press.

University of Joensuu (1998) Annual Report.

  (1999) Annual Report.

  (2001) Annual Report.

  (2001) Performance Agreement Between the University of Joensuu and the Ministry of Education for 2001–2003. Appendix 1. Helsinki: Ministry of Education.

Kuoppala, Kari (2003) Management by Results in Finnish Universities. Paper presented at the 25th EAIR Forum, University of Limerick, 24–27 August.

Vartiainen, Perttu (2000) Introductory Statement: The University of Joensuu. Paris: IMHE General Conference, 11–13 September.

Vartiainen, Perttu and Vieri, Arto (2002) Universities and Their Local Partners: The Case of the University of Joensuu, Finland. *Industry & Higher Education,* April: 83–9.

Chapter 5

Notes

1 Clark (1998): 84–102.
2 A 1995 statement, quoted in Clark (1998): 98.
3 Chalmers University of Technology Annual Report (2000): 32 and passim.
4 Chalmers University of Technology Annual Report (2000): 29.
5 Chalmers University of Technology Annual Report (2000): 44.
6 Chalmers University of Technology Annual Report (2000): 48.
7 Chalmers University of Technology Annual Report (2000): 42–3, 54.
8 Bergqvist (2002): passim.
9 Bergqvist (2002): passim.
10 Chalmers University of Technology Annual Report (2000): 54, 56.
11 Chalmers University of Technology Annual Report (2000): 27.
12 Chalmers University of Technology Annual Report (2000): 30–1.
13 Chalmers University of Technology Annual Report (1997): 3; (1998): 3; (1999): 1; (2000): 7.
14 Chalmers University of Technology Annual Report (2001): 62.
15 Chalmers University of Technology Annual Report (2001): 33.
16 Chalmers University of Technology Annual Report (2001): 32–3.
17 Chalmers University of Technology Annual Report (2001): 62.
18 Chalmers University of Technology Annual Report (1997): 5; (1998): 1–2.

References

Bergqvist, Tuula (2002) How to Create a Win-Win Situation in Partnership With Industry: Experiences From Western Sweden. *Paper given at the 24th Annual Forum of the European Association for Institutional Research (EAIR), Prague:* 8–11 September.
Chalmers University of Technology.
    (1997) Annual Report.
    (1998) Annual Report.
    (1999) Annual Report.
    (2000) Annual Report.
    (2001) Annual Report.
Clark, Burton R. (1998) *Creating Entrepreneurial Universities: Organizational Pathways of Transformation.* Oxford: Pergamon/Elsevier Science.

Chapter 6

Notes

1 Stokes (1997): 74.
2 Spencer Foundation (2001): 5–6.
3 Flyvbjerg (2001); Ragin and Becker (1992).
4 Chalmers University of Technology (2000): 7.
5 On the United States, see Geiger (1986) and Geiger (1993).
6 Johnstone and Shroff-Mehta (2001): 32–54.
7 *Times Higher* (2002) March 22:8.
8 Rhoades and Sporn (2002): 26, in a comparison of university personnel in European and American universities, highlighted the continuous growth of 'non-faculty professionals', specialists who attend to new relationships and duties, and, along the way, acquire status and influence in newly-regularized positions. These 'managerial professionals' are 'factors' of production, working with professors to produce higher education's 'output'.
9 See Geiger (1993) on the role of 'relevant knowledge' in the development of American research universities during the last half of the twentieth century. See also Gibbons *et al.* (1994); Scott (1997).
10 Elzinga (1985).
11 Sundgren (2000): 2.
12 Clark (1998a): 141.
13 Clark (1998a): 143–4. For the original formulation of the concept of organizational saga, see Clark (1998b).
14 Clark (1998a): 145.
15 Clark (1998a): 145. See also Leslie (1996):110; and Leslie and Fretwell (1996).
16 Clark (1998a): 145. Quotation from Stopford and Baden-Fuller (1994): 523; and Leonard-Barton (1995): 28.
17 On incrementalism as organizational theory, see Lindblom (1959, 1979). See also Premfors (1993).
18 Lindblom (1977): 136.

References

Chalmers University of Technology (2001) *Annual Report 2000.* Gothenburg, Sweden.

Clark, Burton R. (1998a) *Creating Entrepreneurial Universities: Organizational Pathways of Transformation.* Oxford: Pergamon/Elsevier Science.

Clark, Burton R. (1998b) The Organizational Saga in Higher Education, in J.V. Van Maanen (ed.) *Qualitative Studies of Organizations.* The Administrative Science Quarterly Series in Organizational Behavior and Theory, pp. 197–206. Thousand Oaks, CA: Sage Publications. (Originally published in the *Administrative Science Quarterly,* 17[2] 1972, 178–84).

Elzinga, Aant (1985) Research, Bureaucracy, and the Drift of Epistemic Criteria, in Bjorn Wittrock and Aant Elzinga (eds) *The Public Policies of the Home of Scientists,* pp. 191–200. Stockholm: Almquist & Wiksell International.

Flyvbjerg, Bent (2001) *Making Social Science Matter: Why Social Science Inquiry Fails and How It Can Succeed Again.* Cambridge: Cambridge University Press.

Geiger, Roger L. (1986) *To Advance Knowledge: The Growth of American Research Universities, 1900–1940.* New York: Oxford University Press.

Geiger, Roger L. (1993) *Research and Relevant Knowledge: American Research Universities Since World War II.* New York: Oxford University Press.

Gibbons, Michael; Limoges, Camille; Nowotny, Helga; Schwartzman, Simon; Scott, Peter and Trow, Martin (eds) (1994) *The New Production of Knowledge: The Dynamics of Science and Research in Contemporary Societies.* London: Sage Publications.

Johnstone, D.B. and Shroff-Mehta, P. (2003) Higher Education Finance and Accessibility: An International Comparative Examination of Tuition and Financial Assistance Policies, in H. Eggins (ed.) *Globalization and Reform in Higher Education,* pp. 32–54. Maidenhead, Berks: Open University Press.

Leonard-Barton, D. (1995) *Wellsprings of Knowledge: Building and Sustaining the Sources of Innovation.* Boston: Harvard Business School Press.

Leslie, David (1996) Strategic Governance: The Wrong Questions? *The Review of Higher Education,* 20 (1): 101–22.

Leslie, David and Fretwell, Jr., E.K. (1996) *Wise Moves in Hard Times: Creating & Managing Resilient Colleges & Universities.* San Francisco: Jossey-Bass.

Lindblom, Charles E. (1959) The Science of Muddling Through. *Public Administration Review,* 19(2): 78–88.

Lindblom, Charles E. (1977) *Politics and Markets: The World's Political-Economic Systems.* New York: Basic Books.

Lindblom, Charles E. (1979) Still Muddling, Not Yet Through. *Public Administration Review,* 39: 517–26.

Premfors, Rune (1993) Knowledge, Power, and Democracy: Lindblom, Critical Theory, and Postmodernism, in Harry Redner (ed.) *An Heretical Heir of the Enlightenment: Politics, Policy, and Science in the Work of Charles E. Lindblom,* pp. 31–50. Boulder: Westview Press.

Ragin, Charles C. and Becker, Howard S. (eds) (1992) *What Is a Case? Exploring the Foundations of Social Inquiry.* Cambridge: Cambridge University Press.

Rhoades, Gary and Sporn, Barbara (2002) New Models of Management and Shifting Modes and Costs of Production: Europe and the United States. *Tertiary Education and Management,* 8: 3–28. Quotation, p. 26.

Scott, Peter (1997) The Changing Role of the University in the Production of New Knowledge. *Tertiary Education and Management,* 3 (1): 5–14.

Spencer Foundation (2001) *Annual Report, 1 April, 2000–31 March, 2001.* Chicago.

Stokes, Donald E. (1997) *Pasteur's Quadrant: Basic Science and Technological Innovation.* Washington, DC: Brookings Institution Press.

Stopford, J.M. and Baden-Fuller, C.W.F. (1994) Creating Corporate Entrepreneurship. *Strategic Management Journal,* 15 (7): 521–36.

Sundgren, Jan-Eric (2000) The Stimulated Academic Heartland. IMHE General Conference 2000. Paris: OECD.

Chapter 7

Notes

1 See Neave (1992), Court (2000), and Musisi and Muwanga (2001): 5.
2 Court (2000): 3; Hyuha (1998).
3 Musisi and Muwanga (2001): 6.
4 Court (2000): 4.
5 Court (2000): 4–5.
6 Mayanja (2001): 11–13.
7 Court (2000): 5–6.
8 Court (2000): 8 (drawing upon Ssebuwufu 1998).
9 Court (2000): 6.
10 Tibarimbasa (1998).
11 Court (2000): 7.
12 Court (2000): 11.
13 Mwiria (1999).
14 Musisi and Muwanga (2001): 18–19.
15 Court (2000): 11–12.
16 Musisi and Muwanga (2001): 24.
17 Musisi and Muwanga (2001): 15 (footnote 34).
18 Musisi and Muwanga (2001): 39.
19 Musisi and Muwanga (2001): 26–8.
20 Musisi and Muwanga (2001): 28–9.
21 Musisi and Muwanga (2001): 29–30.
22 The *Economist* (2003): 30. For in-depth analysis of the Uganda economy, with some attention to governmental and military problems, see Bigsten and Kayizzi-Mugerwa (2001). See also OECD (2002), especially on Uganda's 'unique success in Africa in reducing the spread of HIV-AIDS' – but with AIDS still 'a substantial threat to public health and . . . a significant obstacle to rapid human capital accumulation', pp. 291–302, quotations, pp. 293, 302.
23 Court (2000): ii, 18–19.
24 Musisi and Muwanga (2001): 1.
25 Musisi and Muwanga (2001); Cooksey, Mkude and Levey (2001); and Mario, Fry, Levey and Chilundo (2001).

References

Bigsten, Arne and Kayizzi-Mugerwa, Steve (2001) *Is Uganda an Emerging Economy?* A report for the OECD Project, 'Emerging Africa'. Uppsala, Sweden: Nordic African Institute (Research Report 118).

Cooksey, Brian; Mkude, Daniel and Levey, Lisbeth (2001) Higher Education in Tanzania: A Case Study. Draft of a report. Washington, DC: The World Bank.

Court, David (2000) Financing Higher Education in Africa: Makerere, the Quiet Revolution. Washington, DC: The World Bank and The Rockefeller Foundation.

The *Economist* (2003) *Pocket World in Figures, 2003 edition.* London: Profile Books.

Hyuha, M. (1998) Private Sponsorship and Other Cost Sharing Measures and the Sustainability of Makerere University. Unpublished manuscript.

Mario, Mousinho; Fry, Peter; Levey, Lisbeth and Chilundo, Arlindo (2001) Higher Education in Mozambique: A Case Study. Draft of a report. Washington, DC: The World Bank.

Mayanja, M.K. (2001) Makerere University and the Private Students Scheme. *International Higher Education*, 25 (Fall): 11–13. Boston: The Boston College Center for International Higher Education.

Musisi, Nakanyike B. and Muwanga, Nansozi K. (2001) *Makerere University in Transition, 1993–2000: Opportunities and Challenges.* Kambala, Uganda: Institute of Social Research, Makerere University.

Mwiria, K. (1999) Strengthening Government/University Partnerships in Africa: the Experience of Uganda's Makerere University. London: Commonwealth Secretariat. Unpublished paper.

Neave, Guy (1992) Uganda, in Burton R. Clark and Guy Neave (eds) *The Encyclopedia of Higher Education, Volume I, National Systems of Higher Education,* pp. 753–55. Oxford: Pergamon Press.

OECD (2002) *African Economic Outlook, 2001–2002* (Uganda, pp. 291–302). Paris: OECD.

Ssebuwufu, P.J.M. (1998) Some Experiences for Financing Higher Education: Relevant Courses that Can Sell in the Competitive Market and the Need for Academic Quality as it Relates to Relevance, Effectiveness and Efficiency. Paper presented to the Eastern and Southern African Universities Research Programme, Harare, Zimbabwe, 3–5 August. Makerere University.

Tibarimbasa, A.K.M. (1998) Financial Management of Makerere University: Challenges and the Way Forward. Unpublished paper, Makerere University.

Chapter 8

Notes

1 Bernasconi (2003). All quotations in this chapter not attributed to another source have been taken from this working paper. I am enormously indebted to Andrés Bernasconi for the information and insight he has provided.

2 Levy (1986): 69–70. This volume is the classic in-depth analysis of national systems of higher education throughout Latin American, with special attention to the different deployments of public and private sectors. It described the Chilean system in detail, up to the mid-1980s, as the leading case of private–public

homogeneity. For extended coverage of the development of Chilean higher education up to the late 1980s, see also Schiefelbein (1992): 130–7.
3 Levy (1986): 67–8.
4 Bernasconi (2003): l.
5 Bernasconi (2003): 1–2.
6 Bernasconi (2003): 21.
7 Bernasconi (2003): 21.
8 Bernasconi (2003): 11–12.
9 Bernasconi (2003): 8–9.
10 Bernasconi (2003): 19.
11 Bernasconi (2003): 16.
12 Bernasconi (2003): 19–20.
13 Bernasconi (2003): 12.
14 Castro and Levy (2000): 13–14.
15 Bernasconi (2003): a separate table provided me by Bernasconi, based on World Bank data for 1998.

References

Bernasconi, Andrés (2003) The Privatization of a Private University: The Case of the Pontificia Universidad Católica de Chile, 1985–2000. Unpublished working paper.
Castro, Claudio de Moura and Levy, Daniel C. (2000) *Myth, Reality, and Reform: Higher Education Policy in Latin America.* Washington, DC: Inter-American Development Bank.
Levy, Daniel C. (1986) *Higher Education and the State in Latin America: Private Challenges to Public Dominance.* Chicago: University of Chicago Press.
Schiefelbein, E. (1992) Chile, in Burton R. Clark and Guy Neave (eds) *The Encyclopedia of Higher Education: Volume 1, National Systems of Higher Education*, pp. 130–7. Oxford: Pergamon Press.

Chapter 9

Notes

1 Marginson (2000): 6.
2 For an overview of the development of Australian higher education up to 1990, see Smart (1992): 29–42.
3 Marginson (2000): 11.
4 Marginson (2000): 15.
5 Marginson (2000): 12.
6 Marginson (2000): 21. Quoting from an early law school dean.
7 Marginson (2000): 30.
8 Marginson (2000): 22–7.
9 Marginson (2000): 26.
10 Marginson (2000): 32.
11 Marginson (2000): 55–8.

12 Marginson (2000): 59.
13 Anwyl (1987).
14 Marginson (2000): 64.
15 Marginson (2000): 131–4.
16 Harman and Meek (1988): 120.
17 Marginson (2000): 131–4.
18 Marginson (2000): 141.
19 Marginson (2000): 144–5.
20 Marginson (2000): 144–6.
21 Marginson (2000): 146–8.
22 Marginson (2000): 148–50.
23 Marginson (2000): 148–50.
24 Marginson (2000): 152–3.
25 Marginson (2000): 153–4.
26 Marginson (2000): 154–5.
27 Gallagher (2000): 41–6.
28 Marginson (2002), private communication.
29 Monash University: 2001: 39.
30 Marginson (2000): 182–4.
31 Marginson (2000): 219; 249–50 (Afterword).
32 Marginson and Considine (2000).
33 On modern versions of the research-teaching-study nexus, see Clark (1995), passim, especially chapter 7.
34 *Times Higher* (2002): 10.
35 Marginson and Considine (2000): 238–41.
36 Marginson and Considine (2000): 244–53. Final quotation, p. 253.
37 Marginson (2000): 78–9.
38 Marginson (2000): 86.
39 Monash University (2000): 1–2, 24–31.

References

Anwyl, John (1987) CAEs poised to graduate to full university status. *The Age* 9 June.
Clark, Burton R. (1995) *Places of Inquiry: Research and Advanced Education in Modern Universities.* Berkeley: University of California Press.
Gallagher, Michael (2000) The Emergence of Entrepreneurial Public Universities in Australia. Paper presented at IMHE General Conference 2000. Paris: 13–15 September. 46 pages.
Harman, Grant and Meek, Lynn (1988) Lessons from Recent Experience with Mergers, in Grant Harman and Lynn Meek (eds) *Australian Higher Education Reconstructed?: Analysis of the Proposals and Assumptions of the Dawkins Green Paper.* Armidale: University of New England.
Marginson, Simon (2000) *Monash: Remaking the University.* St Leonards, NSW, Australia: Allen & Unwin.
Marginson, Simon and Considine, Mark (2000) *The Enterprise University: Power, Governance and Reinvention in Australia.* Cambridge, UK: Cambridge University Press.
Monash University (2000) *Leading the Way: Monash 2020.* Clayton, Victoria: Monash University.
Monash University (2001) *Annual Report 2000.* Clayton, Victoria: Monash University.

Smart, D. (1992) Australia, in Burton R. Clark and Guy Neave (eds) *The Encyclopedia of Higher Education. Volume I: National Systems of Higher Education*, pp. 29–42. Oxford: Pergamon Press.

Times Higher (2002) Protests at university closure plan. 9 August: 10.

Chapter 10

Notes

1 For greater elaboration of these characteristics, see: Clark (1987), chapter 3: The Open System; also Clark (1990); and Clark (1995), chapter 4, The United States: Competitive Graduate Schools.
2 *Chronicle of Higher Education* (2002).
3 For extensive coverage of the development of American higher education, especially the university sector, see Geiger (1986, 1993).
4 On these twin headaches for university administrators in the United States, see Duderstadt (2000a and 2000b).

References

Chronicle of Higher Education (2002) Almanac 2002–3. 30 August.

Clark, Burton R. (1987) *The Academic Life: Small Worlds, Different Worlds*. Princeton: The Carnegie Foundation for the Advancement of Teaching and Princeton University Press.

Clark, Burton R. (1990) The Organizational Dynamics of the American Research University. *Higher Education Policy*, 3 (2): 31–5.

Clark, Burton R. (1995) *Places of Inquiry: Research and Advanced Education in Modern Universities*. Berkeley: University of California Press.

Duderstadt, James J. (2000a) *A University for the 21st Century*. Ann Arbor: University of Michigan Press.

Duderstadt, James J. (2000b) *Intercollegiate Athletics and the American University: A University President's Perspective*. Ann Arbor: University of Michigan Press.

Geiger, Roger L. (1986) *To Advance Knowledge: The Growth of American Research Universities, 1900–1940*. New York: Oxford University Press.

Geiger, Roger L. (1993) *Research and Relevant Knowledge: American Research Universities Since World War II*. New York: Oxford University Press.

Stanford University

Notes

1 For the analysis that first fully defined the regional advantage of Silicon Valley, see Saxenian (1994). See also Geiger (1993): 118–35; Lee *et al.* (2000); Tornatzky, Waugaman and Gray (2002): 157–67.
2 Stanford University (1971). The Founding Grant, November 11, 1885.
3 Saxenian (1994): 23.

4 Geiger (1993): 128.
5 Saxenian (1994): 20–1.
6 Saxenian (1994): 23.
7 Saxenian (1994): 23–4.
8 Saxenian (1994): 26–7.
9 Tornatzky, Waugaman and Gray (2002): 163.
10 Tornatzky, Waugaman and Gray (2002): 163.
11 Geiger (1993): 129–31.
12 Geiger (1993): 135.
13 Lombardi *et al.* (2001), passim.

References

Geiger, Roger L. (1993) *Research and Relevant Knowledge: American Research Universities Since World War II.* New York: Oxford University Press.
Lee, Chong-Moon., Miller, William F., Hancock, Marguerite Gong and Rowen, Henry S. (2000) *The Silicon Valley Edge: A Habitat for Innovation and Entrepreneurship.* Stanford: Stanford University Press.
Lombardi, John V., Craig, Diane D., Capaldi, Elizabeth D., Gater, Denise S. and Mendonca, Sarah L. (2001) *The Top American Research Universities: An Annual Report from The Lombardi Program on Measuring University Performance.* Gainesville, Florida: The Center at the University of Florida.
Saxenian, Annalee (1994) *Regional Advantage: Culture and Competition in Silicon Valley and Route 128.* Cambridge: Harvard University Press.
Stanford University (1971) The Founding Grant, November 11, 1885. Palo Alto.
Tornatzky, Louis G., Waugaman, Paul G. and Gray, Denis O. (2002) *Innovation U.: New University Roles in a Knowledge Economy.* Research Triangle Park, North Carolina: Southern Growth Policies Board.

Massachusetts Institute of Technology

Notes

1 Geiger (1993): 62–3.
2 Geiger (1993): 63–4.
3 Geiger (1993): 66–8.
4 Geiger (1993): 67.
5 Geiger (1993): 63.
6 Geiger (1993: 73.
7 Saxenian (1994): 14–15.
8 Saxenian (1994): 16–17.
0 Simha and Snover (1005): 1.
10 Simha and Snover (1995): 4–13.
11 MIT (2003).
12 MIT (2003).

References

Geiger, Roger L. (1993) *Research and Relevant Knowledge: American Research Universities Since World War II.* New York: Oxford University Press.
MIT (2003) *Report of the Office of the Provost.* Sections on: Faculty and Staff; Student Body; Tuition; Research Expenditures; Investments.
Saxenian, Annalee (1994) *Regional Advantage: Culture and Competition in Silicon Valley and Route 128.* Cambridge: Harvard University Press.
Simha, O. Robert and Snover, Lydia (1995) Tradition and Innovation at MIT: A Model for Maintaining Traditional Academic Values and Enhancing the Environment for Innovation in Research. Paper delivered at the EAIR Forum in Zurich, 27–30 August.

University of Michigan
Notes

1 Slosson (1910): ix–x, 182.
2 Slosson (1910): 187–202.
3 Slosson (1910): 199.
4 Geiger (1986): 209–10.
5 Geiger (1986): 210–11.
6 Geiger (2004): 163.
7 Geiger (2004): 163.
8 Geiger (2004): 163.
9 Geiger (2004): 164.
10 University of Michigan (2003): All Funds Budget.
11 Duderstadt (2000a): 304, 310, 312–13. Convinced that we are witnessing the emergence of new 'learning structures', even 'new civic lifeforms', Duderstadt has strongly argued for a nomenclature of 'private-financed public university' and similar terms. His vision, based on the Michigan development, leads to two radical conclusions: that 'America's great experiment of building world-class public universities supported primarily by tax dollars has come to an end'; that 'the autonomy of the public university will become one of its most crucial assets, perhaps even more critical than state support for some institutions'.
12 Lombardi *et al.* (2001): 84, 112, 116.
13 University of Michigan (2002): Recent Rankings for Academic Programs.
14 Duderstadt (2000a): 204, 207.
15 Duderstadt (2000b): passim.
16 Duderstadt (2000a): 266.
17 Duderstadt (2000a): 275, 277.

References

Duderstadt, James J. (2000a) *A University for the 21st Century.* Ann Arbor: University of Michigan Press.
Duderstadt, James J. (2000b) *Intercollegiate Athletics and the American University: A University President's Perspective.* Ann Arbor: University of Michigan Press.

Geiger, Roger L. (1986) *To Advance Knowledge: The Growth of American Research Universities, 1900–1840.* New York: Oxford University Press.

Geiger, Roger L. (1993) *Research and Relevant Knowledge: American Research Universities Since World War II.* New York: Oxford University Press.

Geiger, Roger L. (2004) *Knowledge and Money: Research Universities and the Paradox of the Marketplace.* Stanford: Stanford University Press.

Lombardi, John V., Craig, Diane D., Capaldi, Elizabeth D., Gater, Denise S. and Mendonca, Sarah L. (2001) *The Top American Research Universities: An Annual Report from The Lombardi Program on Measuring University Performance.* Gainesville, Florida: The Center at the University of Florida.

Slosson, Edwin E. (1910) *Great American Universities.* New York: Macmillan. (Reprinted 1977. New York: Arno Press).

University of Michigan (2002) Recent Rankings for Academic Programs at the University of Michigan-Ann Arbor.

University of Michigan (2003) All Funds Budget Table, University of Michigan-Ann Arbor, 1984–2003.

University of California, Los Angeles

Notes

1   Douglas (2000): 112.
2   Stadtman (1970): 215–17.
3   Stadtman (1970): 225–30.
4   Geiger (1993): 138–40.
5   Geiger (1993): 143.
6   Geiger (1993): 146.
7   Geiger (1993): 145–6.
8   Kerr (2001): 342–5.
9   UCLA Today (2002): 6.
10 UCLA (2003a): major funding sources.
11 UCLA (2003a): award dollars by federal sponsors.
12 UCLA (2003a): funding by major campus area.
13 UCLA (2003a): major funding sources.
14 UCLA (2003b): research centers.
15 Carnesale (2002): passim.
16 UCLA (2002): annual financial report.
17 UCLA Magazine (2002): 37–8.

References

Carnesale, Albert (2002) *Perspectives on the Modern Research University.* UCLA.

Douglas, John Aubrey (2000) *The California Idea and American Higher Education: 1850 to the 1960 Master Plan.* Stanford: Stanford University Press.

Geiger, Roger (1993) *Research and Relevant Knowledge: American Research Universities Since World War II.* New York: Oxford University Press.

Kerr, Clark (2001) *The Gold and the Blue: A Personal Memoir of the University of California,*

1949–1967. Volume One: Academic Triumphs. Berkeley: University of California Press.

Stadtman, Verne A. (1970) *The University of California 1868–1968: A Centennial Publication of the University of California.* New York: McGraw-Hill.

UCLA Today (2002): 23(4) October 22: 6.

UCLA Magazine (2002) The New Scientists. Vol. 14 (3) Winter: 37–8.

UCLA Annual Financial Report (2002): 3–4.

UCLA (2003a) Funded Research, Annual Reports 1994–5 to 2002–2003. http://www.research.ucla/edu/ora.

UCLA (2003b) Research Centers, Labs, and Institutes. http://www.research.ucla/labs/index.htm.

North Carolina State University

Notes

1 Geiger (2004): 207–9; see also Tornatzky, Waugaman and Gray (2002): 42–53.
2 NC State (2000): 7–9.
3 Geiger (2004): 207–8; NC State (2002): 1.
4 NC State (2002): 1.
5 NC State (2003): 1–3.
6 Geiger (2004): 209.
7 Geiger (2004): 209–10.
8 Geiger (2004): 210.

References

Geiger, Roger L. (2004) *Knowledge and Money: Research Universities and the Paradox of the Marketplace.* Stanford: Stanford University Press.

NC State University (2000) The New NC State: Becoming the Nation's Leading Land-Grant Institution. Raleigh, North Carolina.

NC State University (2002) Centennial Campus Facts. Raleigh, North Carolina.

NC State University (2003) Centennial Biomedical Campus. Raleigh, North Carolina.

Tornatzky, Louis G., Waugaman, Paul G. and Gray, Denis O. (2002) *Innovation U.: New University Roles in a Knowledge Economy.* Research Triangle Park, NC: Southern Growth Policies Board.

Georgia Institute of Technology

Notes

1 Tornatsky, Waugaman and Gray (2002): 27–30.
2 Tornatsky, Waugaman and Gray (2002): 31.
3 Geiger (2004): 211.
4 Geiger (2004): 212–13.
5 Georgia Institute of Technology (2002): 21; Yamacraw (2002).

6 Geiger (2004): 213.
7 Tornatsky, Waugaman and Gray (2002): passim.
8 Raymond (1996): passim.
9 Tornatsky, Waugaman and Gray (2002): 55–6.
10 Tornatsky, Waugaman and Gray (2002): 129–36.
11 Tornatsky, Waugaman and Gray (2002): 137–8.

References

Geiger, Roger L. (2004) *Knowledge and Money: Research Universities and the Paradox of the Marketplace.* Stanford: Stanford University Press.
Georgia Institute of Technology (2002) *Annual Report 2002: Technological Leadership in a Changing World.* Atlanta: Georgia Institute of Technology.
Raymond, Susan U. (ed.) (1996) *Science-Based Economic Development: Case Studies Around the World.* New York: The New York Academy of Science.
Tornatsky, Louis G., Waugaman, Paul G. and Gray, Denis O. (2002) *Innovation U.: New University Roles in a Knowledge Economy.* Research Triangle Park, NC: Southern Growth Policies Board.
Yamacraw: Broadband Technology (2002) *Annual Report 2002.* Atlanta: Yamacraw.

Conclusion

Notes

1 Herbst, Hagentobler and Snover (2002): i–iv.
2 Clark (1995): 137.
3 Clark (1995): 139.
4 Portes (1987): passim.
5 Rosovsky (1990): 29–36.
6 Herbst, Hagentobler and Snover (2002): iv.
7 Herbst, Hagentobler and Snover (2002): 72.
8 Gumport (1993): 277–85.
9 Herbst, Hagentobler and Snover (2002): 74.
10 Herbst, Hagentobler and Snover (2002): 27.
11 On nineteenth- and twentieth-century versions of the research-teaching-study nexus, see Clark (1995), particularly chapter 1 on Germany, chapter 4 on the United States, and chapter 7 on conditions of integration of the nexus.
12 Herbst, Hagentobler and Snover (2002): 27.

References

Clark, Burton R. (1995) *Places of Inquiry: Research and Advanced Education in Modern Universities.* Berkeley: University of California Press.
Gumport, Patricia (1993) Graduate Education and Research Imperatives: Views From American Campuses, in Burton R. Clark (ed.) *The Research Foundations of Graduate Education: Germany, Britain, France, United States, Japan,* pp. 261–93. Berkeley: University of California Press.

Herbst, Marcel; Hagentobler, Urs and Snover, Lydia (2002) *MIT and ETH Zurich: Structures and Cultures Juxtaposed.* Berne, Switzerland: Center for Science and Technology Studies (CEST 2002/9).

Portes, Richard (1987) Economics in Europe. *European Economic Review,* 31: 1329–40.

Rosovsky, Henry (1990) *The University: An Owner's Manual.* New York: W.W. Norton.

Chapter 11

Notes

1 Shattock (1999): 24.
2 Shattock (2003): passim.
3 Shattock (2003): 12–14.
4 Shattock (2003): 16.
5 Shattock (2003): 14–15.
6 Shattock (2003): 16.
7 Shattock (2003): 17.
8 Shattock (2003): 17.
9 Trow (2003): passim.
10 Smelser and Content noted in a 1980 study of the US academic labor market that competition for academic talent 'is simultaneously a competition *for* individual services and a competition *between* universities trying to advance or solidify their own position in the prestige hierarchy', p. 7. See also Becher (1989); Ziman (1991).
11 Clark (1983): chapter 5, 'Integration', 131–81.
12 Lindblom (2001): 41, 23, 83.
13 Lindblom (2001): 27.
14 PA Consulting Group (2002): passim.
15 McNay (2002): passim.
16 PA Consulting Group (2002): comments by Sir Alan Langlands, 3 pages (unnumbered).
17 Clark (2003): passim.
18 Carnegie Council (1980): 199.
19 Carnegie Council (1980): 203–4.

References

Becher, Tony (1989) *Academic Tribes and Territories: Intellectual Enquiry and the Cultures of Disciplines.* Milton Keynes: SRHE and Open University Press.

The Carnegie Council on Policy Studies in Higher Education (1980) *Three Thousand Futures: The Next Twenty Years for Higher Education* (summarized in *A Summary of Reports and Recommendations* (1980)): 194–206. San Francisco: Jossey-Bass.

Clark, Burton R. (1983) *The Higher Education System: Academic Organization in Cross-National Perspective.* Berkeley: University of California Press.

Clark, Burton R. (2003) Reform That Matters: University-Led Change, in *Creating and Sustaining Entrepreneurial, Innovative Universities,* pp. 1–9. (Lectures given at the University of Strathclyde by Burton Clark and Michael Shattock, September 2002). Glasgow: University of Strathclyde.

Lindblom, Charles E. (2001) *The Market System: What It Is, How It Works, and What To Make of It.* New Haven: Yale University Press.

McNay, Ian (2002) Assessing the Assessment: An Analysis of the UK Research Assessment Exercise 2001, and Its Outcomes, with Special Reference to Research in Education. Paper presented at International Forum of the Association for Study of Higher Education (ASHE). Sacramento, CA.: November.

PA Consulting Group (2002) Higher Education in Scotland: Orchestrating an Adaptive Knowledge-Based System. A Report for the Scottish Higher Education Funding Council. Edinburgh.

Shattock, Michael (1999) The Challenge Ahead: British Universities in the 21st Century. *International Higher Education*, 15 (Spring): 24–6. Quotation, p. 24.

Shattock, Michael (2003) The Entrepreneurial University Model: Factors Which Inhibit Its Realization, in *Creating and Sustaining Entrepreneurial, Innovative Universities*, pp. 10–21. (Lectures given at the University of Strathclyde by Burton Clark and Michael Shattock, September 2002). Glasgow: University of Strathclyde.

Smelser, Neil J. and Content, Robin (1980) *The Changing Academic Market: General Trends and a Berkeley Case Study.* Berkeley: University of California Press.

Trow, Martin (2003) Leadership and Academic Reform: Biology at Berkeley. http://ishi.lib.berkeley.edu/cshe/mtrow

Ziman, John (1991) Academic Science as a System of Markets. *Higher Education Quarterly*, 45 (1) Winter: 41–61.

Index

The Society for Research into Higher Education

The Society for Research into Higher Education (SRHE), an international body, exists to stimulate and coordinate research into all aspects of higher education. It aims to improve the quality of higher education through the encouragement of debate and publication on issues of policy, on the organization and management of higher education institutions, and on the curriculum, teaching and learning methods.

The Society is entirely independent and receives no subsidies, although individual events often receive sponsorship from business or industry. The Society is financed through corporate and individual subscriptions and has members from many parts of the world. It is an NGO of UNESCO.

Under the imprint *SRHE & Open University Press*, the Society is a specialist publisher of research, having over 80 titles in print. In addition to *SRHE News*, the Society's newsletter, the Society publishes three journals: *Studies in Higher Education* (three issues a year), *Higher Education Quarterly* and *Research into Higher Education Abstracts* (three issues a year).

The Society runs frequent conferences, consultations, seminars and other events. The annual conference in December is organized at and with a higher education institution. There are a growing number of networks which focus on particular areas of interest, including:

Access	FE/HE
Assessment	Graduate Employment
Consultants	New Technology for Learning
Curriculum Development	Postgraduate Issues
Eastern European	Quantitative Studies
Educational Development Research	Student Development

Benefits to members

Individual

- The opportunity to participate in the Society's networks
- Reduced rates for the annual conferences
- Free copies of *Research into Higher Education Abstracts*
- Reduced rates for *Studies in Higher Education*

- Reduced rates for *Higher Education Quarterly*
- Free online access to *Register of Members' Research Interests* – includes valuable reference material on research being pursued by the Society's members
- Free copy of occasional in-house publications, e.g. *The Thirtieth Anniversary Seminars Presented by the Vice-Presidents*
- Free copies of *SRHE News* and *International News* which inform members of the Society's activities and provides a calendar of events, with additional material provided in regular mailings
- A 35 per cent discount on all SRHE/Open University Press books
- The opportunity for you to apply for the annual research grants
- Inclusion of your research in the *Register of Members' Research Interests*

Corporate

- Reduced rates for the annual conference
- The opportunity for members of the Institution to attend SRHE's network events at reduced rates
- Free copies of *Research into Higher Education Abstracts*
- Free copies of *Studies in Higher Education*
- Free online access to *Register of Members' Research Interests* – includes valuable reference material on research being pursued by the Society's members
- Free copy of occasional in-house publications
- Free copies of *SRHE News* and *International News*
- A 35 per cent discount on all SRHE/Open University Press books
- The opportunity for members of the Institution to submit applications for the Society's research grants
- The opportunity to work with the Society and co-host conferences
- The opportunity to include in the *Register of Members' Research Interests* your Institution's research into aspects of higher education

Membership details: SRHE, 76 Portland Place, London W1B 1NT, UK Tel: 020 7637 2766. Fax: 020 7637 2781. email: srheoffice@srhe.ac.uk
world wide web: http://www.srhe.ac.uk./srhe/
Catalogue: SRHE & Open University Press, McGraw-Hill Education, McGraw-Hill House, Shoppenhangers Road, Maidenhead, Berkshire SL6 2QL. Tel: 01628 502500. Fax: 01628 770224. email: enquiries@openup.co.uk – web: www.openup.co.uk

Related books from Open University Press
Purchase from www.openup.co.uk of order through your local bookseller

MANAGING SUCCESSFUL UNIVERSITIES

Michael L. Shattock

Michael Shattock is the master craftsman of sturdy self-reliance in modern public universities. Knowing that ministerial steering will not, cannot, do the job in the twenty-first century, he charts an alternative course for continuous change. His liberating lessons will be useful not only in Britain but around the world.

Professor Burton R. Clark,
University of California, Los Angeles

... this important new book strengthens the argument for seeing good management as a necessary condition for effective and worthwhile teaching, learning and research, and its neglect as a serious threat to core academic values.

Professor Sir William Taylor, Former Director,
University of London Institute of Education

Michael Shattock is without doubt Britain's leading authority on the dangerously neglected subject of university management . . . For some his book will not make comfortable reading.

Professor Geoffrey Alderman, Vice-President,
American InterContinental University, London

This book seeks to define good management in a university context and how it can contribute to university success. It emphasizes the holistic characteristics of university management, the need to be outward looking and entrepreneurial in management style, the importance of maintaining a strong academic/administrative partnership and a continuous dialogue between the centre and academic departments, and the preservation of a self-directed institutional autonomy. It draws on the literature of management in the private sector as well as from higher education, and from the experience of the author. *Managing Successful Universities* demonstrates how successful universities utilise the market to reinforce academic excellence.

Contents
Introduction – What are the characteristics of the successful university? – Strategic management in universities – Managing university finance – The academic context: organization, collegiality and leadership – Good governance – Extending the boundaries – Building an image, establishing a reputation – Ambition – Inhibitions to becoming entrepreneurial – Turning round failure or arresting decline – Managing universities for success – Appendix – References – Index.

216pp   0 335 20961 0 (Paperback)   0 335 20962 9 (Hardback)

MANAGING CRISIS

David Warner and David Palfreyman

- Why do crises arise in Further and Higher Education institutions?
- How can these crises be overcome?
- What lessons can be learnt?

There have been several high profile crises in higher education during the last two decades. *Managing Crisis* draws together a number of senior academic managers to prepare, probably for the first time ever, a series of detailed institutional case studies. These case studies identify the nature of the crisis, describe the action taken to resolve it, and consider the lasting consequences. An important chapter gives the informed perspectives of the funding council on higher education crises, and in the final chapter the inimitable Peter Scott draws a series of significant conclusions.

Managing Crisis is the first book to examine crises in higher education in detail and to identify key points on how to overcome or avoid them. Required reading for managers working within UK Higher Education Policy.

Contents
Foreword – Notes on contributors – List of abbreviations – Setting the scene – Crisis at Cardiff – Capital building and cash flow at the University of Lancaster – How one man wove a kind of magic in Ealing – Southampton Institute – The experience of London Guildhall University – Heartbreak ending for a foreign affair – The Lambeth hike – Crisis making and crisis managing – A funding council perspective – Learning the lessons – References – Index.

Contributors
Roger Brown, Vanessa Cunningham, Chris Duke, Sir Brian Fender, Roderick Floud, Lucy Hodges, Marion McClintock, David Palfreyman, Adrian Perry, William Richie, Peter Scott, Sir Brian Smith, Sir William Taylor, David Warner.

216pp   0 335 21058 9 (Paperback)   0 335 21059 7 (Hardback)

MANAGING THE LEARNING UNIVERSITY

Chris Duke

This book debunks prevailing modern management theories and fashions as applied to higher education. At the same time it provides practical guidance for a clear and easily understood set of principles as to how universities and colleges can be re-energized and their staff mobilized to be effective in meeting the growing and changing needs of the global knowledge society. It is anchored in knowledge of management and organizational theory and in the literature about higher education which is critiqued from a clear theoretical perspective based on and tested through long experience of university management and leadership.

Chris Duke offers challenging advice for managers in tertiary and higher education – from self-managing knowledge workers who may feel themselves to be the new academic proletariat, through to institutional heads, some of whose attempts to manage using strategic planning, management-by-objectives and other techniques seriously unravel because they fail to benefit from the talents and networks which make up the rich 'underlife' of the institution. Loss of institutional memory and failure to tap tacit know-how and mobilize commitment through genuine consultation and shared participatory management inhibits organizational learning and generates apathy – or drives staff dedication and creativity into oppositional channels.

Managing the Learning University indicates how higher education institutions can link and network their internal energies with external opportunities and partners to be successful and dynamic learning organizations. It points the way to enabling an enterprising and valued university to thrive in hard times, and to be a community where it is actually a pleasure to work.

Contents

176pp   0 335 20765 0 (Paperback)   0 335 20766 9 (Hardback)

ENGAGING THE CURRICULUM IN HIGHER EDUCATION

Ronald Barnett and Kelly Coate

There is greater interest than ever before in higher education: more money is being spent on it, more students are registered and more courses are being taught. And yet the matter that is arguably at the heart of higher education, the curriculum, is noticeable for its absence in public debate and in the literature on higher education. This book begins to redress the balance.

Even though the term 'curriculum' may be missing from debates on higher education, curricula are changing rapidly and in significant ways. What we are seeing, therefore, is curriculum change by stealth, in which curricula are being reframed to enable students to acquire skills that have market value. In turn, curricula are running the risk of fragmenting as knowledge and skills exert their separate claims. Such a fragmented curriculum is falling well short of the challenges of the twenty-first century.

A complex and uncertain world requires curricula in which students as human beings are placed at their centre: what is called for are curricula that offer no less than the prospect of encouraging the formation of human being and becoming. A curriculum of this kind has to be understood as the imaginative design of spaces where creative things can happen as students become engaged.

Based upon a study of curricula in UK universities, *Engaging the Curriculum in Higher Education* offers an uncompromising thesis about the development of higher education and is essential reading for those who care about the future of higher education.

Contents
Acknowledgements – Introduction – Part I: The possibility of curriculum – Curriculum: a policy vacuum – Understanding curriculum – Higher education for a new age – Framing curriculum – Part II: Signs of curriculum life – Conjectures – Knowing – Acting – Being – Part III: Prospects for Engagement – Engaging the Curriculum – Engaging Students – Engaging Academics – Summary and Reflections – Appendices – Bibliography – Index.

160pp   0 335 21289 1 (Paperback)   0 335 21290 5 (Hardback)

GLOBALIZATION AND REFORM IN HIGHER EDUCATION

Heather Eggins (ed)

As the ability of each higher education system to produce the highly-skilled citizens required in the twenty first century becomes crucial, governments are recognizing and responding to global, as well as local, economic and cultural changes. Moreover, as the effects of globalization spread, their impact upon individual governments and their higher education institutions are becoming steadily more apparent.

This book charts the key issues that are involved in reforming higher education to meet new global challenges. It draws on a team of distinguished international researchers from North America, Africa, Australia and Europe who consider particular topics: the reform of governance and finance, the funding of higher education, managerialism, accreditation and quality assurance, the use of performance indicators, faculty roles and rewards, and the cultural, social and ethical dimensions of change.

The concluding section consists of two case studies: the first is a detailed discussion of the Australian government's introduction of higher education reform; the second assesses the transformation of higher education in South Africa in the face of contemporary global and local change.

Globalization and Reform in Higher Education enables readers to develop a firm grasp of the current state of play in higher education institutions worldwide, issues to be dealt with, and difficulties that have to be transcended. The book is essential reading for academics, senior managers, parliamentarians and civil servants involved in higher education policy-making.

Contributors
Rosemary Deem, Heather Eggins, Elaine El-Khawas, D. Bruce Johnstone, Mary-Louise Kearney, Adrianna Kezar, Elisabeth Lillie, Simon Marginson, Ann I. Morey, Preeti Shroff-Mehta, Barbara Sporn, George Subotzky, William Taylor.

Contents

256pp   0 335 21396 0 (Paperback)   0 335 21397 9 (Hardback)

ASSESSMENT, LEARNING AND EMPLOYABILITY

Peter Knight and Mantz Yorke

Knight and Yorke argue that our assessment practices are often not able to meet students', governments' and employers' expectations. We need to reconsider how higher education can judge and describe students' achievements. This is 'a thinking person's guide to assessment' which makes a compelling case that the challenges facing higher education demand radical changes in assessment thinking, and not mere tinkering with methods.

Peggi Maki, American Association for Higher Education

What is assessed gets attention: what is not assessed does not. When higher education is expected to promote complex achievements in subject disciplines and in terms of 'employability', problems arise: how are such achievements to be assessed?

In the first part, it is argued that existing grading practices cannot cope with the expectations laid upon them, while the potential of formative assessment for the support of learning is not fully realised. The authors argue that improving the effectiveness of assessment depends on a well-grounded appreciation of what assessment is, and what may and may not be expected of it.

The second part is about summative judgements for high-stakes purposes. Using established measurement theory, a view is developed of the conditions under which affordable, useful, valid and reliable summative judgements can be made. One conclusion is that many complex achievements resist high-stakes assessment, which directs attention to low-stakes, essentially formative, alternatives. Assessment for learning and employability demands more than module-level changes to assessment methods.

The text concludes with a discussion of how institutions can respond in policy terms to the challenges that have been posed.

Assessment, Learning and Employability has wide and practical relevance – to teachers, module and programme leaders, higher education managers and quality enhancement specialists.

Contents
Preface – Higher education and employability – Summative assessment in disarray – Formative assessment: unrealized potential – Key themes in thinking about assessment – Diversifying assessment methods – Assessing for employability – Authenticity in assessment – Optimizing the reliability of assessment – Making better use of formative assessment – Progression – Claims making – Assessment systems in academic departments – Developing the institutional assessment system – Conclusions.

224pp   0 335 21228 X (Paperback)   0 335 21229 8 (Hardback)

RESEARCHING HIGHER EDUCATION: ISSUES AND APPROACHES

Malcolm Tight

This book couples an authoritative overview of the principal current areas of research into higher education with a guide to the core methods used for researching higher education. It offers both a configuration of research on higher education, as seen through the lens of methodology, and suggestions for further research.

Contents

Case studies and tables are separately listed after the main contents pages – Part I: Recently Published Research on Higher Education – Introduction – Journals – Books – Part II: Issues and Approaches in Researching Higher Education – Researching Teaching and Learning – Researching Course Design – Researching the Student Experience – Researching Quality – Researching System Policy – Researching Institutional Management – Researching Academic Work – Researching Knowledge – Part III: The Process of Researching Higher Education – Method and Methodology in Researching Higher Education – Researching Higher Education at Different Levels – The Process of Researching – References

417pp   0 335 21117 8 (Paperback)   0 335 21118 6 (Hardback)